BLACKBALLED

BLACKBALLED

The Black and White
Politics of Race on
America's Campuses

LAWRENCE ROSS

St. Martin's Press

New York

www.stmartins.com

Library of Congress Cataloging-in-Publication Data

Names: Ross, Lawrence C., author.

Title: Blackballed : the black and white politics of race on America's campuses / Lawrence Ross.

Description: New York City : St. Martin's Press, 2016.

Identifiers: LCCN 2015026361 | ISBN 9781250079114 (hardback)

Subjects: LCSH: Racism in higher education—United States. | Discrimination in higher education.—United States. | African Americans—Education (Higher)—United States. | African American college students—Social conditions. | College campuses—Social aspects—United States. | BISAC: EDUCATION / Students & Student Life. | SOCIAL SCIENCE / Discrimination & Race Relations. | SOCIAL SCIENCE / Ethnic Studies / Asian American Studies.

Classification: LCC LC212.42 .R67 2016 | DDC 378.1/982996073—dc23

LC record available at http://lccn.loc.gov/2015026361

ISBN 978-1-250-07911-4 (hardcover)
ISBN 978-1-4668-9174-6 (e-book)

Our books may be purchased in bulk for promotional, educational, or business use. Please contact your local bookseller or the Macmillan Corporate and Premium Sales Department at (800) 221-7945, extension 5442, or by e-mail at MacmillanSpecialMarkets@macmillan.com.

First Edition: February 2016

10 9 8 7 6 5 4 3 2 1

For my beloved son,

Langston Ross . . .

who I wish the world

CONTENTS

Eight pages of photos appear between pages 136 and 137.

ACKNOWLEDGMENTS

THEY ALWAYS CAME UP TO ME AFTER MY DIVINE NINE FRATER-
nity and sorority lecture. Hundreds, maybe thousands of African American students, their faces tortured with desperation as they struggled to talk about their situations on campus. They'd speak in whispers, eyes darting, as if talking openly might not be safe. The constant theme? Feelings of isolation, tempered by the idea that their struggles, these "real world" struggles at a predominately white university, would ultimately prepare them for the future. Struggling as a minority in a majority world was one thing, but taking the relentless slings and arrows of racial microaggressions, the daily slights that grind an individual down over time, was another. And at worst, they'd talk fearfully about the overtly racist behavior they and their black friends had to deal with at their schools, where instances of racism were often dismissed by college administrators who should know better as aberrations or isolated incidents.

For almost fifteen years I listened to those stories, wondering if times would get better for these black college students. Maybe their experiences were aberrations, just examples of campus racism in specific geographical areas. Or maybe they were just limited to certain periods of time, like the conservative Bush era or the liberal Obama era. I watched as well-meaning and truly devoted university administrators, faculty, Greek life advisors, and others did their best to make life for African

American students as comfortable and welcoming as possible. But ultimately institutional and systemic racism often sabotaged those efforts, leaving them, and the students, despondent, dejected, and depressed.

And nothing changed. Nothing at all. I watched as campus racism not only continued, but thrived. Yet, to my amazement, people were constantly surprised that it existed. That's when I knew it was time to talk about it, to chronicle it, and thus began the two-year journey culminating in *Blackballed: The Black and White Politics of Race on America's Campuses.*

Books are always disingenuous: the single author's name on the cover never tells the whole story. Yes, I wrote *Blackballed,* but getting the book from an idea to your hands was definitely a collaborative effort. It began with having a great literary agent, and there's none better than Jan Miller, owner of Dupree/Miller & Associates. Not only does she believe in my writing, but she also makes me feel as though my calls are the most important items on her busy schedule. The same goes for all of the Dupree/Miller staff, especially Lacy Lalene Lynch, who did a yeoman's job handling my contract and any neurotic issues I may have had during the writing process.

I always like to say that writers write, and editors edit, and smart writers let smart editors do their work. At St. Martin's Press, I have one of the best in executive editor Karen Wolny. Karen helped me broaden my original idea and tackle campus racism from multiple angles. And you wouldn't have heard about *Blackballed* without the terrific marketing team at St. Martin's Press who *got* what I was trying to do . . . and why it was important to reach as many different audiences as possible.

Of course, I'd like to thank all of the brave people I interviewed for *Blackballed.* It's no easy task talking about racism, particularly when you experience it during one of the most important times in your life, your college years. Often, the psychological ramifications can be long lasting and dismissed by others as being unimportant. But I believe that discussing these issues *is* important, and I feel blessed that I was provided with a platform to allow those voices to be heard.

Most importantly, none of this would be possible without the support of the two most important people in my life: my wife, April, and my son, Langston. They've provided me with nothing but unconditional love and understanding, even as their husband/father walked around the house muttering to himself as he tried to put all of the pieces of the puzzle together into a coherent story.

The brilliant poet, writer, social commentator, and, to me, all-around genius Nikki Giovanni once wrote an essay titled "Campus Racism 101," in which she noted that she taught at the predominately white Virginia Tech "because it's here. And so are Black students. But even if Black students weren't here, it's painfully obvious that this nation and this world cannot allow white students to go through higher education without interacting with Blacks in authoritative positions. It is equally clear that predominately Black colleges cannot accommodate the numbers of Black students who want and need an education."[1]

I agree with that sentiment, and this is why *Blackballed* isn't about predominately white institutions (PWIs) not having a role in educating black college students. For over a century, black students have received invaluable educations at these white colleges and universities and have gone on to change America and the world. And black students will *continue* to enroll, graduate, and change lives, while influenced by their educations at these schools. Hell, *I* have two degrees from a PWI. But providing these opportunities to African American college students does not mitigate the racism that these students will face on nearly every campus in the United States. And we shouldn't confuse the coping mechanisms black students use to survive on these campuses with long-lasting solutions. Campus racism has been at epidemic proportions for decades, and it's time for predominately white colleges and universities to start looking for effective solutions . . . before a tragic event erupts. And be sure, every college and university in the United States is a ticking time bomb due to the unaddressed racism on its campus. The first step in getting healthy is to recognize that you're sick.

Consider *Blackballed* as that diagnosis of societal cancer on the college campus body. Administrators at PWIs are going to have to figure out what's the correct treatment . . . or black students just may start making different choices.

INTRODUCTION

A Century of Isolated Incidents

SPANISH PHILOSOPHER GEORGE SANTAYANA, A HARVARD classmate of African American philosopher W. E. B. Du Bois, was most famous for stating, "Those who cannot remember the past are condemned to repeat it."[1] The phrase has been the go-to refrain directed toward anyone who lacks the depth or tenacity to dive into the tedious waters of true historical analysis. For the most part, the observation has morphed into cliché—something said over a couple of drinks or while watching *Jeopardy!* as you sit on the couch. When it comes to America and race, I'm predisposed to another quote by Santayana, one that I think more fully explains white America's collective historical amnesia regarding the realities of racism and the effects of brutality on African Americans, past and present:

> History is nothing but assisted and recorded memory . . . Memory itself is an internal rumor; and when to this hearsay within the mind we add the falsified echoes that reach us from others, we have but a shifting and unseizable basis to build upon. The picture we frame of the past changes continually and grows every day less similar to the original experience.[2]

For the past 400 years, African Americans tried to assist white America in recording a memory of racism, often to no avail. White America clings stubbornly to a collective narrative, what Gore Vidal famously called "the United States of Amnesia."[3] That amnesia acts like a cloak of ignorance, warm and embracing enough to make the issue of racism a mental no-go zone for those who refuse to acknowledge its existence.

In a post–Civil War world, decade after decade, African Americans have done their best to elicit sympathy for their struggle against systemic white racism. In explaining the day-to-day indignities of state-sponsored second-class life under Jim Crow degradation, along with the domestic terrorism that resulted in thousands of African Americans throughout the United States being lynched for the most captious of reasons, African Americans pointed at the racism and said, "Look."

Today, systemic and institutional racism still plagues African Americans, long after the "Colored Only" signs have been taken down. African Americans are primarily the ones burdened with the task of fixing a race problem they didn't produce or perpetuate, while white America continues to say, "I don't see it."

Even when forced to confront overt racism, white America has been slow, reluctant, and dishonest in recounting that memory, a memory that is deep in their guts, a memory that they know is true. As individuals, white Americans have learned that they can deflect, defuse, and delude as a way to maintain the charade: "This is not a race issue. The people who did this are jerks, but this is not about race"; "This may have been insensitive, but can we move on from this and get back to normal?"; "Because you're talking about racism, you're being racist, and that's the reason why we can't get beyond race in this country"; "This is not who I am. This is an isolated incident."

As the unelected governing body for the purpose of evaluating the validity of racism, white America consistently discounts black witnesses to racism as unreliable, as in *you're playing the race card,* and the falsifying echoes are often those black sophists who ply their trade on Fox

News, or for the Republican Party, eager to comfort the uninformed. Their message? No matter what authentic black voices say, nothing about white racism is worth taking up space in the collective white American memory: "Black people who talk about racism are just trying to be the victim. And that in itself is a form of racism"; "Everything is just fine. Just fine"; "Just don't think about racism, and don't think about color. Feel free to maintain the amnesia."

But everything isn't fine.

Most African Americans live in a world where white racism is an omnipresent entity, an obstacle they attempt to navigate while becoming highly successful, exceedingly mediocre, or abject failures. But pointing out the realities of white racism to America as a black person who lives them, and then having that reality dismissed unheard, logically makes black people question their sanity. When racial inequities around housing, education, jobs, wealth, health care, and a thousand other categories are quantifiably tilted toward the benefit of white Americans, often because of overtly racist public policy, why did a 2013 Rasmussen poll show that 49 percent of white Republicans viewed African Americans, and not themselves or other white Americans, as racist?[4]

It's intentional delusion.

And for most white Americans, the delusion begins with the idea that every child in America begins on an equal footing with every other child, regardless of race. The formula for success, and the formula most often preached to African Americans, is work hard, carry on with your life as though you believe wholeheartedly in the American Dream, and with a little bit of pluck and ambition, you *too* can go far. And for many, including African Americans, you *can* go far. Failure *isn't* a fait accompli when it comes to an African American's life destiny.

But it's also important to note that racism isn't just some "thing" that you overcome. It's omnipresent, like a sea of shit in which you swim, always stinking no matter how many showers you take. But to white America, the inequities of society created by racism are trivial when compared with the opportunities America allows everyone. Racism is simply, in the eyes and ears of white America, an unfortunate but inconsequential aspect of life, like being short or losing one's hair at an early age. An aspect of life to be discounted where the presence of racism is more than balanced by the multitude of mitigating factors.

"I don't see color" is the common refrain for those trying to deflect statements about racism, not knowing that what they're really saying is, "My learned racism, along with my participation and benefit from living in a racist society, has an effect on how I treated you. So in order to counter that, I must pretend that I don't see you or the essence of who you are. And if I don't see you, then I can ignore the facts around your color, and in my mind, the problem goes away."

Racism. It's the great American cat-and-mouse game, with African Americans playing the role of the mouse, desperate to escape from the maze and white society's deadly paw. Racism's genius is its ability to arbitrarily change rules, impact lives, and yet disavow itself, along with its effects on victims. It is the Keyser Soze, or more recently, the Rachel Dolezal, of societal maladies. Real to some, unreal to others, camouflaged in many layers of white privilege, yet always staring us right in the face.

However, in spite of everything, white America and black America have a co-dependent relationship. White America needs to support the illusion that its country's ideals have been realized, at least enough to claim that America is an exceptional nation, where white privilege can be ignored as being an inconsequential advantage *over* blackness—a nation where even the product of a white Kansan mother and a black Kenyan exchange student can rise up to be president of the United States. And African America needs to believe that the journey, one fraught with unwanted, unsaid, and unheard dangers, is ultimately worth it. If not, how else would one remain sane?

And when it comes to college, from the moment African American high school students receive those wonderful large envelopes, the ones with the beautifully written acceptance letters from a predominately white university saying. "Congratulations!," little do they know that despite the brochure showing smiling, happy multicultural faces, they're about to step foot on some of the most racially hostile spaces in the United States. And in their most formative years, when their belief in American ideals is the strongest, or being questioned, these African American students will learn that their white university, their white fellow students, and their white faculty are not automatic allies in their journey toward educational success. And that's been a fact for over a century.

Before they buy their overpriced books, settle into their tiny Spartan dorms, and eat their first bad meal in the cafeteria, they'll learn that overt acts of racism on their campus are often dismissed as a series of disconnected incidents, outside the collective responsibility of the university and always surprising to those who are exposed to them, particularly white university administrators.

"We're surprised and shocked that this would happen on our campus, and we'd like to say that this racial incident doesn't reflect the values of who we are as a university community . . ." is the pro forma response, as we'll see later in *Blackballed: The Black and White Politics of Race on America's Campuses.*

Even more extreme than Santayanna's picture of the past, which gets less accurate by the day, white America never recalls the events of college racism at all, leaving the burden of remembering to eighteen- to twenty-one-year old African American college students. From there, those students are tasked with creating new solutions for old and present problems, often involving white people who refuse to recognize the historical context of racism. And they have to do it every four years, as a new group of black students cycle in and out of the university, while the campus racism always remains. What is the resulting mindset of typical African American college students after they experience episodes of campus racism? Again, it's to question themselves and their sanity: "Are we going crazy, or is there a racist incident on a college campus every day? If so, why are people saying this is an isolated incident . . . again?"

One space where all Americans hoped race would be inconsequential is on America's college and university campuses. As colleges and universities have moved from being the providence of the elite to reflecting the populace of a young democracy, they've long vacillated from openness to the idea of an egalitarian society (as at Berea College in 1850s Kentucky—the first college blacks were welcomed to attend below the Mason-Dixon line *during* slavery) to fighting to keep blacks out (as at southern schools during the turbulent civil rights era of the 1950s and 1960s).

College campuses are supposed to be places where the young elite of all races, sexes, and creeds seek knowledge, a knowledge that throws off the shackles of racism, sexism, and other "isms" in order to create a better, more just society. And that utopian vision is often expressed in Latin, through official school mottoes.

At Amherst it's "*terras irradient*," which translates to "let them give light to the world." At the University of Arkansas it's "*veritate duce progredi*," which means, "To advance with truth as our guide." And Harvard's famous one-word motto is "*veritas*," which translates as "truth."

It's with college students, the future leaders of American society, that we place our dreams, hoping that the ignoble sentiment of racism will erode to the point where everyone can move forward without that burden. New ideas of equality and respect for all will, we hope, trump bigotry and prejudice through a college education. But when you look closely at America's colleges and universities, the veritas, the truth, is much stranger than the fiction we Americans tell ourselves. The truth is that for African American college students, there's a campus racism crisis going on.

And no one seems to recognize that truth.

The University of Oklahoma campus sits in Norman, Oklahoma, a small prairie town about twenty miles south of Oklahoma City. With a population just over 100,000 people, the city is your typical college town, about 85 percent white and only 4 percent of the city identifying as African American. Norman matches, almost to a tee, the student demographics of the university. In the heart of Tornado Alley, that swath of Midwestern volatility where twisters seemingly come out of nowhere to devastate prairie towns, a storm hit the University of Oklahoma on March 7, 2015, rivaling some of the biggest dust devils ever to hit the plains.

And that storm's name was Parker Rice.

By all measures, the Saturday night had been a success. The Oklahoma Kappa chapter of Sigma Alpha Epsilon fraternity had rented a party bus, everyone was wearing tuxedos, and the alcohol flowed like water in the Nile. It didn't matter that some of the fraternity members, like nineteen-year-old Rice, were underage. There was a wink-wink policy, just like on most Greek Rows in America, of ignoring that. What happens in the fraternity stays in the fraternity.

As for the fraternity itself, Sigma Alpha Epsilon was founded in the antebellum South—at the University of Alabama in 1856—and is proud of it. Every fraternity and sorority has heroic lore to exalt early members, and Sigma Alpha Epsilon was no different.

Part of the historical pride within SAE, as it's known colloquially, is that early fraternity members enthusiastically joined the Confederate Army, with many dying for the Lost Cause of protecting slavery in the South. After most of its chapters were devastated by the Civil War, SAE would eventually regroup to become one of the largest fraternities in the country.[5]

So how did SAE's members see themselves in today's society? As "true gentlemen," that's how. The fraternity had always harkened back to that antebellum myth of southern male chivalry among the white slaveholding planter class, with Confederate legends Robert E. Lee and Stonewall Jackson as the ideal role models. But that was then, and this was now, and now the fraternity that proudly proclaimed its Confederate ancestry also stressed that it was open to all, including the great-great-great grandsons of the people its Confederate heroes unsuccessfully attempted to keep enslaved. "True gentlemen" saw no color in today's SAE. Or so some thought.[6]

For Rice, being in SAE was the perfect fit. The camaraderie among the brothers reminded him of the feeling he got while attending a prestigious all-boys Catholic high school, Jesuit College Preparatory School of Dallas. Later, once he'd become a national figure of derision, Rice would describe the Jesuit motto, "Men for Others," the selfless ethos of Jesuit-educated men worldwide, as being his guiding principle in life, while apologizing for what happened on that party bus.[7]

In essence, the party bus was there mainly to keep SAE brothers from drinking and driving, and if that kept the party going, all the better. On the bus were not only the aforementioned tuxedoed SAE brothers, but at least two or three members of Delta Delta Delta sorority, or Tri-Delt. Everyone was in a fine mood, laughing and singing. And everyone on that bus was white.

Rice, now inebriated and fully in life-of-the-party mode, stood in the aisle and led the fraternal singing. With a smile on his face and the confidence of a conductor at the Boston Philharmonic, he began to chant: "There will never be a nigger SAE! There will never be a nigger SAE! You can hang 'em from a tree, but it will never sign with me! There will never be a nigger SAE!"[8]

Those on the bus sang the chant at the top of their lungs, and no one appeared to object to the offensive words. In fact, when someone pointed a smart phone at Rice and recorded, Rice didn't seem bothered in the least. Most sang lustfully, and without hesitation, as though they'd sung the lynching song hundreds of times. The atmosphere had a comfort level that said, "We're among like-minded friends."

While Rice and his fraternity brothers joked about lynching blacks, for African Americans, lynching represents a very real and painful segment of white supremacist history. Black family histories are peppered with stories of real fathers and mothers, sons and daughters, aunts and uncles, grandfathers and grandmothers who were taken from their beds at night and strung up from telephone and telegraph poles. Some were falsely accused of crimes, others just the unfortunate targets of white rage. White mobs strung them up from trees, mutilating them by cutting off their toes, fingers, and genitalia as souvenirs. Many of the victims would be photographed, their images sent around the country as popular postcards, examples of how white supremacy was being enforced not just in the South, but everywhere in the country.

Alice Walker once talked about growing up under the threat of being lynched: "I grew up in the South under segregation. So, I know what terrorism feels like—when your father could be taken out in the middle of the night and lynched just because he didn't look like he was in an obeying frame of mind when a white person said something he must do. I mean, that's terrorism, too."[9]

My grandmother, Willie Lee Johnson, grew up in Texas, with the family migrating between Waco, Temple, and Dallas, as the cotton-pulling season demanded. In her final days, her brain racked by the ravages of Alzheimer's, it was as though her consciousness had been opened to allow suppressed memories to flow back to the fore. And one of the memories that would panic her was some midnight lynching she'd seen as a child.

"Don't let them get me, baby," she'd say to me, her eyes ablaze. "They hung them men in that field, and they buried them underneath that tree."

Lynching wasn't, and isn't, a subject for a drinking song to black people.

But there weren't any black students on the bus, just as there aren't any black members in the current Oklahoma Kappa chapter of Sigma Alpha Epsilon. And more than likely, given the student population on campus, Rice and his friends didn't have many black friends whose memories might have made the frat members think twice about singing this song. So if they sang a song about "hanging niggers from a tree," who would know? More importantly, who would really care?

Little did they know that there was at least one person who would object, and it was that person pointing a camera at Rice. That anonymous partygoer would send the video of Rice and his fraternity brothers singing about hanging "niggers from a tree" to OU Unheard, an African American student group on the University of Oklahoma campus. And by the next morning, OU Unheard would make sure that the world heard what was going on inside that SAE party bus.

But SAE wasn't the only issue for black students on the University of Oklahoma campus, nor the first. In January 2015 OU Unheard sent University of Oklahoma president David Boren a list of grievances, alleging that the university marginalized black students. Those students felt they were ignored, invisible, and subject to the same racist indignities that plague campuses around the country, yet their pleas for a non-hostile atmosphere at OU were not being listened to—hence the name OU Unheard.[10]

But after Rice got through singing, OU Unheard was in possession of a video that would make them heard not only on the University of Oklahoma campus but around the world. And, as happens with all episodes of racism, some would try to characterize the significance of the incident as being limited (in this case, to the University of Oklahoma campus, which was not the case). It was important for people to know that all of those isolated incidents were part of a trend that stretched back for decades, a trend that even those without a recorded memory of racism had to acknowledge.

Blackballed is the book that creates that recorded memory.

The campus racism situation at the University of Oklahoma is neither new nor surprising. What is surprising is that most Americans think it *is* new, and as I said on MSNBC after the SAE incident blew up, "I'm surprised that people are surprised." But that illusion of surprise also gave rise to the usual excuses for Rice and his SAE fraternity brothers and their behavior.

Every time a racist campus event occurs, white privilege explains it as just the act of some immature young white students, who made a mistake of youthful exuberance. In their hearts, apologists say, these white students are not racists. There's always an external reason for their racist behavior, such as being drunk and so not thinking clearly. Or, they didn't mean what they said in a racist way, and so they apologize to anyone who may have been offended.

For many white Americans, the bar for branding students as racist is so high that we'd first have to confirm that they were all dues-paying members of the Ku Klux Klan, wearing white hoods while writing editorials for the John Birch Society *and* using the Nazi Party salute . . . in a Hitler mustache. Only then would we get a "maybe" they're racist. Others would inevitably say that they'd like to get "more information."

And if there hadn't been a video of the SAE party bus full of singing white fraternity and sorority members, you can be sure that the full impact would have been diluted for one of the reasons above.

And this is a problem.

But because there *was* a video for everyone to see in the SAE case, it was increasingly hard for even racism deniers to dispute that what they were seeing was racism. And the SAE case was only a small part of the picture. The real fact is that campus racism is as common as underage drinking at colleges, and just as traditional. For over a century, whether it's overt hostility in the form of racial epithets scrawled on campus walls, or nooses being hung on dorm room doors to intimidate black students, or white fraternities and sororities painting their faces with black paint for Halloween parties, there's been a clear pattern of intimidation, racial hate, and violence that's targeted African Americans on college campuses throughout the country.

There are close to 3,000 four-year universities in the United States, and most have generally stuck their heads in the sand, hoping that the latest controversy would pass them by or be forgotten by a public ever tiring of the issue of race. And when confronted, these universities have been reactive instead of proactive.

And that's not good enough.

Blackballed points out how colleges and universities have historically either been complicit in fostering a campus environment that was friendly to racist behavior, or reacted so superficially that they made the conditions even worse. In other words, racists are more than welcome at PWIs, and they know it.

And it's not like the universities don't know they have a problem. Hundreds of colleges and universities have hired hundreds of staff for their student affairs departments, their equal opportunity programs, and their African American studies departments, and yet . . . these hardworking professionals can only put their fingers in the dike of campus racism.

Why don't their efforts work? For the same reason why antiracism efforts tend to fail in general society: we don't want to take them on honestly, with the full resources available to us. Creating a racism-free environment on campus isn't as large a priority as making sure the donors are happy, the football team is winning, and the tuition money keeps flowing. Everything else is superfluous. And as a result, black students suffer.

Blackballed talks about public policy, including anti–affirmative action measures such as California's Proposition 209 and Michigan's Proposition 2 that have decimated the ranks of African American students at top schools like the University of California at Berkeley, UCLA, and the University of Michigan, creating school segregation that causes black students to despair for their existence while increasing the racial microaggressions black students face each day.

Blackballed also goes back in history, pointing to a time when colleges and universities, feeling the exuberance of the Allied victory over the fascist powers of Germany, Japan, and Italy during World War II, figured that if democracy abroad was worth fighting for, then how about on their campuses, specifically in the racist white fraternities and sororities that dominated there? But as *Blackballed* will show, change can be glacial, and even in the Age of Obama, it may be easier for a black man to sit in the White House than in a University of Alabama fraternity house.

While *Blackballed* documents the racism against African Americans, it's important to note that African Americans have not been passive in confronting the hostile campus environments. The tradition of African American college student activism is strong, and often the civil rights marches that changed society had their beginnings in a main quad at a university. From the militancy of taking over buildings to the demand for African American curricula, black students have demanded changes to the college environment from the early days of integration to the present.

And surprisingly, these black activists weren't protesting the encroachments on their sense of black identity and the need to be heard as college students only at predominately white colleges and universities. I chronicle how activism at historically black colleges and universities was often the point of the spear when those schools' policies skewed too closely to those of the more conservative white schools they emulated.

Finally, *Blackballed* asks whether, given all of the racial obstacles, going to a PWI is really worth it for African Americans. This is not the same as asking whether the education is valuable—we can say definitively that it is—but whether or not that education is worth the psychological damage to the African American student due to racism. That is a question that all stakeholders are going to have to answer.

In the spirit of Thelonious Monk's composition "Straight, No Chaser," *Blackballed* tells the story of campus racism in an unblinking search for the truth, the same word that peppers the mottos of so many American colleges and universities.

This book is a no-holds-barred look at how black students often find themselves at the mercy of white campus racism, both individual and systemic; why the average college and university has turned into a hostile space for African American college students; and why, as a result, black college students feel blackballed from their campuses . . . and American society.

Blackballed doesn't maintain that blacks shouldn't go to college. Today, attending college is vital. But what is the ultimate solution for modern African American college students? Should they give up going to predominately white universities and instead attend black schools? Or should they fight it out and demand a racism-free environment?

As with any answer to a complex question, there are always mitigating factors. Yes, white fraternities and sororities do great work both on campus and off. I have seen that work with my own eyes. Yes, not all fraternity/sorority members agree with the racist views of their brethren, nor do they all participate in racist acts. I have met many wonderful members of predominately white fraternities and sororities on hundreds of campuses. And yes, not all predominately white campuses condone creating uncomfortable racial environments for their black students, and most at least *try* to spend resources to create a comfortable home for black students.

But *Blackballed* isn't about those mitigating circumstances.

Blackballed argues that no number of good intentions, good deeds, nice individuals, or concerned administrations can come close to making up for the racist experiences many African American college students have when attempting to get college degrees from predominately white institutions. What we see clearly, from the sheer volume of racist incidents, is that what colleges and universities are doing to stem campus racism has been a failure.

As a result, *Blackballed* rips the scab off the open secret: that predominately white college campuses, despite the pretty pictures, are now hostile spaces for black students, and they need to do something about it—*now*. This book makes certain that colleges and universities can never say they didn't know or understand past and present campus racism, making it as real for the university as it is for the African American students who live this repeated history year after year.

The great Nigerian novelist Chinua Achebe once quoted an African proverb: "Until the lions have their own historian, the history of the hunt will always glorify the hunter."[11] *Blackballed* is written from the perspective of the lion.

And it's time for the truth.

1

JIM CROW GREEK ROW

"[People should] stop shivering at the word discrimination . . . I love the discriminating tongue, the discriminating eye, the discriminating ear, and, above all, the discriminating mind and . . . soul. The person for whom I can find no love and no respect is the indiscriminate person. To be indiscriminate is to be common, to be vulgar."

—National Interfraternity Conference
chairman, David A. Embury, 1947[1]

THE FALLOUT FROM THE SIGMA ALPHA EPSILON PARTY BUS video was fast and furious, as was the condemnation that came from all corners. The national media, CNN, MSNBC, and Fox News, all converged on the University of Oklahoma, and everyone wanted to get to the bottom of the incident. How could this happen? Where did these students learn the song? Did Sigma Alpha Epsilon teach it to their members? If so, how long had SAE members been singing it? Everyone wanted answers, and they wanted them now.

Universities, being the conservative entities they are, usually react to campus racial incidents slowly, being cautious about placing blame or even identifying the culprits. "We condemn, but need more info," is usually the standard response. "This racist incident doesn't reflect the values of the university." A vague statement is sent out through a press release, and then a university flack is put in front of the cameras to do their best to not answer the questions from the press.

In a surprising move, David Boren decided that he wasn't going that route.

President of the University of Oklahoma, and a former U.S. senator, Boren acted swiftly, and within hours issued a statement that was unequivocal and blunt.

"To those who have misused their free speech in such a reprehensible way, I have a message for you. You are disgraceful. You have violated all that we stand for. You should not have the privilege of calling yourselves 'Sooners.' Real Sooners are not racist. Real Sooners are not bigots. Real Sooners believe in equal opportunity. Real Sooners treat all people with respect. Real Sooners love each other and take care of each other like family members.

"Effective immediately, all ties and affiliations between this University and the local SAE chapter are hereby severed. I direct that the house be closed and that members will remove their personal belongings from the house by midnight tomorrow. Those needing to make special arrangements for positions shall contact the Dean of Students.

"All of us will redouble our efforts to create the strongest sense of family and community. We vow that we will be an example to the entire country of how to deal with this issue. There must be a zero tolerance for racism everywhere in our nation."[2]

By that morning, there were television camera shots of SAE members, most of whom hadn't even been on the party bus, loading moving vans with their personal items. University staff had been dispatched to rip the gold SAE letters from the side of the fraternity house. And when asked if the university would provide assistance to the SAE fraternity members who had to move, Boren responded by saying, "We don't provide student services for bigots." In addition, Boren moved to quickly expel two University of Oklahoma SAE members who'd been featured prominently in the video: Parker Rice and his fraternity brother, the 20-year-old Levi Pettit.[3]

As for Sigma Alpha Epsilon's national headquarters, it was in full Cuban Missile Crisis mode. SAE HQ put out a statement a few days after seeing the video, saying that it was in the process of expelling the entire Oklahoma Kappa chapter from the fraternity, and that Rice and Pettit had learned the song on their own. Their investigation assured the public that the song had been taught only in that Oklahoma chapter, and nowhere else.[4]

The assessment that this racist behavior was seemingly contained within the culture of that particular Oklahoma chapter was buttressed by the discovery of a second video featuring Beauton Gilbow, the chapter's elderly house mom, who, complete with silvery-gray hair, rapped along to the Trinidad James song, "All Gold Everything." Along with the off-camera SAE members filming her, she took particular delight in repeating the word "nigger" at least seven times.[5]

Brandon Weghorst, associate executive director and media spokesman for Sigma Alpha Epsilon, tried to stem the damage the best he could. In interview after interview, Weghorst reiterated that SAE wasn't a racist fraternity and that its internal studies had shown that "based on data gathered since 2013, approximately 20 percent of our members self-identify as a minority or non-Caucasian."[6]

Weghorst's statement pretty much fits the typical response from white fraternities after any racist event: localize the issue as an isolated incident that is reflective of a bad-apple chapter and keep the entire white fraternity clean from the taint of a racist event. Lastly, the fraternity also wanted to impress upon the public that they weren't the predominately white fraternity we thought they were but, in reality, a diverse fraternity with *plenty* of black members.

Actually, the Oklahoma Kappa Sigma Alpha Epsilon chapter hadn't had a black member since William Bruce James II had joined, fourteen years earlier. And when James was interviewed about his reaction to the SAE video, he was blunt.

"I feel like I've lost a family member. That pure bond of brother-hood, I don't know if I'll ever get that back."[7]

Later, on his blog, James' anger was palpable.

"I can have no association with this organization as a black man. I know these were 'kids being kids' and maybe they aren't the hateful ignorant lost little boys I think they are, but I will not stand behind anything that allowed this to happen. They are not just kids being kids. Those boys are sons. Sons of men who failed them, and they failed my son. You failed ME! Member 261–057. Your boys sang in unison. They may not know where the song came from or who made it up or even what all the words really mean, but they sing it so often they know all the words whether they want to or not."[8]

James, a lawyer who still lives close to Norman, remembers a dif-ferent SAE Oklahoma chapter. One that was inclusive—and was also cognizant of the incongruity between the history of SAE's glorification of the Confederacy and James' own black presence. That memory only made the singing incident more painful. For example, he remembered a discussion that took place when he was a pledge; the discussion, which centered on the Civil War and SAE's part in it, provided him an opportunity to see where his new brothers stood on his being in their midst.

"We started learning about the history of the fraternity itself, and the Civil War came up, and SAE was founded at the University of Ala-bama, so it's obvious that they were on the wrong side of the Civil War," James remembered. "And so when that came up, it was interesting be-cause I wasn't sure what to do with that information . . . And so it was kind of one of those deals where I started wondering, 'Do I really want to get too involved with this?' or just get out of it now?"[9]

But to his surprise, his SAE brothers talked about how they were less interested in being tied to that Confederate history than in being brothers to the men in the room. Their words provided James with a level of comfort that allowed him to continue pledging SAE and then have a wonderful four years as a fraternity member. But as it did for James, the SAE video changed everything on campus.

Eric Striker, the All-American linebacker for the University of Oklahoma, had been particularly incensed by what he saw. As with most universities, football at the University of Oklahoma is a combination of black athletes, white fans, and green dollars. And for Striker there was something hypocritical about the singing SAE members being the same people who cheered him on the field. So he let loose on the social media app Snapchat with a no-holds-barred rant.

"I'm so mutherfucking serious right now. SAE just fucked it up for all you fucking white fraternities. Fuck all you bitches . . . [These] are the same motherfuckers shaking our hands, giving us hugs, telling us how you really love us . . . fuck you phony ass, fraud ass bitches."[10]

I spoke with Eric, and while he was sorry about how he'd expressed his emotions, he wasn't sorry for the emotions themselves. The SAE video cut deep with him, and it made him recall his earlier experiences with white fraternities on campus.

"My freshman year, I'd go to the white frat parties, and it was just a feeling," Eric recalled. "When you'd walk in, everybody would look at you like, 'Why are you here?' Or like, 'Damn, we usually don't see this kind' . . . even though we were invited. Eventually, I didn't go anymore because of that vibe.

"A lot of black athletes are afraid to speak out [about racism on campus] because they think that the university, and their team, will think that they're against them," Striker continued. "We're not against them, we just want to put the truth out there. If that's not the truth, then you speak up and say that's not true. I'm just standing up for what's right because you have to stand up for something . . . I'm sure there were people who didn't want me to speak up, but this is bigger than my school, bigger than my sport.

"Football at Oklahoma is more important than bringing a culture of diversity, and trying to bring a positive change to the campus. Football is more important than all that. They could give a damn about race, and racism, and they could give a damn about a culture of change as long as the football team is going good. So I told my football team, 'This is important. We have this power. We have this voice to use to push for what is right, so let's do that. Because I know that if we stop this football, this state would go crazy.'"[11]

For a lot of African American athletes, particularly football players, their existence on campus is designed to isolate them from the rest of the student community. Their schedules are skewed so that football becomes the end-all and be-all. As such, they're seen as being athletic mercenaries, and as a result, when they're in white spaces like fraternities and sororities, there's friction. To white students, their place is on the field, not in the frat house.

After Striker spoke out, all of the Oklahoma Sooners football team, with the full blessing of their coach, Bob Stoops, staged a silent protest on Owen Field to demonstrate against the SAE video.

Meanwhile, the black University of Oklahoma student activist group, OU Unheard, who'd released the racist video, also demonstrated. Two months prior OU Unheard had held a town hall–style gathering to talk about their experiences as black students at the University of Oklahoma and delivered to President Boren seven points they wanted addressed. From the hiring of more black faculty, to greater funding for black student groups, the students noted how they felt isolated on campus and not part of the Sooner family.

"OU prides itself as being a family," said Alex Hall, a junior, mechanical engineering major, and leading member of OU Unheard. "But are black students included in this family?"[12]

"The effort to maintain a black community on campus," continued Hall, "they kinda of dropped the ball on that. The numbers [of black students] was dropping, and tuition was rising . . . I think more could have been done. They didn't see us as a necessity on campus. Things get forgotten, until they're brought up."[13]

In a later January meeting with Boren, the students expressed confidence that the university president, who appeared not to have known about the situation for black students on campus, would help change their experience.

"We feel good about the future of what's happening with the university," OU Unheard executive Chelsea Davis said at the time. "We understand it will take some time to get some of these changes implemented. However, we feel confident in President Boren and his staff."[14]

After the SAE video went national, apparently President Boren's timeline for change shortened, as he quickly announced the hiring of Jabar Shumate, a former legislator and OU alumnus, as OU's vice president for the university community. Boren knew that he had to take decisive action for black students, and he had to do it now.

But then, things got nutty.

As the day went on, more and more people began piping up about the SAE situation, and how and why it could happen. To most, these clean-cut young white guys singing a song about lynching felt like an aberration, a one-off that needed an explanation, like temporary insanity or psychosomatic blindness.

On MSNBC, *Morning Joe* co-host Mika Brzezinski implied that rap music in general, and the lyrics of performers like Waka Flocka Flame in particular, helped create the mindset that led the SAE members to sing about lynching black men. Flame, an Atlanta rapper, who had been scheduled to perform at the University of Oklahoma, was quoted from an Instagram post as saying that he was "disgusted and disappointed in SAE's actions."[15]

"When I first started doing shows it was all hood spots and all black people. Then I had some mainstream success and did some EDM [electronic dance music] and it was all white people at my shows for a while. Now it's white, black, and brown people at my shows. All races partying, having a good time, and enjoying themselves together peacefully. That's what Waka Flocka is all about. For that reason, I must say I'm disgusted and disappointed in the actions of the SAE fraternity at University of Oklahoma and I will be canceling my scheduled performance for them next month. Racism is something I will not tolerate."[16]

Apparently, this was a bridge too far for Brzezinski. Brzezinski read Flame's lyrics, which featured the word "nigger" numerous times, and concluded that Flame was a bad influence on the SAE members. Seemingly finding little difference between Flame's artistic expression and drunken white fraternity members singing the word "nigger," Brzezinski moralized, "He shouldn't be disgusted with them, he should be disgusted with himself."

Conservative commentator Bill Kristol—who, I'd like to remind you, helped bring America Dan Quayle, Sarah Palin, and the Iraq War—agreed with Brzezinski's assessment: "Popular culture's become a cesspool. A lot of corporations profit off it. And then people are surprised that some drunk 19-year-old kids repeat what they've been hearing."

"Exactly," agreed Brzezinski.

Morning Joe contributor Willie Geist tried to provide some rational perspective by saying, "I'd love to never hear that word again . . . but there is a distinction between a bunch of white kids chanting about hanging someone from a tree . . . and this is a term that you hear in hip-hop that African American guys sometimes in certain contexts call each other."[17]

This reaction isn't unusual. For many white commentators, while there's a need to combine a perfunctory disclaimer, "although I find the actions of these [white] students to be reprehensible . . . ," there's an equal need for a reflexive analysis that conflates a white racist action with a black so-called racist action. White cop kills an innocent black man? What about black-on-black crime? Bogus voter fraud allegations as an excuse for voter ID laws that affect blacks and minorities? What about the New Black Panther Party standing next to a polling station? In this case, that always-convenient whipping boy, hip-hop, was used when a false equivalence was needed. Hip-hop, that deep well of badness where all of society's pathologies are explained.

The statements above speak to how white privilege colors America's reaction to campus racist incidents. For Brzezinski and Kristol, the move to blame hip-hop is an unconscious nod to the idea that Rice and Pettit aren't really responsible for their actions. I mean, just *look* at them. With their khaki pants, nice grooming, and Colgate white smiles, they look like *my* kids. And these racist actions, in their minds, couldn't have come from a long tradition *within* white America. White privilege means that Brzezinski and most of the others on *Morning Joe* seemingly believed in the inherent goodness of Rice and Pettit and felt that they couldn't have committed a racist act without being influenced by some outside source. The racist action of singing about hanging "niggers from a tree" isn't something these two bright students should be crucified for; rather, it should be explained. So even when white college students act in a racist manner, black people are, in essence, still responsible for those actions.

The black victim thus gets victimized twice.

Of course, after Brzezinski left the set and felt the wrath of millions of African Americans reacting to the absurd comparison, she came back with a "clarification," saying that the "two students on the video are responsible . . ." and "in no way was anyone else responsible for what they did on that bus." Still, she called for a "conversation" on the "n-word" and its use in hip-hop.[18]

Okay.

Now that hip-hop had been properly blamed, the next move in the campus racism playbook was the heartfelt apology by the two OU students. Admittedly, no one wants to be thought of as a racist, even people who do racist acts, so it's logical that Pettit and Rice would hope to get from under the glare of the national spotlight and offer a sincere-sounding mea culpa to the public. But how those apologies were given speaks to how superficially we treat racism in this country.

Parker Rice, for his part, stayed out of the spotlight for his apology, just as he had since the release of the video. He issued an apology via a written statement, explaining that he wasn't offering any excuses . . . but then, of course, offered a series of excuses, like, "I admit it likely was fueled by alcohol consumed at the house before the bus trip . . ." and "Yes, the song was taught to us . . ."[19] With that, Rice disappeared from public view.

By contrast, Levi Pettit's highly choreographed media strategy included a nationally televised press conference. The mindset? Show your face, take responsibility for your actions, and then urge people to let you put your racist remarks behind you so you can move forward and get on with your life. But performing this apology properly required the time-honored tactic of obtaining some cover from the black community, in the form of cooperation from as many prominent African Americans, ministers, politicians, and students as possible. Fortunately, Pettit and his public relations team found someone willing to help him, someone who was even willing to orchestrate the press conference itself.

Enter Oklahoma state senator Anastasia A. Pittman.

Pittman, an Oklahoma City Democrat and chairwoman of the Oklahoma Black Caucus, turned out to be more than willing, in the words of rapper Common, "to extend a hand of love" to Pettit. And along with the usual cadre of local Oklahoma City black ministers, Pittman gently guided Pettit through the crisis. She arranged for him to meet privately with 25 OU students (none from OU Unheard, by the way) and local black ministers at the Fairview Baptist Church in Oklahoma City, where Pettit would presumably have that "race conversation." And then there was the press conference itself, which Pittman helped set up.

The problem? No one had asked Pittman to be the representative of forgiveness for black people. But none of that mattered, not to her, and not to Pettit. So there she stood with him.

"Let me start by saying that I am sorry, deeply sorry," Pettit said, looking directly at the camera. "I am so sorry for the pain I have caused, and I want all of you to know that directly from me. Although I don't deserve it, I ask for your forgiveness . . . Now, before I take a couple of your questions, let me just say this: All the apologies in the world won't change what I have done. So I will spend the rest of my life trying to be a person who heals and brings people of all races together. That is what I hope and pray will come out of this."[20]

If you were the average white American, you saw a young man who recognized that he'd made a mistake, wanted forgiveness, and wanted to move forward. After all, it was just a silly mistake. He sang a song he shouldn't have sung, and now he was promising to never sing it again. Move on, people, nothing to see here.

If you were African American, the optics was terrible.

As Pettit spoke, African American ministers stood behind him, with facial expressions that reeked of opportunism. And there was Pittman, right at Pettit's elbow, her arm intertwined with his, as if to say, "We're in this together." In fact, it *was* to say, "We're in it together." As Pettit spoke, the ministers periodically comforted him by patting him on the back. It was a perfect fraudulent scene of superficial racial healing.

After he finished, reporters asked him about how and where he learned the song, and Pettit deflected the question, saying, "I'm not here today to talk about where I learned the chant or how it was taught. I'm here to apologize for what I did."[21]

Of course he wasn't. He was there to say his piece and get the hell off the stage. And when he was asked about this incident during his post-graduation job interviews, he could point to this press conference as a sign of his humility and, ultimately, bravery. White privilege preserved for young Mr. Pettit.

Afterward, Pittman walked to the microphone and triumphantly declared that Pettit's apology represented "a wonderful time for us and our community" and that it showed "how a village can heal a child."[22]

A wonderful time. It was almost Monty Pythonesque in its ridiculousness, except the Monty Python actors would have stopped the press conference on account of it being too silly.

Yet, the *Dallas Morning News* opinion blogger Rudolph Bush was effusive in his praise of Senator Pittman, writing, "We need people like Pittman in our public life. We need leaders who are willing to unite us, who are willing to see past our mistakes and our differences to see that we can be something better than we are. And we need leaders who won't leap to every opportunity to point out how wrong the other guy is to show how right they can be."[23]

African American social commentator Earl Ofari Hutchinson also backed Pettit and Pittman, saying, "Despite the lambaste of him and the racial put downs and myopia of the detractors, this is an important step forward. Pettit did the right thing when he spoke out and so did the black leaders who stood behind him, encouraged and ultimately embraced him. For that, I applaud and will continue to applaud Pettit."[24]

Others, to say the least, were decidedly less pleased with Pettit's apology and Pittman's role in offering "forgiveness."

"I think what she did was primarily for publicity," said Chelsea Davis, a leader in OU Unheard. "She's up for re-election soon, and a lot of what she did was to get the white vote. In no way, shape, or form did she consult us about what she was doing . . . We were the catalyst for all of this happening. She did ask us to be at the press conference, and they never said what was going to happen, and I'm so glad that we didn't go, because the media has torn them apart. I don't think she was doing this in the best interests of the black community here at OU. The community [Pettit] should have been apologizing to was the OU community, and not the Oklahoma City community."[25]

"We do not get gold stars or extra credit for forgiving those who hate us," Kirsten West Savali wrote angrily for the African American website TheRoot.com. "Somebody lied. Our worth and our humanity shouldn't be inexplicably tied to our capacity to forgive. And our response to prejudice and bigotry should not be a carefully modulated tone. There has to be room for black rage, black frustration and black discontent if we are ever going to move forward as a country. If white tears were going to work, this racism thing would have been fixed a long time ago."[26]

From Facebook to the social media community on Twitter better known as "Black Twitter," African Americans savaged Pittman as being an "Uncle Tom," a "Mammie," and other derisive terms traditionally aimed at African Americans who are deemed to have sold out to white racists. And while it may be harsh to call Pittman an Uncle Tom, plenty of black people saw a lot of tomfoolery in her actions.

On Pittman's Facebook page, one commenter, under the pseudonym Troy Da Fisherman, wrote, "Your public acceptance of Levi Pettit's apology was very premature . . . If Levi Pettit wanted to apologize to you personally in a private setting and you chose to accept his apology would have been perfectly fine, but to host a press conference where you accept it was quite offensive."[27]

A poster identified as Sparkell Adams posted, "Have a seat Senator Anastasia and I can't believe all those black preachers and or so-called 'black state leaders' skinning and grinning to get their possible 15 mins of fame . . . Unbelievable!"[28]

In response, and as a way to start a "conversation," Senator Pittman asked her Facebook followers to send her stories about racial discrimination. One poster identified as Christopher Porter refused, "I want to say no to your offer Miss Pittman . . . Because you showed me that a white person can say and do whatever . . . So I'm good on that, because you don't really care no way."[29]

Just as Brzezinski tapped into her white privilege in order to provide an excuse for Rice and Pettit's actions, many African Americans recognized that Pittman had fallen into a classic white supremacist trap.

White racism needs willing black apologists to help show that racist acts are individualized, not systemic. Of the moment, not tied to anything from the past.

More importantly, Pettit used Pittman as a pressure valve, allowing white society to avoid confronting the realities of the situation, both for black students at the University of Oklahoma and in society in general. It's over, right? Move on. And by getting a prominent African American like Pittman to play along, the individual gets the bonus prize of being forever cleansed of the taint of being dubbed a racist, because didn't the black people standing behind him forgive him? Why are *you* still judging him? Ms. Pittman probably thinks she did the good thing, a Godly thing, but in truth, Pittman's coordination of an apology doesn't help eradicate racism. It only helps perpetuate it.

"Most [white] students here didn't think it was that big of a deal anyway," Davis recalled. "They didn't mean it, it was just a song. So I think everything she did that day did not help the situation at all. I think that it has limited the conversation, because as a white student, you see a black woman essentially saying, 'We stand behind [Pettit]. It's okay, let's move forward,' then the conversation stops because there's nothing left to talk about because he's apologized. Everything is handy dandy, and that's not what should have happened. I just really wished she'd consulted us, to get our thoughts, because we pretty much have been the spokespeople for the black community at OU since this happened."[30]

Pettit used Pittman's prominent position as a legislator to create the assumption that he was apologizing to all African Americans, with Pittman willingly playing the role of the "Magical Negro." The Magical Negro, an archetypal black character often seen in Hollywood films, typically redeems the flawed white protagonist, and in Oklahoma City that day, fantasy met reality. While her intentions may have been genuine, coming out of a Christian sense of love and redemption, Pittman still acted as an unwitting stooge in the latest campus racism incident and, as a result, helped grease the wheels for the next one.

Because if redemption is as easy as a carefully crafted apology with black faces nodding, who would ever learn that it's hard to come back from the act?

If history is our guide, no one ever does.

"What Senator Pittman did was show that white men can do things, and present this type of [racist] behavior, and all they have to do is say, 'Sorry' on camera, with five black pastors, the president of the black student association, and a black senator from the city, and it's okay . . . For us as a people, it does set us back," said Davis.

"It starts as a chant," Davis continued. "It starts as a song. Until someone's dead. So for them to say, 'Oh, he didn't mean to . . .' only lays the foundation for more things to happen, and more things to come. As we can see, they're still happening."[31]

As for the song itself, Sigma Alpha Epsilon would later admit that the chant hadn't been learned only within the University of Oklahoma chapter, but taught four years earlier during a six-day national leadership retreat. So this was a tradition learned by *multiple* SAE chapters. But despite being wrong about the chant having been only a University of Oklahoma SAE chapter tradition, the executive director of SAE, Blaine Ayers, nevertheless reassured the public that the *second* investigation "to date shows no evidence the song was widely shared across the broader organization."[32]

Still, Sigma Alpha Epsilon was trying to figure out how to limit the damage. And that meant contacting the last black member of the Oklahoma chapter of SAE, William James. "The head of their leadership school is actually an alumnus of Oklahoma Kappa [the Oklahoma SAE chapter], and he called to express his disappointment, because it's his chapter too . . . And so he was remorseful because it happened under his nose.

"Here's what they did," James continued. "They offered me a faculty spot in August at leadership school. I asked, 'What's the criteria?' Because there's an application process for it, and the deadline had already expired. And it was basically, 'We won't put any restrictions on what you do. You can come up with whatever you want.' And it felt to me very odd. Because why would I do this? What would I talk about? I can sit there and give them some speech, and some anecdotal story about how we can do this or that for the future, and me being the guy who happened to be the guy who was African American in the chapter where it happened, why would I do that?"[33]

Unlike state senator Pittman, James refused to be the show pony for SAE. "I felt like it was, 'If we bring you in here, and we get all of these photo op moments, then the face of the offense accepts our contrition, this is over.' There was no way I could do this. Any good I could do by speaking to the kids as a faculty member would be negated by what nationals could do with the photo op, and thus, providing them with an out. This stuff needs to be addressed. It's not going away, unless it goes away. It stays that way because no one wants to acknowledge that there are issues, because if you can sweep them under the rug, quickly, then it saves everyone the headache. As a business decision, that's the way to go, but as a cultural one, it's crushing."

James ultimately turned down SAE's invitation, and while he has not formally renounced his membership, he effectively thinks of himself as an ex-member. His fraternity brothers, the ones he grew to love while in the Oklahoma chapter, respect him enough to not give him the fraternity grip or sing hymns in his presence. They've even stopped introducing him to others as a fellow fraternity brother. And James is okay with that.

"I don't claim it, and I don't talk about it," James said.

• • •

As with most campus racist incidents involving mostly white fraternities and sororities, as the weeks went on, and other news events dominated the headlines, this episode began to fade from the public's consciousness. Just another incident to be forgotten . . . until the next one.

But one question persisted. How could white millennials, a so-called postracial generation who'd never experienced the separate-but-equal world of Jim Crow segregation, sing a song about "lynching a nigger from a tree?" Not just that song in particular, but any racist song full of imagery designed to dehumanize and humiliate African Americans? America thrives on the idea that each generation moves us that much closer to a nation without racism. But we can prove that when it comes to racism at colleges and universities, this theory is demonstratively untrue. Racism is as common at America's universities as pretty cheerleaders.

And while Rice and Pettit are to blame for their actions, it *is* unfair to believe they alone are responsible for campus racism. In fact, Rice and Pettit's act is reflective of how campus racism is normative, and not outlier, behavior. And each time we come up with simplistic solutions for white racist behavior like "We must teach children not to be racist," or "These guys said something racist, but they didn't mean it this way," we fail to realize that getting rid of racism isn't as simple as wishing it away.

You can't just hope each generation of white students gets more sensitive to racism, because as we see with campus racism, it's just not true. Campus racism is the visible tumor on that American social cancer that is systemic white racism. And despite many well-intended attempts to the contrary, this societal cancer has been in America's university bloodstream for over a century.

Rice and Pettit are just the ones who got caught this time. But the circumstances under which they got caught, as members of a mostly white fraternity system, says a lot about how campus racism is propagated and perpetuated. And more importantly, why it's not being addressed effectively.

• • •

To talk about campus racism, we're going to start in post–World War II America and the optimism that democracy could be the savior of the world. For African Americans, democracy was a half-promise. Jim Crow was the law of the land, and the hope was that change would happen after the war. During World War II, African American newspapers took the "V for Victory" slogan used by the Allied nations in their fight against the fascist powers of Germany, Japan, and Italy, and transformed it into the "Double V" campaign. The Double V, meaning Victory Abroad and Victory at Home, postulated that if the United States could make the world safe for democracy abroad, then it should be able to do the same on the domestic front after the war. This was the African American dream of racial barriers being knocked down, of access to all of society being the norm in postwar America.

After the surrender of Germany and Japan, however, the reality was that separate-but-equal Jim Crow laws were still the law of the nation, whether de facto in the American South, or de jure in the rest of the nation. Slowly but surely, though, the nation was changing. Jackie Robinson broke the color barrier in baseball in 1947, when general manager Branch Rickey brought him to play for the Brooklyn Dodgers. In 1948 President Truman issued Executive Order 9981, desegregating the armed forces. And some colleges and universities thought about their own campuses. How could they be progressive and help create an America where integration, and not segregation, was the norm? On their own campuses, what would be the best method to get students of all races to interact? The university administrations soon turned their attention to the most segregated segment of their student bodies and the most resistant to change: white fraternities and sororities.

The history of white fraternities and sororities begins prior to the Civil War, with the establishment of literary societies like the Phi Beta Kappa Society at William and Mary and the Skull and Bones society at Yale, formed in the late eighteenth and early nineteenth centuries, respectively. Designed to be spaces where white male students could debate the issues of the day, literary societies gradually turned into social fraternities, where the focus turned from literary pursuits to fellowship and brotherhood for white Christian men. They became very popular, spreading from Union College in the early nineteenth century, and establishing chapters throughout the country.[34]

As America recovered from the destruction of the Civil War, fraternities and sororities were initially devastated by the huge loss of men killed during the war, but they flourished anew as white men beyond the ranks of the elite began attending college. And as white women started attending colleges in greater numbers, women's fraternities, or what would later be called sororities, flourished as well. As a matter of rule, fraternities and sororities in the nineteenth century were almost exclusively white and Protestant. But going into the twentieth century, as African Americans became a larger presence on predominately white campuses, white fraternities and sororities needed added protections to keep their organizations racially pure, which necessitated the need for "white only" or "Aryan only" clauses.[35]

African Americans, for their part, had been attending American colleges, particularly in the Midwest and Northeast, in sporadic numbers since the late-eighteenth century. In 1799 the Presbyterian minister John Chavis became the first black to attend what is now Washington & Lee. Middlebury College, in Vermont, awarded an honorary masters degree to Lemuel Haynes, a prominent black religious leader and anti-slavery advocate, in 1804. Nearly twenty years later, in 1823, Alexander Lucius Twilight would be the first African American to graduate from college in the United States.[36] And over the next decade, a handful of black students would graduate from Northeastern schools like Amherst College, in Massachusetts, Bowdoin College, in Maine, and Dartmouth College, in New Hampshire. Most of these schools were willing to make exceptions for the occasional black student who showed promise, but it wasn't until 1833 that a school made it policy to not discriminate against blacks.

Oberlin College, in Ohio, declared from its founding that it was to serve both whites and blacks. George B. Vashon, in 1844, would become its first black graduate. Vashon would later go on to be a founding professor at the historically black Howard University. Also at Oberlin, in 1850 Lucy Ann Stanton would go on to be the first black woman to graduate from a college, even though she wasn't given a bachelor's degree.[37] And in 1855, Berea College, in Kentucky, became the first interracial college south of the Mason-Dixon line.[38]

However, the backlash against the presence of African American college students began around the same time. In 1850 Harvard admitted three black students to its medical school but had to rescind the admissions after white students protested. It was a precursor of campus racism to come.[39]

The end of the Civil War meant the theoretical end of the restrictions on education for blacks, especially in the old Confederacy, as colleges tied the mission of creating an educated African American elite with the ultimate uplift of the African American race. Fisk, Howard, Morehouse, and Hampton joined Wilberforce and Lincoln universities as black schools meant to educate black students. And while thousands of blacks were educated in these newly formed black institutions, many others attended PWIs, particularly Northeastern Ivy League institutions.

In 1870, twenty years after rescinding their admission to three black students, Harvard graduated its first black student, Richard Theodore Greener, who would later become a faculty member at the University of South Carolina, the first black to get a position there. Later, Greener would become the dean of the Howard School of Law.[40]

Through the latter part of the nineteenth century and the early twentieth century, African American students flooded historically black colleges and universities and peppered the predominately white universities of the West, Midwest, and East (Jim Crow laws excluded them from schools located below the Mason-Dixon line). However, African American students' being allowed into these northern schools didn't mean that they felt welcome. Black and white social interaction on campuses was generally restricted, with many white students protesting over being forced to eat and live with black students.

For a study undertaken in 1909 by W. E. B. Du Bois and Atlanta University, *The College-bred Negro American,* Du Bois sent a survey to predominately white colleges and universities throughout the country, asking them whether or not they had admitted black students and, if so, how those black students had been treated on campus. The schools broke down into two camps: those that couldn't foresee having black students on their campuses because of the backlash from white students, and those nominally integrated schools that felt their black students were treated just like white students. The replies were telling. The first came from Princeton: "Princeton University has never had any graduates of Negro descent."[41]

It isn't altogether surprising that Princeton hadn't admitted any black students, as it had long ago earned its reputation as the Ivy League school for the white southern aristocracy. Virginian Woodrow Wilson had been the president of Princeton before ascending to the U.S. presidency, and only five years after Princeton announced that it had never graduated any blacks, President Wilson declared after a private screening of the Ku Klux Klan–glorifying film *Birth of a Nation,* "It is like writing history with lightning, and my only regret is that it is all so terribly true."[42] Along with President Wilson's allowing the federal government to be segregated, this should provide an insight into how Wilson viewed African Americans who wanted to attend Princeton.

And Princeton was by no means alone. St. Vincent College in Pennsylvania replied, "I cannot tell what the attitude of the student body should be towards Negroes, but we shall not risk a trial of it. Applications are very rare—one during the last four years. We do not think it wise here under the prevailing conditions to accept any distinctively colored students into the college."[43]

Carleton College of Missouri was even more blunt. "We have never had any Negro or any person with Negro blood graduate from Carleton

College in its history. I have not found a student in the state that would tolerate a Negro in the college. And it is even worse since the Johnson-Jeffries fight."[44]

The respondent from Carleton College was referring to African American heavyweight boxer Jack Johnson's defeat of the previously unbeaten Jim Jeffries, aka the "Great White Hope," in 1910. Before the fight, the *New York Times* had declared, "If the black man wins, thousands and thousands of his ignorant brothers will misinterpret his victory as justifying claims to much more than mere physical equality with their white neighbors." Johnson's victory sparked white race riots throughout the country as whites felt humiliated by the loss.[45]

Conversely, there were other white schools that felt they treated their African American students fairly. Union College in Nebraska: "We have had several Negro students in the past and accept them in our school at the present time. As far as we are able to judge there has not been much distinction made among our students between the Negro students and the others. It depends very largely upon the student himself how he is received by the student body."

Simpson College in Iowa: "The sentiment of the students seems to be along the line of being willing to help these students in any way possible and, of course, we are far enough North so that race prejudice is not very manifest."

Occidental College in California: "So far as I know a Negro applying for admission would receive a cordial welcome from the student body. We have Japanese, Koreans and Chinese, and there is no race prejudice in this school so far as I know. The question has never been raised."

The University of Nebraska: "We have had a number of Negro graduates and so far as I know the general student body feels very kindly towards them and towards our Negro undergraduates. On commencement days a Negro usually receives a little more applause than a white boy when he walks over the stage. I presume some things happen in his personal relations with his fellow students that are not entirely pleasant, but they never come to the surface. I doubt if there is a school in the country which is freer from race prejudice than the University of Nebraska."[46]

And that's how many white colleges liked to see themselves in relation to black students: either as spaces from which black students were excluded or utopias where black students were judged by the content of their character and without prejudice to the color of their skin. It's important to note that white students were never expected to change their attitudes about race; instead, the black student was expected to conform to the standards of the university and assimilate to the norms of the white student body. That meant not making waves when it came to the social norms of the day; assimilate or leave the school.

In 1923, long past its days of rejecting black students, Harvard considered itself liberal and progressive because it declared that in the rules for admission, "Harvard College maintains its traditional policy of freedom from discrimination on the grounds of race or religion."[47]

But when it came to the idea of black and white students eating and living together, well, that was another thing altogether. The Harvard Board of Directors voted that "men of the white and colored races shall not be compelled to live and eat together, nor shall any man be excluded by reasons of his color."[48] The classic concession to white racism, made by those declaring that they are not bound by it. This is a regular tactic of colleges and universities, where the idea of conceding fully to the demands of African Americans is generally frowned upon, even to this day. As a result, universities try to give the appearance of change without actually changing, acting as though the compromise is designed to leave everyone happy. But the real-life impact of such rules meant that black Harvard students had to find boarding houses in town that accepted African Americans.

Earlier, in 1906, at Cornell University, the founding members of the first African American fraternity, Alpha Phi Alpha, found themselves in a similar situation, renting space in boarding rooms open to blacks in Ithaca, New York. And Kappa Alpha Psi fraternity founding members at Indiana University noted the discrimination black students felt both on the campus and in the town. Kappa Alpha Psi, the second black fraternity, founded in 1911, was originally named Kappa Alpha Nu. But because of white students' calling them "Kappa Alpha Nig," the members decided to change to Kappa Alpha Psi.[49]

The nine African American fraternities and sororities were formed at both white and black colleges: Alpha Phi Alpha Fraternity at Cornell in 1906, Alpha Kappa Alpha Sorority at Howard University in 1908, Kappa Alpha Psi Fraternity at Indiana University in 1911, Omega Psi Phi Fraternity at Howard University in 1911, Delta Sigma Theta at Howard University in 1913, Phi Beta Sigma Fraternity at Howard University in 1914, Zeta Phi Beta Sorority at Howard University in 1920, Sigma Gamma Rho Sorority at Butler University in 1922, and, decades later, the ninth organization, Iota Phi Theta at Morgan State in 1963.[50]

As for the establishment of African American fraternities and sororities, it would be a mistake to think that they were formed in the early twentieth century simply because black students were excluded from white fraternities and sororities. Those founded on white campuses were formed because of the hostility blacks felt from white college students at the time *and* the desire to create Greek-lettered organizations that reflected their own African American history and culture. Black spaces on white campuses.

The founders of Sigma Gamma Rho Sorority, a group of teachers, also faced racism on the campus of Butler University. Since its founding, in 1855, Butler had been open to African American applicants; however, at least one Board of Regents member supported the KKK. The school itself practiced de facto segregation in numerous ways. In 1927 the university adopted a quota system that admitted only ten African American students annually. As a result, the university's black enrollment declined from seventy-four in the 1926–27 school year to fifty-eight, including nine entering freshmen. In 1925 the university yearbook, the *Drift*, placed photos of black graduating seniors in the back of the book, away from the alphabetical listing and pictures highlighting other seniors. These realities suggest that African Americans on the campus were met with a degree of hostility.[51]

So the general campus racism that touched all African Americans was simply well organized when it came to white fraternities and sororities. It was in these organizations that Jim Crow was enforced to maximum effect.

After World War II, universities were flooded with ex-GI's who were flocking to fraternities. While many white fraternities and sororities struggled during the pre–World War II Great Depression, with closed chapters and waning interest, from 1946 to 1956 the number of national fraternity chapters jumped from 2,600 to 3,500, with undergraduate memberships up 60 percent, making the total number of Greek men in the United States greater than two hundred thousand.[52]

By 1946 the Greek system had solidified around strict segregation lines, with blacks almost exclusively joining black fraternities and sororities and whites joining white fraternities and sororities. In fact, white fraternities and sororities tried their best to exclude *other* whites, including Catholics, Jews, and non-Christians. Most included in their constitutions restriction clauses for membership, including Phi Delta Theta, founded in 1912, which required that "only white persons of full Aryan blood, not less than sixteen years of age, should be eligible." Others specified that students had to be "Christian Caucasians" while banning "the black, Malay, Mongolian or Semitic races."[53]

Later, in 1953, Phi Delta Theta would suspend its Williams College chapter for pledging "non-Aryans." This caused such a blowback that Phi Delta Theta was forced to change its "full Aryan blood" constitutional clause to "socially acceptable." But the suspension against the Williams chapter stood.[54]

However, the growing numbers of African American, Jewish, and other minority college students, along with mandates from universities, meant that white fraternities and sororities increasingly felt the pressure to integrate their ranks. There were some success stories, with Dartmouth College's Interfraternity Council leading the way toward integrating all-white fraternity and sorority chapters. And in 1949 Elmer W. Henderson, the director of the American Council on Human Rights, a coalition of seven black fraternities and sororities, urged the National Interfraternity Conference, the umbrella organization for white fraternities, to end their racial restrictions. In a letter to the NIC's chairman, Judge Frank H. Myers, an associate judge of the Municipal Court in Washington, D.C., Henderson wrote: "We feel that a racial bar in an organization which owes its existence to a community of interest among college and university students is an anachronism which cannot possibly be reconciled with the great aims and purposes of higher education in America."[55]

Henderson, a major civil rights attorney and a member of the African American Kappa Alpha Psi fraternity, was responsible for integrating black workers in wartime industries, and his successful lawsuit against the Southern Railroad's Jim Crow accommodations was an early victory against the principle of separate but equal.[56] He concluded his letter by asking: "Can we expect those among us less advantaged to progressively do away with their racial or religious prejudices if those educationally advantaged cannot do away with their own?"[57]

There is no record of whether Judge Myers responded to Henderson, but earlier in the year Myers, a member of Kappa Alpha Order, the white fraternity that considers Robert E. Lee its spiritual founder, attended an interfraternity conference where he noted that he was "opposed to any type of 'Hell' Week," and that fraternities needed to improve their scholarship. But he said nothing about the integration of the all-white fraternities and sororities.[58]

Judge Myers wasn't alone in his ambivalence to racial integration. Most white fraternities and sororities weren't happy about these calls to integrate, and the resistance to integration became particularly fierce, and overt, as universities demanded that the organizations integrate or be disbanded on their campuses. In 1954 L. G. Balfour, the past president of Sigma Chi and the leading manufacturer of fraternity and sorority jewelry, thought that if the colleges required the fraternities to stop discriminating, it would lead fraternities "involuntarily into regimentation and control." At the time, Sigma Chi restricted its membership to white male Christians.[59]

Balfour and sixty-one other white fraternity officials met in 1954 to discuss their plan of action against universities pressing for their chapters to integrate. The plan? A resolution that said "that various institutions apparently contemplate restricting the traditional freedom of fraternities to choose their own members . . . a more unified action, as the withdrawal of all charters at an institution, may be necessary or desirable as a means of self-preservation."[60]

But four months later *The Teke,* published by one of the NIC's largest members, Tau Kappa Epsilon, strongly protested against such a boycott: "For the NIC fraternities now to boycott colleges frowning on discriminatory clauses could have only one result—suicide of the fraternities participating in such action. It is hoped that the pitfalls of such unwise procedure will be recognized before it is too late."[61]

As it turns out, 1954 would prove to be a pivotal year in America's fight for integration. The landmark U.S. Supreme Court decision *Brown vs. the Board of Education* would declare the concept of "separate but equal" to be unconstitutional in public education, effectively overturning the Jim Crow laws supported by the 1896 decision in *Plessy vs. Ferguson.* And feeling the tide turning against them, white fraternities and sororities would do their best to appear to be inclusive without actually being so. The official policy of the National Interfraternity Conference was that each organization was autonomous and therefore had the right to change or modify its constitution as it saw fit. Yet the organization's opposition to integration of its ranks was as solid as ever. "Elimination of 'clauses' is only the beginning. Next in line is a system of quotas, whereby you prove your purity and adherence to a new social order, all in the name of freedom!" Phi Kappa Psi fraternity president W. Lyle Jones said in 1957.[62]

Despite the fierce opposition, colleges continued to insist that white fraternities and sororities integrate or risk losing their privileges on campus, with penalties for refusal ranging from expulsion from university-owned housing to the decision not to recognize their chapters. Still, the national offices of fraternities and sororities fought tooth and nail to keep their chapters white. The National Interfraternity Conference unsuccessfully sued the College of New York in the early 1950s over their efforts to desegregate fraternities and sororities. Meanwhile, local chapters sometimes tried to defy their organizations by pledging black students.

Thomas Gibbs, a young African American student at Amherst College, was asked to pledge the up-to-then all-white chapter of Phi Kappa Psi in 1948. His membership became a cause célèbre, with the *New York Times* devoting six news items and an editorial to his case. Gibbs, who was a member of the Amherst Student Council and the Freshman Orientation Committee, had originally pledged and then depledged once the national organization of Phi Kappa Psi said that they hadn't been given the proper amount of time to evaluate Gibbs' application.

But the Amherst chapter was under the impression that if they gave all of the Phi Kappa Psi chapters proper notice, they would repledge Gibbs, which the Amherst chapter decided to do on its own. The national office of Phi Kappa Psi then gave an ultimatum, stating that it would revoke the charter of the Amherst chapter because of "unfraternal conduct," unless the white students rejected the future theologian. The students rejected that ultimatum and a year later formed their own nondiscriminating local fraternity, Phi Alpha Psi, as a result.[63]

Alfred Rogers, an African American student at the University of Connecticut, is thought to have become the first black to integrate a white fraternity when Phi Epsilon Pi accepted him in 1950. A predominately

Jewish fraternity, Phi Epsilon Pi initially rejected Rogers on account of his color. But they eventually relented when the Connecticut chapter protested and threatened to secede from the national organization.

"The experience with Phi Epsilon Pi was an example of a team of committed Americans who were determined to strike a blow to intolerance and bigotry on their watch," Rogers told a University of Connecticut audience in 2006. "But the lessons I brought away from it were: You can never judge a man by the color of his skin and if you want to achieve something, make a plan, establish objectives, analyze resources, establish strategies and give it your best shot."[64]

In general the 1950s and 1960s were a period of very little successful integration into white fraternities and sororities. Even as the civil rights movement swept the country, local white fraternity chapters would attempt to pledge black students, only to have their national organizations almost universally reject them.

In the early 1960s, while a member of Sigma Nu fraternity and president of the University of Mississippi Interfraternity Council, future Senate majority leader Trent Lott would lead the fight to keep Sigma Nu all white. "He was the leader of his chapter and a very strong voice in the national fraternity," said Tom Johnson, former president of CNN and fellow Sigma Nu member at the University of Georgia at the time. He voted with Lott and later regretted it. "He certainly took a major role in leading the opposition to integration."[65]

On the other hand, there were outliers when it came to having clauses against pledging nonwhites. Tau Kappa Epsilon fraternity, the fraternity of Ronald Reagan, bucked the restrictive-clause trend and encouraged ethnically diverse chapters. TKE never had an exclusionary clause, either written or unwritten, at any time during its existence.[66] But this didn't mean that TKE was immune to racism, as we'll see later.

After the passage of the landmark 1964 Civil Rights Act and the federal government's threat to cut off funds to universities unless fraternities and sororities stopped discriminating, white fraternities and sororities tried to hide their discrimination by removing clauses forbidding "non-Aryans," instead requiring chapters to submit pictures of potential pledges. This allowed them to use a visual test to pick out the "non-Aryans."[67]

On the converse side, white students began joining African American fraternities and sororities in the 1940s, 1950s, and 1960s. Like white fraternities and sororities, most African American fraternities and sororities had their own exclusionary racial clauses in their constitutions, limiting membership to black students. But by 1945 most had begun eliminating those clauses and pledging white members.

Dr. Bernard Levin, then a 22-year-old Chicago native, pledged Alpha Phi Alpha at the University of Chicago in 1946 and would be the first nonblack member of the fraternity. Levin was featured in the African American magazine *Ebony,* which showed him as a pledge, polishing the shoes of his Alpha big brothers. In a world of overt white supremacy, in which a large portion of the African American working class held jobs in which being subservient to whites was a way of life, the image of a subservient white pledge—who in reality was doing the same task as any black fraternity pledge—had to be a satisfying role reversal to *Ebony* magazine's black readers.[68]

As the civil rights movement continued to grow, African American fraternities and sororities began taking a leading role, participating in sit-ins, marches, and campus demonstrations, all the while attracting more and more white students. In the words of Levin, "The other fraternities had nothing to offer except social affairs. Thus, Alpha was the only logical choice for a fraternity."[69]

Joan T. Mulholland, a white Virginian transfer from Duke University to the all-black Tougaloo College in Mississippi, became a member of the African American sorority Delta Sigma Theta in 1962, attracted by the activism of the Deltas. Mulholland went on to become a prominent Freedom Rider during the civil rights movement, working to integrate the interstate bus system, and is still active in Delta today.[70]

The battle to integrate predominately white fraternities and sororities continued through the next fifty years. In the late 1950s, a fraternity member at the University of Virginia was heard to say, "The only way a black man will ever get in this house is if he's a bartender or plays in a jazz band."[71] But eventually, the national organizations of predominately white fraternities and sororities dropped their racial clauses, sometimes under the threat of being made to vacate university-owned housing, as President Boren ordered the SAE to do after the video surfaced. Many fraternities and sororities actually made diversity a goal, at least in theory, and began adding small numbers of black students and other minorities to their ranks. Yet their membership always remained predominately white, and the struggles to integrate their ranks is still a steep one. And nothing illustrates that like Greek life at the University of Alabama, where the conspiracy to keep white fraternities and sororities as white as possible is a well-oiled machine.

On some campuses in America, things haven't changed one bit since the 1950s.

2

THE MACHINE

"White supremacy is the conscious or unconscious belief or the investment in the inherent superiority of some, while others are believed to be innately inferior. And it doesn't demand the individual participation of the singular bigot. It is a machine operating in perpetuity, because it doesn't demand that somebody be in place driving."[1]

—Professor Michael Eric Dyson

REMEMBER WHEN I SAID THAT RACISM HAS A WAY OF MAKING black people feel like they're crazy? As if there's an ongoing racist conspiracy that black people can see and feel, and yet when they turn around and tell white people about it, white people look at them as if they're paranoid? And because racism is as much an unseen as a seen phenomenon, it's sometimes difficult for black folks to point at something and say, "Here's the racism. See?" and have people recognize it. But at the University of Alabama, we may have found the one place in America where even white racism deniers will say, "Yeah, you just might have a point."

According to Cornell University, only 2 percent of America's population is involved in fraternities, yet 80 percent of Fortune 500 executives, 76 percent of U.S. senators and congressmen, 85 percent of

Supreme Court justices, and all but two presidents since 1825 have been fraternity men.[2] To have influence that extensive, you need to have a Greek organization that starts on the undergraduate level and then operates as a powerful network once you've graduated. And at the University of Alabama, that organization is known informally as the Machine.

With more than 8,600 members, the Greek system at the University of Alabama is the largest in the country. The Machine is a coalition of twenty-eight white fraternities and sororities that uses its collective power to run the University of Alabama student government, determine which monies go to which campus activities . . . and sometimes influence matters off-campus.[3] It's one of those college organizations that purposely live in the background. Unseen, rumored about, but rarely acknowledged publicly, the Machine keeps its core operations known only to the small cadre of those comprising its inner circle. The idea behind the Machine, as with the infamous secret fraternity at Yale, Skull and Bones, is that a strict discipline forbidding discussion of its very existence is the key to effectiveness—then no one is encouraged to poke around and see what you're actually doing. Let them be curious about you, but wield your power in silence as needed. Where the Machine does its most effective work is in campus politics. And it has been wielding that political power for nearly a century.

According to a 1992 *Esquire* magazine article, the Machine started in the nineteenth century as a chapter of the Theta Nu Epsilon fraternity, which "believed that secrecy guaranteed selfless leadership." Today it acts as the political arm for a coalition of white fraternities and sororities on campus.[4] Most of what we know about the Machine is shrouded in mystery, rumor, innuendo, and some great reporting by the University of Alabama student newspaper, the *Crimson White*.

In 1989 the Machine put out a pamphlet that stated, "One standard we base our membership on is the future usefulness of newcomers to our union and its members. We are proud of our history at the

University. Theta Nu Epsilon has elected an SGA [Student Government Association] president 68 times in the 75 years of the SGA's existence. This is because the SGA is ours. Our brethren formed it in 1914."[5]

In 1928 an open letter from William J. Cabaniss to the *Crimson White* first named the coalition of sororities and fraternities a "political machine" for its efficiency in dominating campus politics. Cabaniss, whose son would go on to be ambassador to the Czech Republic under President George W. Bush, warned that because "this organization and some of the things it has promulgated [are] unfair and subversive of the best interests of the students, we call upon all members or former members to give all aid in their power . . . to expose and eliminate such vicious and unfair political practices from this University."[6]

It is that subversive nature, closely resembling white privilege in the larger society, codified through white fraternity and sorority membership, that is the foundation of the Machine. So much so that in 2001, *USA Today* noted, "'The Machine' is the linear successor to [former Alabama governor George Wallace], who proclaimed during his 1963 inaugural address: 'Segregation now, segregation tomorrow, segregation forever.'" It is that Wallace "stand in the schoolhouse door" racial legacy that hangs over everything at the University of Alabama and stunts the progress that many if not most students want to see.[7]

The Machine has been termed "a farm club system where those who aspire to public service or politics get their training." Many of the Machine's former members are now important members of Alabama's political hierarchy. People like Alabama senator Richard Shelby, congressmen Jack Edwards, Walter Flowers, Carl Elliott, Albert Rains, and William Dickinson have been rumored to have been members of the Machine, as are prominent members of Alabama's top law firms.[8]

As one former member of a Machine-affiliated sorority explained to the *Crimson White,* "The goal is to run campus politics, but the real reason they want to run campus politics is so they themselves can run politics in Alabama."[9]

In 2011 the *Crimson White* published an exposé of the Machine, confirming that the organization controls twenty-eight white Greek houses through two house representatives each, one older and one younger. The houses fund the Machine through a fee of $875 each semester. Some of the money goes toward paying the bar tabs of Machine representatives, supporting Machine-backed candidates, and funding an annual beach party.[10]

The Machine has an internal structure that replicates a typical fraternal organization, with an executive board that includes a president, vice president, and treasurer. Potential nominees for student government are brought to the Machine for possible endorsement; the Machine then makes decisions on whom to secretly endorse for SGA offices, often supporting the candidates with campaign funds.[11]

David Wilson, a former SGA vice president for student affairs and a member of Phi Gamma Delta fraternity who eventually turned against the Machine, recalled in an interview how he was given money as a freshman for his first campaign: "I received 50 dollars for my senate campaign. [It was] delivered in an envelope, cash. My Machine rep gave it to me . . . and I knew who it was from. It said 'David Wilson, Phi Gamma Delta' on there."

Wilson said that he'd seen early on the way the Machine operated and didn't think it was right. "I always told myself, what I'll do is I will become SGA president, work with the Machine, change the Machine internally and try to get them to follow me and then speak out against it when I'm done."[12]

What Wilson failed to understand was that being resistant, even hostile, to change is one of the tenets of the Machine. The goal is to control as much of the campus as possible, by being as conservative as possible.

Like most university property leased by white Greeks for their fraternity and sorority houses, the properties at the University of Alabama are deeply subsidized. Back in 2001 *The Journal of Blacks in Higher Education* detailed how the state of Alabama rents prime real estate in the middle of the university campus to segregated fraternity and sorority houses for a token fee of $100 per year. Estimates of the fair market rental value of this real estate are $600,000 annually.[13]

Because these predominately white fraternity and sorority houses are on university land, the state also pays for maintaining the grounds surrounding them. And because the fraternities and sororities belong to the Interfraternity Council, a student organization that has free office space on campus, they have access to free secretarial services, office supplies, and administrative support.

According to estimates of officials at the University of Alabama in 2001, at least $50 of each student's comprehensive annual fee went to supporting the racially segregated fraternity system.[14]

"They'd come to the house saying, 'Voting's coming up. Yes, we're part of the Machine. The rumors are true,'" Melanie Gotz, a member of Alpha Gamma Delta sorority, remembered. "You know, they would kind of make it like a funny thing. This was before I hated everything about them. 'So tonight at voting, candidate is so-and-so, and so he's a really great guy, or she's a really great girl.' And they'd give a little background on her, and be like, 'And we're doing this.' Blah, blah, blah, and that was it. For me, either way, it didn't make a big deal because I didn't know anything about the candidates, so I was like, 'Alright, cool. Friend of a friend.'"[15]

"They have the executive board . . . president, vice president, treasurer, etc., and have two representatives from each house, an older one and a younger one," Wilson told the *Crimson White*. "The older one is the one that gets to make a choice and gets to say, 'This is who I support.' The younger one can make a case for people, but when it comes to questions of who you want for SGA president [or] who you want for homecoming queen, the older one is the only one who decides. Each house gets one vote."[16]

The Machine is good at what it does, in part because of the strict discipline it enforces among its members. It has been known to assess fines of $25 to $50 per member for not voting and, in particular, not voting along the Machine party line. When one sorority member tried to vote for an independent SGA candidate, her fellow members tried to get her pin taken away.[17]

Back in 1992 a Machine opponent, Chuck Hess, noted, "Vans hired by the Machine take voters to the polls. Someone sticks a beer in your hand and says, 'These are the people you're supposed to vote for.' At least we have gotten them to remove the kegs from the vans." And is the Machine effective? One year an independent student ran for SGA president, and even though he lost a close election, the Machine was so angered that it organized a boycott of the student's father's pizza shop, causing it to go out of business.[18]

As a result of the Machine's activities, students who aren't part of the Greek system, black or white, have had a difficult time fully participating in the administration of student life. Often their voices are drowned out by the sheer enormity of the Machine's bloc voting and power. But not always.

For example, the Machine assumed that the position of campus homecoming queen would always be held by a white sorority member, until two black women won the position in the mid-1980s. To prevent this from happening in the future, the Machine backed Bill 25, which was, ironically, an SGA bill designed to break up bloc voting, the Machine's main weapon. The bill was so odious that the *Crimson White* dubbed it "The Negro Queen Exclusion Act."[19]

But the Machine has been blamed for more than bloc voting. When things haven't gone their way, particularly around elections, it has been rumored that the Machine will go to more extreme measures, especially against black students.

Back in 1976, Cleo Thomas became the first black independent candidate to win the SGA presidency, by organizing a coalition of blacks, independents, and, ironically enough, white sorority members.

"The university was responding to larger forces around it at the time, and there was, really, this spirit of inclusion," Thomas remembered in a 2006 article for *Tuscaloosa* magazine. "Certainly, the African-American students themselves were deeply interested in claiming the university as their own. During my four years there, at least two of the homecoming queens were black, and I remember one of those years, my sister was in the homecoming court.

"That whole sense of 'our university' was that it was our university. That coupled with that zeitgeist and the spirit of the age to which I refer, I think, led to the level of participation and the level of success that students had at that time."[20]

At the time when Thomas was at the University of Alabama, white sororities hadn't been added to the Machine yet, although they would be soon afterward. Apparently, the Machine quickly learned that sexism could mean lost elections, so why not co-opt their natural allies?

Thomas went on to graduate with honors in 1977 from the University of Alabama and then attend the University of Oxford, where he received an advanced degree in philosophy, politics, and economics. He also earned a law degree from Harvard and was appointed to the University of Alabama board of trustees at the unusually young age of twenty-seven. But before all that, soon after his SGA election, an eight-foot-tall cross was burned in front of the Kappa Kappa Gamma sorority house, presumably to display displeasure for their support of the black student.

"Climbing the mountain to beat the Machine was high enough, adding more feet of elevation to it with thought of race and all of that would have just been too much. I never thought much about the racial aspect of it. I was always trying to come up with a winning strategy to beat the Machine. Who needed the further complication of race . . . After the election . . . somebody burned a cross, which was almost a benign act of terror. It was so uncreative . . . at least to me."[21]

While Thomas was able to brush aside the cross burning as being almost cliché, that didn't stop the acts of intimidation. In 1999 another black SGA candidate, Fabien Zinga, received death threats he suspected were related to the Machine, and his campaign ads were marred with racist graffiti. A student from the Republic of the Congo, Zinga received anonymous phone calls from a male who Zinga recalled saying, "We are going to hang you from a tree."[22]

The key to winning elections wasn't just getting voters to the polls but keeping non-Machine candidates from even getting a chance to win a vote. In 2002 the Machine held an important pre-election cookout under the innocuous name *Students for a Better SGA* and invited candidates to speak . . . except for Mario Bailey, the independent black candidate, who wasn't allowed to participate.[23]

But from time to time, a non-Machine candidate *has* figured out a way to win. In 2015 Elliot Spillers, an independent candidate for SGA president, became only the second African American to win the job. He succeeded by forming a coalition of independents and African Americans, while also gaining the support of some Machine Greek houses. He won by over 2,000 votes, the largest margin in SGA history.

"It was a very positive campaign, no backhanded deals, all out in the open," Spillers said, who credits being a military brat for his ability to build coalitions across all lines. "It was a unifying campaign."[24]

Like all other independents who somehow got past the Machine, he faces fierce opposition to all of his moves. For example, his first two nominations for chief of staff were shot down by the Machine, which then attempted to push through its *own* chief of staff appointment for Spillers. Eventually, Spillers got his way, but it's been a struggle.

"I now have a greater appreciation for the job President Obama does," Spillers said with a laugh.

For Spillers, the Machine is an organization stuck in time, as the rest of the University of Alabama progresses as an international university, not just a relic of the George Wallace–era South. But he still thinks he'll be able to work with the Machine, even as it obstructs his every move.

"I'm willing to work with them, but not for them," he told Al.com. "I've always said this, but not everyone in the Machine is the same. But there is that small minority in there who want to keep this campus the way it's been for the past 40 years."[25]

"It is the training ground for what we suffer now," Thomas, UA's first black SGA president, said about the Machine after Spillers' election. "What we learn here, at the University of Alabama, affects how we govern Alabama. It is predictive, it is a forecast. It is more than just child's play."[26]

And just to show that it isn't playing, the Machine has demonstrated that its influence doesn't end at the campus' gates. In 2013 the Machine injected itself into the local Tuscaloosa school board elections by endorsing two candidates, former Machine members, offering sorority members free drinks at local bars and limo trips to the polls to encourage them to vote for the Machine-backed candidates.

"They would really appreciate/need your vote to win this election," a sorority stated in an email to its members. "It's going to be really tight, and it is SO IMPORTANT that they get the Greek Vote. I told both of them that I would do my best to make sure that I got every Chi O that was registered to the polls. There is a big incentive for you going as well!!"[27]

The sorority said that it had rented out a local bar, and that anyone who showed up with an "I Voted" sticker would get one free drink. The Machine was successful, as both candidates won by slim margins, even though local television station WVUA uncovered potential voter fraud when it investigated one fraternity house that ten members listed as their residence, despite the fact that "they didn't live there."[28]

Paul Horwitz, whose wife, Kelly Horwitz, lost to one of the Machine's candidates, had had enough. Horwitz, who also happened to be a Gordon Rosen Professor of Law at the University of Alabama, wrote a scathing letter to the UA Faculty Senate, stating, "Simply put, the question is whether the university is going to be a modern institution that honors fairness and the rule of law, or whether it will, in important respects, retain remnants of the kinds of views and behavior that this university has been burdened with and failed to definitively address for at least fifty years.

"Both the Greek and Machine questions have of course come up many times before. But they have not been addressed with clarity, tenacity, and a willingness not to stop until the issue is fully and completely aired in the open and addressed forcefully . . . In important ways, our university is corrupt. It seems to me that it is the duty of the Faculty Senate to arrest this corruption."[29]

"We need people graduating from this university with a belief in the values of human beings as individuals, in the ability of a democratic system to work, with a belief that the people of Alabama can solve their own problems," reporter Chuck Hess said in an *Esquire* article. "The people that are graduating from the political system here don't see any problems. There are none to solve. But the problems in our state are so basic that it shouldn't take a Rhodes scholar to explain to people that we need educational reform."[30]

The Machine is simply the best-known consortium of white students wielding power on a college campus, but in reality, most campuses don't need all of the mystery and secrecy. The Machine is about making sure that the great majority of resources that are divvied up go toward *their* interests, while blacks and others have to scrape for the scraps. It provides an illustration of how power is created, maintained, and used, one that serves as a good lesson for black college students who hope to fight Machine-like power in regular society. And then there were the Machine's historic efforts to keep the white fraternities and sororities on Greek Row white.

In some ways, the University of Alabama's Greek Row represents an idyllic version of fraternity and sorority life, that of a bygone era—the Ozzie and Harriet 1950s—but ready-made for those born after 9/11. Tradition is what makes the UA Greeks who they are. A conservative tradition, in which things may change, only not too much. It's that continuity that both attracts and repels those who interact with it. And for UA Greeks themselves, nothing that breaks that continuity is welcome.

For two straight years beginning in 2001, the Machine allegedly helped to keep a black University of Alabama student, Melody Twilley, from joining a white sorority. According to a *USA Today* article, "The university officials lobbied the white sororities to open their doors—if not their hearts—to Twilley, who has a 3.85 grade-point average and sings first soprano in the school choir."[31]

That lobbying fell on deaf ears.

This case in particular is puzzling, because when you talk to Melody Twilley, now Melody Twilley Zeidan, you instantly think, "Who could possibly not like her?" From the minute she greets you, Zeidan's soft Alabama accent drips with a friendliness as sweet as any iced tea in Tuscaloosa. Perfect even for the world of Alabama's predominately white sororities, who pride themselves on their civility.

Before arriving at the University of Alabama, Zeidan grew up in Camden, Alabama, population 2,257, one of those one-stoplight southern towns where the opening of a Wal-Mart is cause for a school holiday. Wilcox County, where Camden is located, is one of the poorest counties in Alabama, and "our claim to fame is that we're the poorest county in the country that has the highest gas prices in the country because we're so isolated," Zeidan said with laughter.[32]

Demographically, Camden is split almost evenly between African Americans and whites, and like most small towns in Alabama, it is characterized by de facto segregation, especially when it comes to education. There are two high schools in Camden: Wilcox Central High

School, the public school that most of the black students attend, and Wilcox Academy, a private school, where all of the white students go. Wilcox Academy is one of hundreds of private high school segregationists throughout the South created as a way to circumvent the integration of public schools. As a result, many southern towns continue to operate a separate-but-equal educational system, long after *Brown vs. Board of Education* was supposed to have eliminated it. And until the tenth grade, Zeidan attended Wilcox Central High, which was all black (except for one white student, who couldn't afford to go to Wilcox Academy).

"Going through Wilcox Central High School, where I've gotten straight A's, and I've not been challenged yet. I just wanted to get out of there. I didn't want to live in Camden my whole life, and I don't know many people who do. I was trying to escape on the first train headed out, so I applied to the Alabama School of Math and Science, which is a residential public high school. It's a boarding school where everything is college prep. You take your entrance exams to get in, and there are interviews with your teachers. And your parents have to vow that you won't go wild and burn the place down," Zeidan said with a chuckle. "This is where I ended up for the eleventh and twelfth grade."

Having grown up in Camden, Zeidan was amazed by her new white classmates' surprise over segregation. "That was my first time being around people that when you said the word 'segregation,' their lips curled, because they think of it as a bad thing. Where I'm from, it's just the way it is. It's just how it is."

What makes segregation insidious is that it can create an atmosphere in which racial separation is considered normative behavior, accepted by all, both black and white. And while there's no intrinsic benefit for black people from being around white people, there *is* an advantage if the resources of a community are concentrated in one (white) area. So while Zeidan didn't see segregation as a bad thing for her sense of identity and self-esteem as a black person, in which she is very secure, it was a bad thing for most black people in Camden, as the black poverty levels and the quality of the black high school would tell you.

The Alabama School of Math and Science was the first place where Zeidan had not been in a majority-black setting, but it didn't seem to faze her. After all, the only white person at her old segregated school had been her friend.

"In the eleventh grade, I'm surrounded by all of these white people, but I'm not freaked out . . . I know they're not aliens, it's just, whatever. That was literally the first time that I'd been in the minority. I was fifteen years old, and that might have had something to do with the fact that I didn't really notice that I was in the minority. And because I was used to being in the majority, I'm thinking of these people as 'people.' We're in classrooms, not ballet studios, so we're not surrounded by mirrors, seeing myself and thinking, 'Oh my gosh, I stand out.' We're a bunch of teenage smart people, who are all dorks."

Zeidan was sixteen years old when she graduated from high school. The University of Alabama wasn't her first choice; she wanted to leave the state for school. But her parents thought she was too young to do so, and she was happy enough heading to Tuscaloosa. But there was a problem. She didn't make her decision on UA until the middle of the summer, after most of the students she knew had already paired up for roommates. That meant she was going to be a bit socially isolated, almost a panic situation for a sixteen-year-old heading off to college where everyone is eighteen years old and more connected.

Lacking a guide for making friends in college, Zeidan turned to the one source that seemed to make the most sense.

"The Sweet Valley University books," Zeidan said, laughing. "I was like, yeah, we've got a tutorial here about what college is all about. So I'm reading *Sweet Valley University*, and one of the characters decides to join a sorority, and I'm like, 'Bam! That's what I'm going to do! I'm going to join a sorority, and that way, I'll have about fifty best friends before classes even start.'

"I had no previous experience with sororities, because remember, in Camden, if you went to community college, you were most likely the most educated person there. People weren't in sororities, so I didn't know Greeks of any kind, of any color."

Remember, she was sixteen. But as young as she was, Zeidan was a perfectionist. "When I'm going to do something, I want to do it right, do it correctly, and do it really, really well. I don't like leaving boxes unchecked."

So Zeidan went into the sorority rush with gusto. Rush is a series of social events at which young women pick the sororities they would like to join, and the sororities make their own picks. After each round, the sororities cut people from their lists, and the rushees do the same. The process is about getting through each round with as many choices as possible, so that theoretically, at the end of all the rounds, the sorority and rushees will all find the right match.

Zeidan read the University of Alabama rush book, which provides tips for what to do and what not to do when rushing the sororities. "The shoes have to match the dress. I've gotta get my earrings and makeup just right. I'm going to get my highlights touched up, and I'm going to rush!

"So before I get to Alabama, I think, 'Okay, you get to meet all the sororities, you go to all the houses, meet sisters in every house, and they'll invite you to parties and give you ice water, because it's 147 degrees out there,'" she recalled. "Afterward, people asked me why I didn't join an NPHC sorority, and it was because they didn't have a unified rush. You sorta have to know what you're gonna do before you do it."

For a person as outgoing and approachable as Zeidan, rush was a blast. "I'm going through rush, and I'm having the best time. I'm sort of a social butterfly, so I'm making friends. I thought this was one of the best things ever. When rush was over, most of my friends were like, 'My god, I'm so glad that's over.' I'm like, 'Aw man, rush is over?'"

Maybe it was her naiveté, maybe it was just being young, or maybe it was just because Zeidan had always looked at people as people, but she hadn't thought much about being the only black person going through rush.

"I literally didn't notice that there weren't other black students. Everyone else probably noticed, but I'm just like, there were like a thousand people, this is awesome.

"The first go around, I went to fifteen houses, and I was in love with a bunch of them. I would have been very happy to accept a bid from all of them," Zeidan recalled.

As for how she was treated, "You have to remember that rush is all about being polite. If there's something ugly to say, they'll just smile and nod at you. And if you think about it, there's not feedback exactly. At the first round, you go to all the houses, and then whichever ones invite you back, you go. The others, you never talk to again, so you don't get any feedback."

In the South there's a rich tradition known as "nice nasty," in which smiling people create the façade of being genteel and welcoming, all the while despising you. So you can be met with a broad, toothy smile, a vigorous and firm handshake, and a soft "bless your heart" that can mask the fact that you never had a chance. The nice-nasty tradition isn't exclusive to white fraternities and sororities or even to the Greek system as a whole, but it *is* very difficult in Greekdom to figure out upon first contact who truly likes you and who is against you from the start.

"So after the first cycle, I got dropped by eight, and asked by seven to come back." On the surface there was nothing unusual about that ratio of dropped houses to callbacks. Most rushees get rejected by some and invited back by others. But almost everyone gets to the second round, which is focused on bonding around an activity, usually some type of arts-and-crafts project for a charity.

"We made boo-boo bunnies at one sorority," Zeidan recalled. "This is about seeing how creative you are. Team building. How you interact with your teammates. If you're freaking out, they probably don't want you to come to their house. The next round would have been skits, but I didn't make it that far."

Zeidan hadn't been invited back to any sororities for the next round, but she had no clue why. "I thought everybody loved me. I loved myself." Her attitude was, "I don't know what you're doing over there, but I'm over here being awesome," she said. "I figured that if they didn't like me, there were some really amazing girls accepted into the sorority. Good for them."

While only a tiny handful of women who complete the process get no invitations to join sororities, nearly 90 percent receive bids, with most of the other 10 percent usually dropping out voluntarily after finding that the rush and sorority life are not for them. Zeidan thought that it was just not to be.[33]

And like others who got rejected, Zeidan got on with her life as a University of Alabama student. "I've already overloaded on classes, and I'm busy. By that time, I'd already made friends outside of sororities, my roommate was an old [high school] classmate, and I'm going to parties, trying to not flunk out of school and head back to Camden. That would have been embarrassing."

And there she was, not particularly interested in rushing again, mainly because "they don't like sophomore or juniors, they like freshmen." But sorority life came back into focus during her second semester. It was during an almost annual sit-in protest of the Machine at the SGA offices, where Zeidan just happened to be on an SGA committee, that matters took a sudden turn.

"One of the girls protesting, I think she was a Delta, was friends with my boyfriend, now my husband. And she asked, 'Didn't you go through rush?' And I was like, 'Yeah, it was fun, did you go through it?' And she looked at me like I was an idiot. She then says, very seriously, because obviously I'm a moron, 'You know they don't let black people into the white sororities, right?'"

That hit Zeidan like a thunderbolt.

"'What? This is 2001, how is that even legal?' That was the first I'd ever heard of that, eight months after I'd gone through it. And I'm finally hearing about it. And that was the first time I thought, 'Oh my gosh, you're right. There weren't any other black people there, were there?'"

Zeidan paused, with a soft, wry chuckle. "I felt so dumb. I had to sit in my room for a while and think how stupid I am. I'm so oblivious. How had I not gotten hit by a bus yet? You should notice these things."

What Zeidan didn't know is that the white sororities at the University of Alabama had *never* knowingly rushed a black student. Gamma Phi Beta had been snookered earlier when, in the middle of rush, a sophomore named Christina Houston—whose mother is white and whose father is black—had come forward to reveal, after joining Gamma Phi Beta in 2000, the truth about her racial makeup. It wasn't that Houston had purposely kept her parents' races a secret; she just didn't volunteer the information. And from the way her sororities talked about blacks, it was clear that they weren't aware of her mixed race.[34]

Houston said that her sorority sisters pretty much accepted her, but "lots of times they would forget what they were talking about, and n-words would go flying like bullets. When I asked them about it, they would say, 'Oh, we don't think of you like that.' Well, you should, because that's what I am."[35]

Zeidan's own story would have ended with her belated discovery about segregation in sororities, if not for an article about the Machine in the *Crimson White,* which has been the most consistent chronicler of the Machine and a thorn in its side for years. This article about the organization attracted a letter to the editor from a student. That letter is what angered Zeidan and moved her to action.

"The black students are all up in arms about this Machine thing keeping them out of government," Zeidan remembered the letter saying, "but if they want to be in government, why don't they just join a Machine fraternity? But we never get one who comes through rush that's qualified. Qualified black people don't go through white rush." "And I promise you," Zeidan said, "that I wouldn't have said a thing, except that he said that. So I did the ladylike thing and wrote back."

Her letter read: "I, an African-American female, participated in Fall Rush 2000, and I have the T-shirt to prove it. I was dropped from rush after the second round of events, and I will leave it up to the reader to decide why."[36]

Her response led the *Tuscaloosa News* to pick the story up locally, after which it went national. The item caught the attention of John Patrick Hermann, a professor of English at the university, now retired, who'd been fighting to integrate the University of Alabama Greek Row for decades. Just ten years earlier, in 1991, Hermann had helped create a new accreditation system that was designed to desegregate the UA Greek Row, which then, as now, makes up about 21 percent of the campus.

According to the *New York Times,* the accreditation program called on the Greek chapters to make a "commitment to the university's stated ideal of an inclusive campus" and to demonstrate "good-faith efforts to achieve and maintain a racially and culturally diverse chapter management." Hermann recognized that the statement was vague, and he wanted to mandate that white Greeks at UA rush black students. He realized, however, that that wasn't going to be possible. The accreditation program mandated only that the white Greeks fill out various surveys and perform other self-assessments, whereupon each chapter would be reviewed by the university, with the penalty for noncompliance being loss of certification.[37]

"The only thing they care about is that it doesn't happen this year. It's a brilliant, self-perpetuating system," Hermann told the *New Republic.* "I don't present myself as a proponent for integration," he says. "I only present myself as an anti-segregationist, as someone who's fighting a struggle against taxpayer-supported segregation . . . I've never spoken out in favor of integration in the Greek system."[38]

The desegregation of the white Greek Row was an all-consuming mission for Hermann, his own quest for Moby Dick. Greek Row itself was divided between Old Fraternity Row, exclusively white and filled with million-dollar mansions, and New Fraternity Row, a side street for less-prestigious white fraternities and sororities, along with Alpha Phi Alpha fraternity and Alpha Kappa Alpha sorority houses. To Hermann, this divide was symbolic of how the University of Alabama consolidated power in white hands.

"Anyone who thinks the Greek system is silly or a foolish thing that can be satirized is seriously underestimating the success of a racist structure that allows not particularly bright young men and young women access to worthy mates," Hermann noted.[39]

But not all students were convinced these changes would work, including the black students, who tended to be skeptical.

Jennifer Turner, a senior history major from Birmingham, Alabama, who is social chairman for Delta Sigma Theta, told the *New York Times* back in 1991, "If their goal is to really integrate, I don't think that's going to be successful, not to the extent that they want. If the goal is to bring the chapters closer together, maybe."[40]

Turner had a right to be skeptical, since, as noted earlier, no black student had yet broken the color barrier when the white sorority knew the applicant was black. But Hermann read Zeidan's letter to the editor and persuaded her to give it another try.

"Pat Hermann was the ringleader. He grabbed me and took me around town. He helped me get some recs [recommendations], but first he had to persuade me to rush again. Because I was like, 'No.' And he was like, 'Yes, you are.' And so I rushed again. And that was in 2001."

Not everyone thought this was a good idea, including the president of the University of Alabama campus NAACP, Dave Washington. Washington, a member of the African American fraternity Kappa Alpha Psi, held a press conference, surrounded by white Greeks, as he said, "There are some things that are more important [than Greek integration], and I stand by that. I've gotten overwhelming support from people on campus and in Tuscaloosa. The university's Faculty Senate and the news media should quit interfering with Alabama's Greek system." He said the Faculty Senate should concern itself with "more serious racial issues," adding that Greek integration "is going to occur. But we want to be properly prepared to accept all that comes with change."[41]

This caused a harsh response from Hermann, who said of Washington, "There is in Alabama what I call, for the lack of a better term, an Uncle Tom approach. There is a group of administrators and faculty who know how to work within and benefit from the racist system, but they don't want to rock the boat. I don't see any of the prominent blacks on campus struggling to end state-supported segregation. There have always been blacks who would sell out their people for personal advantage. Dave Washington, by his recent remarks, has put himself in that category."[42]

Yet Washington was praised in the *Tuscaloosa News* in a letter to the editor by Eric N. Baklanoff, a conservative professor emeritus of economics, who suggested that the university host a "a series of scholarly symposia focusing on race relations and reconciliation" and that "my short list of black intellectuals who could invest such a dialogue with both substance and balance would include: Thomas Sowell, Walter Williams . . . Ward Connerly . . . John H. McWhorter, and Shelby Steele." The black individuals he listed are known for their conservative views, thus making them, in Baklanoff's eyes, perfect choices to lead a discussion on race.[43]

It was this backdrop that made Zeidan's second attempt at rush a bit of a circus. Her name was now well-known by all of the white sororities at UA, and the press was literally following her around the campus as she went from sorority house to sorority house during rush.

"The *LA Times* sent somebody, and they followed as I went down the street. I didn't talk to him or anything because I thought that wouldn't be good as I went through rush, but he followed me as I walked down the sidewalk. There was a camera following me as I went down the street."

Despite all of the hubbub on campus and her knowledge that white sororities weren't accepting black members, Zeidan was still rather hopeful that she'd have better luck this time. Her heart was still in it.

"It really was. I still wanted to be in a sorority, and I was kind of pissed off that I lost a year. So this time, I'd get a bid, and bygones would be bygones."

That optimism had served her well throughout her life, but this time was a bit different. Recognizing that she was the only black student going through rush "felt weird," she said.

"I tried to get it out of my head that this was the second time around. By now, I was taking a lot of classes with these girls, so when I saw someone I knew, I'd go over and give them a hug, and check out how they were doing. It helped me to not think like I was the odd person out."

But as weird as it felt, she rolled through the first and second rounds. She was excited that she'd gotten to the third round, the skit round, with at least one sorority, Alpha Delta Pi. She later found out that while she'd gotten one sorority interested in seeing her for the third round, other white rushees were getting interest from multiple sororities. Still, she was happy to receive a final bid from Alpha Delta Pi.

"Alpha Delta Pi is the only sorority out of the nine to invite me to the third round skits. Everybody I knew was turning down houses because you're allowed six. Some people after the first round were invited by all fifteen houses, and were only allowed to go to ten, so they had to cut five. And for the second round, you were only allowed to go to six, so you had people who'd have to cut at least four or five.

"The skit was cute. We were doing something about Peter Pan, and having to find the land of ADPi. I thought it was adorable. I liked ADPi, a lot. You know how some sororities are going for their Mrs. degrees, and they're going to be just like their moms? Sometimes those types of sororities were fun, but ADPi was not like that. ADPi sisters are very real. They're sweet and genuine, but if they don't like you, they're not going to smile in your face and then sleep with your boyfriend.

"So I'm at ADPi skit, and a girl who's friends with my boyfriend came up to me, and we're talking. She's interviewing me for the sorority, but it's comfortable because we know each other, and I assume that's the reason why they had her speak to me. But that's also why I know they put her up to asking me if I was only there [going through rush] to prove a point.

"And that was a legitimate question, everyone was wondering. So I told her the truth. Yes, I wanted to be in a sorority, but it was not because I wanted to be the first black person, because I don't want that kind of responsibility. I'm here for me, and I'm here for sisterhood. So, that was that. Apparently, my answer wasn't good enough, because I was released from rush again that night."

Rejected again.

Bid day was on September 10, 2001, and while Zeidan was hurt again, she simply decided to do a little bit of "retail therapy" with the money she'd reserved for the sorority. White sororities can cost upwards of $5,000 per year at the University of Alabama, so it's no small economic feat even if you make it. Zeidan would go on to found a multicultural sorority, Alpha Delta Sigma sorority, "but after the nine of us graduated, it was kind of hard to keep the momentum going. So it lasted about another five years, and then petered out."

Often when people read these stories, even if they're sympathetic to the plight of the African American victim, they tend to think, "Big deal. It's just a silly little sorority filled with immature young women. Get over it." But that's not all of it. Racism leaves wounds that run deep.

"You know, if I don't speak about it in a detached way, I'll cry," Zeidan said slowly. "Because sitting here, my feelings are still hurt. It's very hard to get over a rejection to that extent. Because if you think about the percentages of people who don't get bids versus those who do, and keep in mind that the 10 to 20 percent who don't get bids may be

partly those who went through rush and thought these girls were mo-
rons and dropped out."

Today, Zeidan is a corporate lawyer, and while joining a sorority
was not ultimately a make-or-break experience in her life, the episode
still haunts her. She still wonders if she could have done something different, something that would have allowed her to transcend her race and
the racism that the sorority members demonstrated against her.

"If I could go back and change some things, it would have been to
go back and do some more research before freshman year. Not about the
race relation aspect of it, but to be better prepared. I read the rush book,
but the rush book is what they tell everybody. When it comes to getting
into a highly competitive sorority, it's more about the things that you do
know than the things you don't know. I needed recommendations from
alumnae. I needed more expensive designer shoes. It's the things that are
unspoken that I wish I'd known beforehand. I think it was a systemic
[racial] thing, but I wish I'd had all of my ducks in a row."

"As far as consolation, I don't have anything to say. I'm still hurt,
and it's been ten years," Zeidan said in 2011 to the *Crimson White*. "For
encouragement, accept that that's maybe a part of life. Being rejected
just means that somebody couldn't appreciate how great you are. It's
not really something that you get over easily . . . to say that I don't care
anymore would be a total lie. Even ten years later, looking back on it,
I'm still very upset. There's nothing I could have done. That whole lack
of control over the situation is . . . heartbreaking. It's like saying a person
is born not good enough."[44]

The Machine is important not just because black college students
aren't allowed into white fraternities and sororities, but because it's a
real-life symbol of white privilege and white supremacy, all under the
genteel canopy of fraternalism. And white supremacy is about denying
access to power, by any means necessary.

Periodically, the University of Alabama administration attempts to
change things. In 2003 the Machine, under pressure from the university

to integrate its ranks, decided it had the solution. It would secretly rig
the game by promising a so-called "lesser" sorority, Gamma Phi Beta,
added benefits if they bit the bullet and initiated Carla Ferguson, an
African American student.

"I think a slot in the Machine was promised," said former Gamma
Phi Beta social chairwoman Stephanie McGee, a junior in the College
of Arts and Sciences, who resigned her sorority after the scandal. "It
supposedly would also get us more parties and swaps and that kind of
thing."[45]

A poster on a Greek message board, Greekchat, read, "The Machine is getting sick of everyone telling them how racist they are, so
they decided to de-segregate the sorority system this year. However,
none of the 'top' chapters wanted to risk their reputations by bidding an
African-American, so they wanted one of the not so prestigious sororities to do [so] instead. They promised Gamma Phi entrance into the
Machine as a bribe, which would theoretically raise their social standing
on campus."[46]

The phrase "risking their reputations" is often heard when it comes
to white fraternities and sororities. There's the fear that the presence
of African Americans in the ranks of a chapter will result in fewer invitations to parties from other white fraternities and sororities, reducing the chapter's prestige. This thinking mirrors the racist idea that the
presence of black homeowners in a neighborhood reduces home values
for the white neighbors. This idea that whiteness comes with a value,
prestige, and reputation that can be eroded by blackness is at the core of
how white racism operates.

And that thinking didn't end with Melody Zeidan. In 2011 Sherles
Durham came to Alabama from Douglasville, Georgia, with a 3.6 high
school GPA. Durham was vice president of her senior class and regularly
volunteered at her community's local Special Olympics. Like Zeidan,
Durham rushed to make friends, but said she didn't expect to pledge.
"I just wanted to make friends out of the experience," Durham said,

"which I did." That fall 1,711 women participated in rush, according to a University spokeswoman. Of those, 77 were released without a bid. Durham was one of them.

"I've been trying not to look at it this way because, you know, sometimes when it's brought into question, some people get offended, but I think race might have come into play," Durham said. "If all the girls who went into rush week were completely covered or blocked from view in some way, I think the outcomes could be completely different."[47]

Unfortunately for Durham, everyone could see the faces of the rushees. But then, one brave white sorority woman decided that she would speak up when others were quiet.

• • •

"Are we not going to talk about the black girl?"

Melanie Gotz didn't enter her Alpha Gamma Delta sorority rush meeting imagining that she'd later be a catalyst for a discussion of black women in predominately white sororities on the University of Alabama campus. In fact, that was the furthest thing from her mind. She, like all UA students, knew the university had a tinderbox history when it came to race, beginning with the infamous stand-in-the-schoolhouse-door stance. And she knew there had been periodic racial incidents through the years that made life at UA uncomfortable for many black students. But that was in the past, right?

Gotz herself came to the University of Alabama from Dallas, Texas, which made her an outsider on a campus that typically had a heavy contingent of instate students.

"My friends were going to universities in Texas, and I kind of felt like I was going to just be hanging out with the same kids I did in high school, so I wanted to go out of state. My uncle had just moved to Alabama, but I actually wanted to go [to college] on the East Coast. So when we were traveling to schools, we stopped in Alabama. My dad twisted my arm into visiting it because they give great scholarships," Gotz said with a laugh. "But I loved it. It was beautiful, I liked the culture; it was like nothing I had ever seen before. So, it was a pretty easy choice for me after that."[48]

As for joining Alpha Gamma Delta, Gotz did so the way many people join white fraternities and sororities: because of a friend.

"I had a friend two years older, and she was like the only person I knew in any sorority, and she was an Alpha Gamma. I really had no other reason other than that, so I joined it. Everyone that I met was super down-to-earth, but even when I went [to the Alpha Gamma Delta house], I wasn't sure I wanted to join a sorority. I thought to myself, 'I can go through it, and if I didn't like it, just drop out.' But rush was the weirdest thing I've ever been through. Like, these girls open their doors and sing in your face. All these girls trying to stay cool in the 100-degree heat. It was something weird and exciting about it, though."

Eventually, Alpha Gamma Delta accepted Gotz. Once she was a member, she realized that the sorority liked to emphasize diversity, just not the racial type.

"So you basically kind of had geographic diversity in the sorority, which is to be expected because the University of Alabama is a pretty international university, and a flagship. I ended up finding three other girls who were also from Dallas, they called us the Texas Girls, because there were so many girls that were from Alabama, and the sororities at the time [only had members] from Alabama, or maybe Mississippi, so we were like foreigners my freshman year.

"But it changed a lot since I was a freshman. By the time it was my senior year, there were girls from all over. Our university had expanded so much, so there were girls from California, there were Jersey girls, and, you know, [out-of-state girls] were like a quarter of the sorority. That's because the school got a lot more money from people coming from out-of-state."

But Gotz soon realized that through these rushes, one type of University of Alabama student wasn't being accepted by her sorority: black students.

"Now, in terms of ethnic diversity, no one really kind of thought about African Americans being in the sorority."

Gotz found out that when black women went through rush, there were many ways to reject them without getting tagged with overt racism. You did it subtly.

"Once you get on the other side of it, it's pretty shocking and eye-opening that it happens. You're oblivious to a lot of things, and it's a well-kept secret, too. The [black] girls kind of came through, but it was never mentioned. Looking back now, the [sorority members] would just say things like, 'Oh. She was an academic risk,' and immediately drop her during rush. They would find something, score her low on points, and be merrily on their way because nobody knew the African American girl. The reason this case was different is because everyone knew [the black girl]."

When it comes to rush, there's a template for the type of young woman you want to add to your sorority ranks: connected. From Tuscaloosa. Easy to get along with. Popular. And if you found that combination in a rushee, you offered her membership quickly, mainly because you knew that twenty-one *other* sororities on campus were going to do the same. In some ways, rush begins with the rushee trying to impress the sorority sisters, but ends with the sorority trying to impress outstanding applicants. Great candidates are simply not allowed to get away if the sorority has anything to do with it. And that's why one particular black girl's omission was so startling.

Kennedi Cobb was from sorority-rushee central casting. Having been her high school's salutatorian, she walked into the University of Alabama with a 4.3 grade-point average. A local Tuscaloosa girl, which was usually a huge plus in the white Alabama sorority world, she was connected, an even more important attribute on a campus where connections were everything. Her step-grandfather, John England Jr., was a member of the University of Alabama board of trustees. You don't get more University of Alabama than that.

"It was kind of the perfect storm when Cobb came through because she was from Tuscaloosa," Gotz said. "She knows people not just in our sorority, but every single sorority. She'd been coming to rush parties, knew girls in my sorority, so she knows the game. So she knows you had to have a letter of recommendation."

Unlike Zeidan, who a decade earlier hadn't made it past the third round, Cobb was now at the final stage: voting night. By now Gotz was an old hand; as a senior, she wasn't paying that much attention to what was going on with rush. To her, Cobb was a no-brainer, though she hadn't really been following the young woman's progress through rush. But she did want to hear the scuttlebutt from her sisters.

"So me and my roommate go downstairs, and I see all these sopho-mores and juniors bundled up in groups. So I was like, 'So, any drama goin' to happen tonight?' And in the past it was like, you know, 'Sarah has a sister coming through, and her sister's weird, so we might drop her.' That type of drama. But I go up to one of the groups, and she's like, 'You know, they're gonna drop that black girl tonight.' And I was like, 'Whoa, whoa, what? What are you talking about?' And they're like, 'Yeah. We're serious.'

"[My sorority sister] Anna's over there crying because she doesn't know what to do about it. She feels very close with her. Cobb had a great time every time that she was there. There were girls crying in that vot-ing room that night because they had gotten so close with her. I asked one more person about it, and I was like, 'Some of this is so messed up.' And then, as we're walking down to the voting room, I see Anna bawl-ing on the phone, talking to her mom. She's like, 'I don't know. I don't think this is something I want to do.' And I just like grab Anna and I was just like, 'Dude. We got this.'

"So we walk down, sit down in the voting room, and we sit by level of seniority. So I'm right front and center," Gotz recalled. The alumnae members of Alpha Gamma Delta had arrived unexpectedly, and they tried their best to make it seem as if nothing was wrong.

"I'm right next to the alumnae and the president and stuff. And all the sophomores, the ones that really care about Cobb, are in the back. I can hear girls sniffling behind me. Multiple girls were really upset about this.

"OK! Great news. We don't have to do voting tonight," Gotz remembered the alumnae saying. "We got rid of all the people who aren't eligible."

"So you know," Gotz says, "this is normally awesome news, because I've been in voting rooms where we've sat there until one or two in the morning. But this time, it just seems sketchy and kind of messed up. So she reads the list, and then says, 'OK. Be here tomorrow.'"

Kennedi Cobb was not on that Alpha Gamma Delta list of invitees.

To Gotz, the omission was as though Big Al, the famous University of Alabama elephant mascot, had plopped himself in the middle of the room and set himself on fire, and no one was going to say anything about it. Some of her sisters were still crying about Cobb's omission, while others raged quietly. But no one had the courage to question the decision, and more importantly, no one said what everyone knew: that Cobb had been rejected for being black.

As the alumnae continued to talk about who would be included on their completely white list of invitees, Gotz gathered her courage and thought, "What the hell?"

She said aloud, "Are we not going to talk about the black girl?"

The alumnae suddenly became very quiet.

"They just froze and everyone just kinda looked to the president. I think everyone was kind of flustered, and they're like, 'Well?'"

"The girls had informed me earlier," Gotz told the alumnae, "that one of the reasons why we're meeting is because we were going to vote on it. And another girl told me that it's just not even up for voting.

So that's why I asked that." The alumnae responded, "Well? Do we need to?"

When Gotz said yes, the answers she got from the alumnae made her even angrier.

"Technicality," one answered.

"Letter of recommendation not proper."

"Another girl behind me raises her hand," Gotz remembered, "and was like, 'Um, she's from Tuscaloosa. She should definitely have a letter of recommendation.' There's a Jewish girl behind me, and she's like, 'You know, back in the day, there were Jewish separations, between Jewish sororities and fraternities, and look at me!' She was high up in the sorority. Then she asked, 'What if I had never gotten into the sorority?'

"Then so I raised my hand, 'Look, I don't know what's going on, but this should be talked about and voted on. At least we should see what's going on, because, I feel like everyone here wants her and there's girls crying in the back that are so upset about this; can we at least hear what is going on?'"

According to Gotz, the alumnae's faces were getting red.

"It doesn't matter," they kept saying, "her letter of recommendation doesn't work."

The Alpha Gamma Delta sisters, the ones who liked Cobb and wanted her to be admitted, asked if the decision could be put off for a day in order to get the technicality straightened out. One even produced a photo of Cobb's letter of recommendation on her phone.

"No."

The vote was final, and Cobb was dropped that evening. To Gotz, nothing about the process felt right.

"It was all so fishy and we all knew that they were lying. But there was nothing we could do. Girls are still crying and giving speeches and the alumni are just pissed because they have to sit there and listen to it. There were a couple girls who tried to do prayers at the end of it, and I'm just like, man, this is bullshit."

The lies her alumnae sisters had given for excluding Cobb; the fact that she thought race wouldn't have anything to do with who was brought into her sorority, and finding out that race had everything to do with it: Gotz decided to do something about it.

"Honestly, I was livid days after this," Gotz recalled. "I felt really defeated. Like I think I faked being sick the next day for rush, just because I was just so disappointed in everything about it. I thought about dropping the sorority, but then I was like, 'What point does that serve, though?' I was more proud of the girls in my sorority more than ever. It was just those three [alumnae]. Then one of the girls in my sorority was like, 'Mel, you're gonna love this. Did you hear that Abby Crane is thinking about doing an article?'"

Gotz was contacted by the *Crimson White* and told her story. "I just thought to myself—everyone is being a coward, you can't be one of them," she said.[49]

"I was really nervous. [Abby's] an old friend of mine, so I was just like, 'Abby, I'm really scared that you might twist this in a way that seems like I, our whole sorority is, you know, racist or something. I don't want people walking around saying, "Those are the Alpha Gammas. The racist ones." But I still want to tell you the story because I feel like it needs to be told.' And she was like, 'OK. I understand. I'm going to do the best I can.'"

Once the story was published, all hell broke loose.

For their part, Alpha Gamma Delta issued a statement saying, "Alpha Gamma Delta policy prohibits discrimination on the basis of race in all of its activities including recruitment. We take seriously any allegation that recruitment policy was not followed."[50] But as the national media descended, including CNN and the *New York Times,* they soon found out that Cobb's rejection wasn't unusual, or even surprising, on the University of Alabama Greek Row.

Right after the *Crimson White* story was published, the Machine's twitter handle sent out the following tweet: "The first rule of rush is you don't talk about segregation to media. The second rule of rush is you don't talk about segregation to media."[51]

"I had the [chapter] president call me [to] say that 'the ladies from the nationals are coming tomorrow,'" Gotz recalled. "They said, 'Please don't do any more news stories.' When they get there, I sit down with them, and they just seem disappointed in me, kind of mad at me, which is opposite to everyone else's reactions. Most people I met after the article were proud of me, cool with what I did. So it just seemed really messed up that the people that could have made it awesome were just kinda like, 'You need to shut up and not say anything else.'

"'Why did you do it?'" they asked, as Gotz recalled. "'Why did you feel the need to do this?' I said, 'This has been happening for years. The alumnae do crappy stuff like this and nothing is done to change it.' But they were like, 'Well, we were about to come down and take action.' And I was like, 'Were you? I don't know that for sure. Bad things happen here every year and nothing has changed. Maybe you were going to slowly come down and say, "Don't do that again," but I don't know that. I can't say that for sure.' You know, [I think] they just didn't like being in the press.

"It was just really frustrating because they could have been a part of something so awesome to change the school. But they were like 'Shush, shush, shush. Shut up. Don't say anything. We're looking bad.' So they, I guess, they were looking at their own picture and weren't looking at the bigger picture.

"I kept thinking, 'Can we think about this girl Kennedi? Like, for one minute? Don't you think she'd like to be heard? Can you imagine what it would be like to be eighteen years old, and trying to get into a sorority, but you can't because you're black? No. You can't. Because you're old, wound-up women from Minnesota, or wherever you're from.'"

As it turned out, one year after that major uproar, when it was revealed that no African American women were offered bids to join sororities at the University of Alabama, the university established reforms to encourage fraternities and sororities to select African American students. The new policy, the first substantial reform of the rushing process in decades, was called open bidding.

The open-bidding process meant that in 2014, all 21 black women who registered for sorority recruitment received bids to join Greek organizations, and all 21 women accepted their invitations. All 16 sororities on campus offered bids to African American women, who accepted offers at 10 different sororities. Among those women was Kennedi Cobb, who eventually joined Alpha Chi Omega.

The university has a long way to go. In 2014 there were 2,276 women who registered for sorority recruitment, and 2,054 were accepted into membership. Thus, the 21 new black sorority members make up just 1 percent of all new members, while African Americans make up 13 percent of the undergraduate student body at the university.

"We have taken the first steps toward removing barriers and ensuring access and opportunity throughout our Greek community," University of Alabama president Judy Bonner said in a video statement in 2013. "I am confident that we will achieve our objective of a Greek system that is inclusive, accessible and welcoming to students of all races and ethnicities; we will not tolerate anything less. The process of continuous open bidding is already yielding positive results."[52]

Gotz wasn't very impressed with the university's response.

"It was like, 'Oh crap, we'd better do somethin' about this!'" Gotz laughed. "But they weren't going to. Then they realized I could do more national news stories, so that's the only reason they began to act. You know, I'm happy that they have the whole open-bidding process, that was their doing, but I don't know. But this is not the first time [a black student was rejected], and after the story came out, I had so many people share their stories with me, people who'd been completely, blatantly, discriminated against, and they didn't do anything about it."

Gotz, who would face blowback not only from her sorority members but from others on the UA Greek Row, would later receive an award at the Southern Christian Leadership Conference's annual Realizing the Dream: Living Together in Peace legacy banquet.

"It was still one of the best decisions I've ever made," Gotz said. "I mean, to come forward. I kind of always look back at this, and just say, 'You know, a lot of people disagreed with me, but I've still never been prouder of something I've done.'"

In a 2014 interview with *Marie Claire,* a couple of white University of Alabama sorority members talked about why black women weren't picked. "We were told we do not take black girls, because it would be bad for our chapter—our reputation and our status," said Yardena Wolf, twenty, a junior and a member of Alpha Omicron Pi. Her experience underscores the view of whiteness as having a value that blackness doesn't possess. "There was a list of girls who were to be dropped from rush," said a senior, Caroline Bechtel, twenty-one, a member of Phi Mu. "Anyone who was a minority was automatically added to it. Sometimes they'd say things like, 'Oh, she wore an ugly dress,' but it was so obviously wrong, so obviously racism."[53]

And it wasn't just at Alpha Gamma Delta that a qualified black candidate was rejected. An anonymous Chi Omega member told the *Crimson White* that her sorority had rejected a black candidate even though the chapter had wanted her, all because their rush advisor, Emily Jamison, had rejected her.[54]

Jamison issued a statement saying, "As a private membership organization, Chi Omega's membership selection process is confidential; however, our criteria for membership is simple, we seek women who reflect our values and purposes. Our recruitment processes and procedures were followed, and while I cannot take away the disappointment a potential new member or chapter member may feel, I can share that all women were treated fairly and consistently in our process."[55]

As a result, the Chi Omega philanthropy chair resigned from the sorority, disgusted by the black candidate's rejection, which appeared to the chapter to have been completely due to race.

"Our philanthropy chair really wanted her and was rooting for her and left before the parties and everything when she found out [the recruit was dropped]," the anonymous Chi Omega member said. "She was living in the house—she just packed up all her stuff and left the house and left rush."[56]

After the results of the 2014 bid process were announced, a member of the Chi Omega sorority posted a photograph online showing three white women. The caption of the photo read, "Chi O got NO Niggers!!!!!" In reality the sorority had asked two black women to join the organization. The national organization of Chi Omega quickly expelled the woman who posted the offensive photograph and caption.[57]

The Machine wasn't broken by any means. Like most malignancies, it had just metastasized. "They know they don't have the majority on campus. It's an apartheid system," said "Emma," a university alumna who was a freshmen member of Delta Zeta sorority in 1986. "It's a bunch of kids with too much power trying to get even more, and that's the contradiction of democracy."[58]

So why is the Machine important? It's important because it represents the type of systemic racism that black students will face as college students. The Machine provides a rare chance to see how exclusionary racist power works, and how it must be fought. The point is not whether you agree that black students should join predominately white sororities or fraternities, but whether or not there are barriers to those groups based on race. As I noted at the beginning of this chapter, white Greek members are in every field, and to allow a segment of the population to act in a discriminatory manner between the ages of eighteen and twenty-one is to see that behavior codified when those young people reach adulthood. A white fraternity or sorority member of the Machine becomes an adult who makes decisions in law, business, and society in general with Machine values as his or her bedrock principles.

What the existence of the Machine says about American campuses is that an organization dedicated to the preservation of white supremacy—one whose members wear khaki pants instead of white hoods—can not only exist on a college campus, but can thrive.

But there have been victories. Women in both black and white sororities have spoken up to protest against the discrimination. Khortland Patterson, a member of Alpha Kappa Alpha, the oldest African American sorority, helped lead a group of Greek women in support of Cobb. And in 2014 African American twin sisters, Hillary and Halle Lindsay, decided to pledge sororities at the University of Alabama. Hillary pledged the African American sorority, Alpha Kappa Alpha, while Halle successfully rushed Alpha Gamma Delta, the predominately white sorority that had rejected Cobb just a year before.

Both are ecstatic with their choices.

3

NOT BITTER, NO APOLOGIES

"I'm a forgiver. I might not forget, but I forgive. My mother, father and older brother always told me: 'Don't hold grudges. If you do that, you lower yourself down to your adversary. Just treat people the way you want to be treated.' I honestly think that's why I was able to survive and have some success."

—Monte Irvin

ONE REASON WHY RACISM PERSISTS IS BECAUSE ITS VICTIMS tend to be passed over as faceless, one-dimensional historical footnotes. Voices often get lost as a series of dates and places, so it's easy to think that the ramifications of racism are a temporary condition that people should get over. That the pain is not significant, that there's a statute of limitations during which the victim is allowed to be hurt.

This is wrong.

Racism has deep, long-lasting psychological implications for the victim. Racist incidents transform lives, change points of view, and create a sense of insecurity in a world where every human being looks to be as secure as possible. In other words, the victims of racism are real people, and the pain doesn't go away.

Patricia Hamilton, now Patricia Hamilton Gyi, and Keni Washington were both college students in the early 1960s, right in the heart of the optimism of the civil rights movement. Gyi was a student at tiny Beloit College, in Beloit, Wisconsin, while Washington studied at Stanford University, in Palo Alto, California. And even though they didn't know each other, they were similar in many respects. Both grew up in small Midwestern towns during the Eisenhower years of the 1950s, Gyi in Madison, Wisconsin, and Washington in Gary, Indiana, with Madison being a predominately white community and Gary being relatively integrated.

"I grew up in a 90 percent white environment," Gyi recalled of her early days in Madison. "All of my early education, all of my teachers, all of my neighbors, all of my world was. I was the exception to the rule. So, it was logical and normal for me to be thinking primarily of attending predominately white schools [for college]. But there was also, somewhere buried in me, that desire to get out of this box and maybe see what the rest of the world was like. Also, socially I had been so isolated as a black female, or a little colored girl as we were called then."[1]

Gyi remembers being under the considerable sway of her parents prior to college. "I was still not particularly an independent person on the surface, not seemingly very assertive at times . . . I don't think there was any indication that I was rebellious."

While Madison was the embodiment of a *Happy Days* 1950s America, white-bread and conformist, Gary, Indiana, represented something completely different.

"Gary, as a 1940s, '50s, '60s American town . . . was ahead of the curve," Washington remembered. "In fact, I have an *Ebony* article right here that was written in 1956, and it features my father and my uncle . . . 'Gary turns its back on Bias.' It's a very interesting article about how Gary is ahead of the nation in integration."[2]

As part of that move toward integration, Washington would go on to be the first black graduate of the Howe Military Academy in

Howe, Indiana, the high school where he soon found out that his new fellow students, unlike those in Gary, didn't accept his skin color automatically.

"I had to basically fight my way through the first part of my first few months I was there, and by the end of my sophomore year, they elected me president of the class. So, you know, I won them over, and they won me over, too. Most of the students wanted me to be there, but there were a few clearly racist students, and that caused my fights. You know, you get to call me nigger once, [but never forget] I'm off the streets of Gary," Washington said, laughing.

When it came to picking colleges, both Gyi and Washington thought about attending Fisk University, one of the more prominent historically black colleges at the time, before settling on Beloit and Stanford, respectively.

"My brother was attending Beloit when I was applying to colleges so it was really an easy call for me to make," Gyi recalled. "Why not just go where he is and, you know, continue the family tradition?"

That family tradition was a hefty one, as Gyi's mother, Velma Bell, had graduated from Beloit College in 1930, magna cum laude, after only three years. She'd also become the first black woman at Beloit to be elected into Phi Beta Kappa. In her senior thesis, titled *Race Prejudice,* Bell's words would speak to the dreams and desires of African Americans of every generation.

"The cry of the Negro is one with that of all the darker peoples," she wrote. "They want freedom from economic exploitation; they want to participate in whatever economic system touches them on the basis of their merit as individuals; they want freedom from political dominations; they want their real interest represented in whatever government rules; they want an education, not one which will fit them for a certain subordinate status, but an education that will fit them to make a living in the world as it is; they want the stigma of inferiority lifted from them so that they may be able to walk down the streets of the world and into the common gathering places of mankind free from contempt. They ought to have unfettered opportunity for the realization of these hopes. Should such attitudes and desires be treated with unreasoning, intolerant prejudice?"[3]

Gyi entered Beloit in 1959, while Washington entered Stanford in 1964, having chosen it over Brown and West Point as well as Fisk. Both noted that when they first came to campus, the black student populations were nearly nonexistent.

"I think my entering freshman class was somewhere between eight and nine hundred students," Washington recalled. "Of that, roughly twenty of us were black. Of the twenty, probably seven from Africa."

The situation at Beloit was around the same for Gyi. "My brother, when I started at Beloit . . . he was a senior. Count that one," Gyi laughed. "There was an African male who was in his class, and there was an African student, a Nigerian student, in my class. There was one black female, not in my class, couple of years older than I was . . . That's it. The population, I mean the enrollment, was probably about, I want to say one thousand students.

"But the point is, I was not quite the only one, but close to it. And in my class, I would say I was certainly the only black female in my class. After the first year, [I was] probably the only black female enrolled at Beloit."

But despite the lack of black students on campus, both Gyi and Washington got along well with their fellow students. And Greek life was prominent at both campuses, especially at Beloit.

"I want to say 80 percent belonged to fraternities and sororities," Gyi said. "It was very little social life on the campus that didn't involve the sororities and fraternities. And that was the context in which most social activities occurred. There were certainly, let's say 20 percent of the students, who didn't belong to it, a fraternity or sorority, probably mostly by choice. And they were, now you would call those people geeks, I suppose."

Washington, for his part, didn't come to Stanford with the intention of participating in Greek life. He only got involved because it was convenient.

"It was really quite an accident. My roommate was a white guy and Sigma Chi was rushing him. This is my freshman year, and they would come to our room every day, over and over, and take him to the frat house. I would be sitting there doing my homework and stuff, and so we struck up a conversation a couple of times and they said, 'Why don't you come to the frat house, too?' I was thinking that, 'I'm not really a fan of fraternities' . . . But I said, 'OK.'"

While Gyi, as she noted, was not rebellious, Washington was. And he thought that joining a fraternity just might serve a future purpose: to get an inside view of what fraternity life was, and then renounce it.

"My motivation was sort of nefarious. I was thinking, 'OK, at some point or another I might want to run for student body office, maybe president or something, on an anti-fraternity stance, because I really don't like fraternities.'"

Sigma Chi, one of the oldest predominately white fraternities in the country, was founded at Miami University of Ohio, in Oxford, in 1855, following a split among the members of the Delta Kappa Epsilon fraternity. At the time that Washington went to the Sigma Chi house at Stanford, Sigma Chi still had a clause in its constitution that stated, "No person shall be eligible to membership in Sigma Chi fraternity who is not a bona fide white, male student in the college or university in which the chapter proposing his initiation is chartered." The whites-only clause was so strictly observed that a black foreign exchange student, Hegos Yesus, wasn't even allowed to live temporarily at the Sigma Chi house at the University of Illinois in 1961.[4]

Gyi and Washington both were familiar with fraternities and sororities, specifically African American fraternities and sororities, as their parents had been members of them. Gyi's mother, Velma, had belonged to the Alpha Kappa Alpha sorority, while her father was a member of the

Alpha Phi Alpha fraternity. Washington's father had joined the Kappa Alpha Psi fraternity, which wasn't on the Stanford campus during Washington's years there, so there was no chance that he could pledge it. Attending schools where there were no African American fraternities or sororities meant that the options were white groups or nothing. It was in that context, as Gyi remembered, that she was introduced to Delta Gamma sorority.

"I had met some of the members of Delta Gamma, and a couple of them said, 'Oh! We would just love to have you in the sorority.' Well, as an innocent high school kid, I just thought, 'Oh! That's kind of cool!' Then I get to campus and you have your schedule of activities here, your orientation there, a picnic over there, and rush for fraternities and sororities starts, next week. And so they had all the rules whereby you could go visit each house for ten or fifteen minutes and then move on to the next one and the next one, etcetera. So I participated in the rush activities as a freshman and went to each house, and was part of the group."

Delta Gamma was founded in 1873 in Oxford, Mississippi, at the Lewis School for Girls. One of the oldest predominately white sororities in the United States, it helped establish the National Panhellenic Conference, the umbrella organization for predominately white sororities. Early growth was concentrated in the South, but Delta Gamma quickly became a national sorority, with chapters in the West and the North, including Beloit College.

The local Delta Gamma and Sigma Chi chapters embraced Gyi and Washington, respectively, and these two black students grew to like the members of their chapters.

"I went to the fraternity house and I got to know these guys, and I actually liked them," said Washington. "They were nice guys, you know, earnest in their own way, and were sincere. The guy who kind of headed up bringing me into the fraternity was a guy named Frank Olrich. He was probably a junior or senior at the time, and I was a freshman. Frank was just a sweetheart of a person, and so, I [thought to myself], 'Do I really want to turn against these guys and stab them in the back?' And that was kind of the way I left it. But anyway, they asked me to join . . . and then all hell broke loose."

For Gyi, on the other hand, things went differently. "The process is probably the same as it always was, you wait until you get a letter inviting you to come back to pledge, and if you don't, you're out. Anyway, I went through rush, and that was the end of that. And so, I proceeded with my life at college. Because it's such a small place, it's kinda hard for some things not to be shared. And so, I knew from early on, probably even that first year at Beloit, that there were members of Delta Gamma who would have liked to have had me pledge, but they couldn't do it, but they were working on it."

And although Gyi didn't get that magic letter, she also remembered that no one came up to her and said that she hadn't been invited to join Delta Gamma because of her race. "They were very, very careful," she laughed. "For a couple of years, I was getting more invested in this idea. And perhaps hoping, wanting for this to happen."

It wasn't until her junior year that she received an invitation to join Delta Gamma, "and then it was not too long after that, maybe, that the national Delta Gamma office discovered, lo and behold, wonders of wonders, that the Beloit chapter hadn't done everything to procedure, [at least] according to them," Gyi said.

According to the Delta Gamma national headquarters at the time, the local chapter, Alpha Mu, had violated a number of sorority rules, including communicating with headquarters in a timely manner and following proper procedures with regard to rush. As a result the chapter was placed on probation.

"Council has voted unanimously to place the chapter on fraternity probation immediately and has instituted the procedures necessary to follow as provided in article 18 of the fraternity constitution before the council can determine whether or not to suspend the chapter's charter."[5]

Placing chapters on probation was a scare tactic many white fraternity and sorority headquarters (Delta Gamma, like a lot of early white sororities, referred to itself as a "women's fraternity") used when trying to prevent blacks from joining. Usually, headquarters used that cover in conjunction with the objections of alumnae members, who held veto power over the local chapters. By citing a technicality, they could stop a black pledge from being initiated. The national organization accused the Alpha Mu chapter of having broken its oath of secrecy because some members had talked to their parents about pledging Gyi. Gyi herself suspected that it was the Delta Gamma alumnae who objected to her being pledged, and that they had alerted Delta Gamma sorority national headquarters.

"Had every single person in the chapter wanted to pledge me? Well, actually, I cannot even with certainty say that's true. There could have been a vote where 90 percent said 'Yes' and 10 percent abstained. But nobody said 'No.' But the way sororities and fraternities operate, you not only have to be acceptable to all the active people [in the chapter], you have to be acceptable to all the alumni."

But none of this prevented her rejection from being a national story.

"Girl Pledge Stirs Ruckus in Sorority" was the headline in the *Sarasota Herald-Tribune*. "Negress Pledges, Sorority Punished," the *Milwaukee Sentinel* proclaimed.

And Gyi's hunch was right, as it was an Iowa Delta Gamma alumna who had been told about her potential initiation and who had alerted Delta Gamma's national headquarters.[6]

When asked for a comment, the national president of Delta Gamma, Helen H. Million, tersely told reporters, "This is a private organization." In fact, the national organization instructed the Beloit chapter that "if questioned by anyone outside of your own group, you are to reply 'no comment.' If, however, you are questioned by your college administration, you are to refer them to the president of the fraternity."[7]

The directives from Delta Gamma national headquarters didn't placate the local chapter.

"Oh, [they were] terribly frustrated, angry, upset, and for the most part," Gyi said, "I don't think anybody, for a minute, misunderstood why it was happening. So they, of course, extended all kinds of comfort and support to me. And the college administration responded very appropriately, with indignation. I'm very proud of the way the college handled their end of the deal."

Over at Stanford, the decision to pledge Washington was met with immediate action by Sigma Chi national headquarters, especially the national president, Harry V. Wade, who said that he hadn't known that the Stanford chapter was going to pledge Washington. The chapter was put on probation for its "contemptuousness for the fraternity and the ritual."

"It was crystal clear that the chapter was not particularly interested in carrying on the ritual, standards and traditions of the fraternity," Wade said about the probation. Washington heard that Wade, who was the president and chairman of the Standard Life Insurance Company in Indiana, said something different. "The way he put it was that 'if we had maybe a higher quality negro, we'd consider it.'"[8]

The Sigma Chi brothers at Stanford fought against their national headquarters on Washington's behalf. "We plan to fight this thing within the fraternity," Sigma Chi member Frank Olrich said. "We have violated no constitutional provisions or regulations and we have no intention to get out."[9]

The chapter president, Gary Kerns, was even more resolute. "We have pledged a Negro . . . We will not give up the pledge to stay in the national but we intend to try to convince the national organization that we should stay affiliated."[10]

Prior to pledging Washington, Olrich had sent a letter to Sigma Chi national headquarters, saying in part, "Not only are we losing many outstanding Negro athletes and scholars, but many well qualified

Caucasian students are avoiding our house because of their overt distaste for our discriminatory policy."[11]

At least two Stanford Sigma Chi brothers were active in the civil rights movement as volunteers for the Mississippi Freedom Project, better known as Freedom Summer, for which they did the very dangerous work of trying to register African Americans voters in Mississippi. That work would result in Freedom Summer volunteers James Cheney, Andrew Goodman, and Michael Schwerner being killed by the Ku Klux Klan in Philadelphia, Mississippi.

In fact, it was because the civil rights movement was rapidly dismantling Jim Crow segregation, both in the streets and by law, that the reaction from Sigma Chi national headquarters actually surprised Washington. Stanford, even with its small black population, did have at least one African American member of a predominately white fraternity, with Stanford student Haldane King a member of Alpha Tau Omega, so there was a precedent.

"I mean you had these kinds of barriers breaking down. By this time, the civil rights legislation, Civil Rights Act of '64, had passed, the Voting Rights Act of '65, it passed, and so you had segregationist barriers everywhere just dropping. It didn't seem like a big deal to me, so I had no inclination that this was going to happen. Not at all.

"To be frank with you, I didn't know exactly how to react. Should I just let it go, or go ahead and push and be a martyr slash role model? Pushing forward has always been my inclination. If somebody says, you've got a racist out there that says you can't do it, then I'm gonna do it. That's always been my parents' attitude, and so after discussion with them, that was what we decided to do. You know, just go ahead and push it."

For Gyi and Delta Gamma, the reaction was the same, as the national organization brought down the hammer on the Alpha Mu chapter. The chapter members were instructed to return all of their official documents, including "officer's notebooks, manuals, constitutions,

Fraternity forms and instructions, Fraternity and chapter materials on file, song books, ritual equipment and ceremonies, roll books, chapter minutes, and such other items as may be classified as Delta Gamma Fraternity property."[12]

For Gyi, who never wanted to be the eye of the integration storm, the controversy was a bit too much. Her brother Henry demanded that the university make sure that his sister hadn't been rejected because of her race. The Madison community, which supported Gyi, was outraged that one of their local daughters had been treated unjustly. But Gyi wasn't interested in continuing the fight.

"After a period of time with this circus . . . I felt was just ridiculous, and unnecessary . . . I said, 'OK. You win! I de-pledge.' And so I basically told Delta Gamma that I wasn't interested in being in Delta Gamma at that point.

"The whole incident had a lot of fallout that was very hard on some Delta Gamma members. My classmates and members of the sorority, some who'd invested so much emotion in those first couple years . . . I think, well I'm sure, some felt betrayed when I took the action . . . they had put themselves on the line with Delta Gamma on my behalf . . . but I was just emotionally exhausted from all of this."

Plus, by her junior year, joining Delta Gamma had become less of a priority than looking toward her future. She had studied in Europe during her sophomore year in what she hoped was a precursor to a career in international relations. By the time she came back, being a Delta Gamma member seemed less important than it had before. She was no longer the shy eighteen-year-old interested in fitting in, and more the twenty-year-old who was thinking beyond Beloit.

"It was not going to change my life in the way that joining a sorority or a fraternity does when you're a freshman, when you're just making new friends, getting involved in what it means to be in college. By the time I was a junior, I was just way beyond that in a lot of ways. I had many friends in Delta Gamma, probably my closest friends, and some of them are still close friends to this day. I just didn't feel the need to be part of the sorority life."

But that didn't placate the Delta Gamma national headquarters. They voted unanimously to not reinstate the Alpha Mu chapter, so the women all decided to disaffiliate with the sorority. They were allowed to remain Delta Gammas as *individuals,* but not as a chapter.

"After I made my decision the [Alpha Mu] members said, 'You know what? We're just going to be a local sorority.' So, they became Theta Pi Gamma sorority, and never applied for reinstatement."

Theta Pi Gamma was a local sorority founded on the Beloit campus in 1896; through fits and starts, it had maintained a presence on the campus. And once Delta Gamma ceased to exist on campus, Gyi joined the others and pledged the local sorority. But as for Delta Gamma and its discrimination, the issue was not over. Instead, it was spreading.

The University of Wisconsin's faculty committee recommended that the sorority be booted from campus for failure to comply with the school's antidiscrimination policies. The Delta Gamma national headquarters promised that it would eventually comply.[13]

At Stanford, the Sigma Chi situation was coming to a head, and as with Delta Gamma, the situation spread beyond the campus. At the University of Colorado, the administration demanded that its Sigma Chi chapter prove that it hadn't discriminated against African American students, and when the chapter couldn't, it was placed on suspension.[14]

And once suspended by HQ, the Sigma Chi chapter, like the Beloit Delta Gammas, decided to go independent. It stayed that way for nearly ten years before coming back to campus after the discriminatory clauses had been removed from the Sigma Chi national constitution. But for Washington, like Gyi, joining the fraternity had started to become less a priority than other events of the time, such as the antiwar movement. But the fraternity episode did have an impact on him personally, as his grades started to slip while he fought against Sigma Chi's policies.

"I had nowhere to turn, no one who I could really talk to," Washington recalled about his time as a symbol of integration. "My parents, God bless them, they would have listened to what I had to say, but I didn't have the presence of mind of how to bring them into that conversation in a meaningful way. I mean, their answer to everything, which was appropriate for their time, which was that you just try harder. In the '30s and '40s, my mother went to Fisk, and also went to Smith in Massachusetts. You know, that was certainly no cakewalk for her. And my dad went to Indiana University Medical School when they had what was called a three-three-three unwritten rule, where they'd let in three blacks, three women, and three Jews. And that was kind of the practice in many, many schools across the country. I would say the vast majority of white schools who allowed any blacks or any women in at all would have a rule similar to that. They expected the women to be gone by the end of the second year, and maybe half the blacks, if any, that was their expectation. That's kind of how they ran the schools. So my father, he would have said, maybe rightly so, 'Buck up and get over it!' But this was a different circumstance. Different time and a different circumstance. Dealing with the stuff that I was dealing with, I just wasn't, as I look back, equipped to do it all successfully."

Washington eventually left Stanford for a time, then returned for his senior year, during which he joined protests against the Vietnam War. Then Dr. Martin Luther King Jr., whom Washington had met while in Gary, was assassinated in April 1968; the tragedy solidified a rebellious streak that would define the rest of his life.

Washington and other members of the Black Student Union disrupted a Stanford memorial service for King by "taking the mic" and insisting on ten improvements on behalf of blacks at the school. With this action, along with his antiwar activities on campus, Washington was ruffling the feathers of Stanford bigwigs.

"I actually got a letter of high complaint [about his antiwar activities] from Leland Stanford, the grandnephew of the founder of

Stanford, Leland Stanford Jr.," Washington laughs. "I remember that I checked with the administration to confirm that it really was a relative of the founder of the university, and they confirmed that it was. He was very disappointed in my actions."

The experience of being rejected because of the color of their skin had profound effects on the lives of both Gyi and Washington. In some ways, the rejection removed the veneer of politeness that surrounds racism, showing them—in stark relief—the world as it is, not as they wanted it to be.

"I started to have a paradigm shift in my own thinking, and my own values, things that I thought were important," Washington said. "Even questioning whether or not I should even be at Stanford. Maybe I would have been happier at Fisk?"

Similarly, Gyi questioned whether or not staying at Beloit was the right thing, and she briefly considered transferring to American University. Talked out of doing so by a Beloit counselor, Gyi graduated from Beloit and then headed to Washington, D.C., where she worked in government for a time. But her experience with the world of sororities had shaken her.

"I'm not trying to be cute about it because I know it affected me. There's no doubt about that. I suspect that it was probably a good experience for me to have. In a sense, my life has been lived within the context of the kind of community that I was seeking in college. But I think the experience, the sorority experience, also was a wonderful learning experience for me in terms of race. Having been in this little bubble all of my life, it taught me things that my parents probably thought they were teaching me, but were also protecting me from. I ended up, many years later, working for twenty-something years at a university where I didn't start out, but I ended up in affirmative action."

Gyi became a fixture at Ohio University, where she worked to implement affirmative action policy at the medical school, seeking to increase diversity. Gyi guesses that she would have been an archeologist if not for the sorority experience. In any event, being rejected by Delta Gamma allowed her to see how racism operated in the United States.

"I guess I felt like it contributed to my ability to understand institutional racism. That's what fraternities and sororities have. It's beyond the personal, it's institutionalized."

For Washington, music became a respite. He dropped out of Stanford only a month before graduation; an accomplished tenor saxophonist, he sought a career as a professional musician. But that dream was cut short after the tragic death of his wife. He had a family to support.

So he gave up that dream and worked in business for twenty years before returning to his passion. Today, he plays music and also operates Earth-Solar Technologies, a company he founded, which is focused on renewable energy products. "I want to see us do as much damage to the fossil-fuel world order as possible," he said.[15]

The *Stanford Alumni Magazine,* in an article about the Sigma Chi incident, asked Washington about the effect the fraternity rejection had had on him. Washington was blunt. "I would imagine," he said, "that no sane person enjoys being rejected for reasons that have nothing to do with your achievements and capabilities in life. That's what racism does. It questions your humanity, your basic humanity.

"I'll tell you the part that I appreciate," he added. "It's the sacrifice by the white Sigma Chis at Stanford, who wanted so much to be part of their national fraternity. They sacrificed being embraced by the national fraternity on behalf of integrating. And I've come to respect and honor those guys because they are the ones who really sacrificed that organizational brotherhood and fellowship."[16]

The same can be said by Gyi, who still returns to Beloit College for reunions and was delighted to see the fully integrated Theta Pi Gamma sorority still flourishing.

"The little blue [former Delta Gamma] house on campus is still right there," she said. "I was on campus almost two years ago, believe it or not, for my fiftieth reunion. The members, several members of the sorority, introduced themselves to me. It's just so heartwarming to meet this group of young women now, who are just so diverse! It's amazing . . . I feel wonderful about that! I just have to keep going back to the point that, it was not my goal to integrate something, any more than when I went to elementary school, and I wasn't integrating it. I was just being me."

But even after all these years, the one thing that neither Gyi nor Washington has received is an apology from a fraternity's national headquarters. And that still stings.

Washington has an unclear fraternity status, as a quasi-brother of Sigma Chi, which frequently asks him to participate in various events.

"They have invited me to attend something next month. I guess I would say I'm kind of a member of Sigma Chi," Washington said uncertainly. "I don't identify as a member of Sigma Chi, but I don't renounce it either. And so, it's kind of an odd feeling that I have about it. I don't know if you understand what I mean by that.

"I mean the local [Sigma Chi] guys have always been, 'Hey man. We're sorry this happened.' They've done that. They sacrificed their own membership in the national Sigma Chi on behalf of bringing me in. I don't know if they would have done it with just any black guy, but a lot of them said, 'Keni, you're the guy we wanted in this fraternity.' So they don't owe me one thing. They've done it. It's the national organization who owes them, and me, all an apology."

Gyi has had no contact with Delta Gamma. But she did find some recent research about the sorority that made her reflect that as much as things change, they also stay the same.

"There was a recent incident at the University of Maryland, relating to Delta Gamma," Gyi said, referring to a 2014 incident in which a white Delta Gamma member posted a photo of a three-tiered cake on Instagram. The birthday girl smiled next to the cake, which was loaded with cheap wine, beer bottles, and tiny cupcakes and emblazoned with the words "Suck A Nigga Dick."[17]

"In this article, there was a statement from the national sorority in response to this racial incident, and it just cracked me up," Gyi said. "The sorority issued a statement that read, 'We have become aware of an unacceptable Instagram post by a member of our chapter.' Delta Gamma Fraternity. I'd forgotten they call themselves a fraternity. Then there's this quote, 'Delta Gamma is a dynamic organization committed to diversity that does not discriminate.'"

Gyi chuckled ruefully as she read the last sentence. In her eyes, the more things changed, the more they stayed the same.

4

THE GREAT AMERICAN HALF-BAKED SALE

"I had no need to apologize that the look-wider, search-more affirmative action that Princeton and Yale practiced had opened doors for me. That was its purpose: to create the conditions whereby students from disadvantaged backgrounds could be brought to the starting line of a race many were unaware was even being run."

—Sonia Sotomayor

EVERY FEW YEARS, THE UC BERKELEY COLLEGE REPUBLICANS host a very special bake sale. Setting up the event in the main quad, Sproul Plaza, for maximum exposure, the young conservatives pack a table full of items necessary for a successful fund-raiser—cakes, cookies, brownies, cupcakes—and sell them to students who pass by. The problem? This particular bake sale isn't designed to satisfy any Cal student's sweet tooth. Instead, it's designed to put a sour taste in their mouths.

You see, the UC Berkeley College Republicans have a unique price list for their baked goods, one on which price is determined by one's race (and, in some cases, gender). So if you're white, the price of a slice of cake is $2.00, the highest of any race. If you're Asian, the price is

$1.50 (unless the College Republicans want to avoid any suggestion that they're being racist, in which case they'll make the Asian price the same as the white price; for them, it's a sign that the so-called model minority has essentially reached equality with the downtrodden white students in terms of merit). For Latino students, the price is $1.00, while for blacks, the price is even lower, somewhere around seventy-five cents. If they remember to add Native Americans, those individuals can get the baked goods for about a quarter. Women? They receive twenty-five cents off the price for any goods, regardless of their race.

So what's the point of the different prices for different ethnicities? According to these millennial future low-tax, free-market Republicans, the bake sale prices illustrate the injustices of affirmative action, or, as they like to term it, racial preferences, in college admissions. And in the eyes of these students, it is unfair to white students applying to Berkeley that affirmative action includes race as a factor.

"The purpose of the pricing structure is to cause people to disagree with this kind of preferential treatment," said Shawn Lewis, president of the Berkeley College Republicans. "We want people to say no race is above another race, or no race is below another one. Why put one over the other? Why rank them that way?"[1]

Obviously, I beg to differ. This "Increase Diversity Bake Sale" wasn't designed to start a dialogue about affirmative action, despite the protestation of young Shawn Lewis. Instead, it is intended to provoke a response from supporters of affirmative action on campus, specifically minorities. And at other campuses, where they've conducted "Anti-Affirmative Action Bake Sales," that response has been almost universally negative.

At Bucknell University, in Pennsylvania, officials shut down a similar bake sale. Officials at the College of William and Mary in Virginia cut off a cookie sale, saying they were "shocked and appalled." The University of California, Irvine, shut down a bake sale on campus, saying it was discriminatory. And a bake sale at Southern Methodist University in Texas was shut down after forty-five minutes because of what officials called an "unsafe environment."[2]

These bake sales may seem silly and laughable, and most write them off as minor distractions on the part of immature politicos. But they're more dangerous than that. They're disingenuous, ahistorical, and meant to intimidate African Americans and other minorities via a philosophy that says, "You're not good enough, and we're the ones to who set the standards." It's another form of racism that hopes to make inequity generational and systemic, and it contributes to the real pain minority students feel on campus.

At some point political conservatives began wondering: if they couldn't destroy the historical legacy of Martin Luther King Jr., what if they could do the next best thing and co-opt it? So over the years, affirmative action critics have enjoyed pointing to one line, delivered as part of King's "I Have a Dream" speech during the 1963 March on Washington for Jobs and Freedom, as summing up America's color-blind ideal. And since America's historical memory has been reduced to 140 characters, this quote serves as a kind of Cliff's Notes to King's entire political philosophy, warped for the benefit of conservatives: "I have a dream that my four little children will one day live in a nation where they will not be judged by the color of their skin, but by the content of their character."[3]

It's the money quote. The quote children are given to study, understand, and then regurgitate as King's ultimate vision for America. But it's incomplete. Conservatives never seem to quote *another* section of the speech, in which Dr. King says, "It is obvious today that America has defaulted on this promissory note insofar as her citizens of color are concerned. Instead of honoring this sacred obligation, America has given the Negro people a bad check, a check which has come back marked 'insufficient funds.'"[4]

And for all their newfound love of Dr. King, conservatives have failed to read his book *Why We Can't Wait*, published a year later, in which King wrote, "Whenever this issue of compensatory or preferential treatment for the Negro is raised, some of our friends recoil in horror. The Negro should be granted equality, they agree; but he should ask for nothing more. On the surface, this appears reasonable, but it is not realistic. For it is obvious that if a man is entering the starting line in a race three hundred years after another man, the first would have to perform some impossible feat in order to catch up with his fellow runner."

"If a man is entering the starting line in a race three hundred years after another man, the first would have to perform some impossible feat in order to catch up with his fellow runner."[5]

Puts those bake sale prices in perspective, doesn't it?

And while the words of Dr. King were inspirational, it was the words of President Lyndon Johnson that put meat on the bones of affirmative action policy. During a commencement address at Howard University in 1965, he laid out the reasoning behind it.

"Thus it is not enough just to open the gates of opportunity. All our citizens must have the ability to walk through those gates. This is the next and the more profound stage of the battle for civil rights. We seek not just freedom but opportunity. We seek not just legal equity but human ability, not just equality as a right and a theory but equality as a fact and equality as a result.

"For the task is to give 20 million Negroes the same chance as every other American to learn and grow, to work and share in society, to develop their abilities—physical, mental and spiritual, and to pursue their individual happiness.

"To this end equal opportunity is essential, but not enough, not enough. Men and women of all races are born with the same range of abilities. But ability is not just the product of birth. Ability is stretched or stunted by the family that you live with, and the neighborhood you live in—by the school you go to and the poverty or the richness of your surroundings. It is the product of a hundred unseen forces playing upon the little infant, the child, and finally the man."[6]

The UC Berkeley College Republicans fail to realize that given the historical context, their menu pricing is off . . . by a lot. To be truly fair, they'd first have to realize that American society already puts one race over another, and has for over four hundred years. And that fact didn't just go away when blacks could eat at integrated Woolworth lunch counters. But let's keep to the bake sale analogy.

Prior to affirmative action, white students were given nearly unlimited preference, a white-skin subsidy that came with a near-monopoly to purchase any baked good on the table, no matter the price. African Americans were allowed to purchase the baked goods, but only while public policy suppressed their wages, which made the baked goods hyper-expensive. Also, since the white-owned baked goods industry didn't value the black dollar, blacks would have to go longer and farther to even get the opportunity to buy the baked good. And even when they did, they'd be denigrated by being asked to buy from the back.

But forget purchasing the baked goods. Whites also controlled the means of production, dictating who was employed and who wasn't. That meant that whites made the life-and-death decision about who ate and who didn't, or, in the case of education, how many blacks were given an opportunity to build enough wealth so they could even consider participating in higher education. And artificial quotas further limited African Americans, to the extent that only a certain number of blacks were allowed to purchase the baked goods, while generations of mediocre white students were given free access to the beneficial properties of the baked goods.

The white-skin subsidy also came in the form of the inherent value of white skin in America. This subsidy provided societal protection from violence, like the overt violence faced by James Meredith as he tried to integrate the University of Mississippi, or the microaggressions black students face every day, on the basis of skin color. Approaching the baked goods table sometimes meant being assaulted by ravenously angry whites, who believed that they, and they alone, had a right to the goods. And this has gone on not for years, or decades, but for *centuries*.

What's the price for that?

You have to look at racism as not just an "ism" of inconvenience, but also one of substantial depth and cruelty. One that encompasses slavery, the legacy of slavery, black code laws, domestic terrorism, segregation, disfranchisement at the polls, health and housing discrimination, banking discrimination, job discrimination, just to name a few things. And they all have an effect down to the present day, since racism has never gone away. Have things gotten better? Sure. But as Malcolm X once said, "If you stick a knife in my back nine inches and pull it out six inches, there's no progress. If you pull it all the way out that's not progress. Progress is healing the wound that the blow made. And they haven't even pulled the knife out much less heal the wound. They won't even admit the knife is there."[7]

The UC Berkeley College Republicans deny the existence of a knife.

Noam Chomsky once noted, "Racism is a very serious problem in the United States. Take a look at the scholarly work on it, say, George Fredrickson's study of the white supremacy, comparative study. He concludes, I think plausibly, that the white supremacy in the United States was even more extreme and savage than in South Africa."[8]

Still, even if you took the Berkeley College Republican price list at face value, with whiteness as the end-all, be-all standard for non-preferential admission to college, you'd be wrong. College admissions include a lot of variables.

In a 2004 study of nineteen elite schools, including Harvard, Middlebury, and Virginia, former Princeton president William Bowen and two other researchers discovered that a recruited athlete was 30 percentage points more likely to be admitted than a non-athlete. A black, Latino, or Native American student was 28 percentage points more likely to be admitted than a white or Asian student. And a legacy applicant received a 20-percentage-point boost over someone whose parents hadn't attended that college.[9]

It is an open secret that even if you looked at college admissions, and racism itself, ahistorically, white students and others *still* could receive a preference. It's just that only minorities are asked to explain themselves. You can't be an average black student, like a substantial number of white students are, and be admitted to colleges and universities every year. At top universities, the black student needs to be extraordinary, even if she comes from a community that has disadvantages that are hard-baked because of race. That said, conservatives have successfully made the idea of race-based affirmative action the one segment of affirmative action policy that is not politically acceptable.

"Those liberals who have defended affirmative action have not been able to popularize even the most uncontested arguments in its favor: for instance, that preferences of various sorts are often used in selection processes, such as, benefits for veterans, or college admission for athletes and the children of alumni and alumnae," wrote political scientist Jean Hardisty.

"What makes those practices acceptable, especially in the case of veterans and athletes, is the widely held judgment that these recipients are 'appropriate' and 'legitimate.' Most white Americans do not extend the same benefit of the doubt to 'average' people of color."[10]

Even before President Johnson's Howard University speech, there were some colleges who made overt pleas for the recruitment of African American students via affirmative action measures. In a 1944 editorial to the black newspaper the *Afro American,* Antioch College wrote, "It is our belief that we can never secure interracial understanding until we get children, high school and college students of all races working and playing together. It is difficult for people to start to co-operate with one another in middle age. We consider exclusively one-race schools an abnormal situation unlike the outside world, and therefore to be avoided."

To help foster this idea of integration, Antioch formed a Race Relations Scholarship Fund and asked *Afro American* readers to contribute.[11]

Another advocate for racial integration on college campuses was Felice Schwartz. When Schwartz was a junior at Smith College in the late 1940s, she "saw Smith's six Negro students hurt by chance remarks, by the snobbery of the townspeople in the socially alive college town." Schwartz thought, "This sort of thing will keep happening until there are enough colored students in school to give their group a feeling of security and companionship. Why don't more Negroes go to college anyway?"[12]

Schwartz would go on to found the National Scholarship Service and Fund for Negro Students, one of the first agencies to fight for the inclusion of African American students on college campuses while also providing financial assistance. Schwartz would later become a stalwart of the women's movement, identifying ways that employers could better support working women by providing services like day care and flexible work hours, in what eventually became known as the "mommy track."[13]

But none of this matters, because the College Republicans know that they're winning the affirmative action battle in terms of the public policy of *today*. Not because they have the right argument, but because they've been able to convince white voters that fixing the inequities of society through affirmative action somehow violates the civil rights of white students.

But white anti–affirmative action proponents knew that it would be politically impractical to have someone white make the argument initially. What they needed was a willing black face, one who just happened to be on the Berkeley campus helping sell cupcakes for the College Republicans.

A black man named Ward Connerly.

Actually, Connerly uses the term "black man" to identify himself very reluctantly. Mr. Connerly considers himself black "because blackness is an experience and others have thrust that experience upon me."

He takes great pains to explain that his ethnicity goes beyond being black. "One drop of blood does it," he said, reviewing the computation: "25 percent black plus 37.5 percent Irish plus 25 percent French plus 12.5 percent Choctaw equals 100 percent black," Connerly said in a 1997 *New York Times* article. "I suppose I could claim to be Irish, but who wants to stand there and argue the point every time? So I'm black."[14]

Connerly, a Sacramento businessman, was appointed to the University of California Regents by Governor Pete Wilson, after ironically making his fortune through affirmative action set-aside programs. The *San Francisco Chronicle* reported that Connerly repeatedly listed his land-use consulting company as a minority contractor with the California Energy Commission, which guaranteed his firm, which he co-owned with his wife, at least three contracts to carry out energy conservation training worth $1.2 million. Connerly's firm was hired by fifteen California communities, which used his minority status to take advantage of affirmative action regulations.[15]

Connerly continued to be seen as benefitting from affirmative action. The first time was in 1969, when he was added to the California State Housing Committee by his longtime political benefactor, then state legislator and future California governor Pete Wilson. And then in 1993, when Wilson again chose Connerly to be on the University of California Board of Regents. It's no surprise that Connerly had donated more than $100,000 to Wilson's campaign.[16]

And yet, once Connerly had risen to prominence, he suddenly thought affirmative action was a bad thing, and it was his job to kick away the ladder that had allowed him to rise so high. It's as old as America. Delude yourself into thinking that your achievement came only from your own enterprise and pluck, and that justifies denying to others all of the instruments that were responsible for your success.

For African Americans, this is a particularly pernicious and egregious manifestation of self-hate. But Connerly isn't alone in being an

African American against affirmative action. One of conservative radio commentator Rush Limbaugh's favorite quotes is from Condoleezza Rice, the former U.S. secretary of state and an African American woman: "I tell you what affirmative action is, soft bigotry, low expectations. Affirmative action is a racist insult disguised as social justice by the Democrats."[17]

Black conservative social commentator Thomas Sowell once wrote that affirmative action is "one of the few policies that can be said to harm virtually every group in a different way . . . Obviously, whites and Asians lose out when you have preferential admission for black students or Hispanic students—but blacks and Hispanics lose out because what typically happens is the students who have all the credentials to succeed in college are admitted to colleges where the standards are so much higher that they fail."[18]

Connerly soon began working to dismantle affirmative action in the state. And when Proposition 209, a voter initiative, was drafted by Cal State anthropology professor Glynn Custred and California Association of Scholars executive director Thomas Wood in 1996, it amended the California constitution to include a new section: "The state shall not discriminate against, *or grant preferential treatment to,* any individual or group on the basis of race, sex, color, ethnicity, or national origin in the operation of public employment, public education, or public contracting."[19]

But contrary to popular myth, affirmative action in admissions continues to be a popular concept, as the American public understands that the disparities in K-12 are not just economic, but racial. But to move the needle, the Proposition 209 proponents knew they had to present the initiative in a way that tapped into the white voters' racist DNA, without making it appear that they were *acting* racist. It was akin to Tom Sawyer getting his friends to whitewash the fence; instead anti–affirmative action proponents were whitewashing their flagship campuses of black students.

In a Pew Research Center survey conducted in 2014, "63 percent of people said [affirmative action] programs aimed at increasing the number of black and minority students on college campuses were a good thing, versus just 30 percent who called them a bad thing."[20]

The Orwellian language in the initiative, *or grant preferential treatment to,* equates the remedies used to fix the past and present discrimination against African Americans as somehow being discriminatory against whites, thus making them the victims. It would be like preventing a surgeon from using a scalpel to operate on a patient dying from knife wounds, all because one equates knives with being bad in all contexts. The argument was a perversion of the 1964 Civil Rights Act.

But it was effective.

Connerly became the black face of the initiative, which was backed by big money from right-wing activists, including media mogul Rupert Murdoch, who contributed $750,000; Howard F. Ahmanson Jr., who contributed $350,000; and Richard Mellon Scaife, who contributed $100,000. Altogether, Yes on Proposition 209 raised $5,239,287, while its main opponent, the Campaign to Defeat 209, raised $2,185,086. The anti–affirmative action side was able to convince white Californians that it was okay to vote against a public policy that was falsely portrayed as a "quota" for African Americans when it came to college admissions.[21]

Using a black man as the face of the proposals, as even Connerly admitted, allowed whites to protest affirmative action "without having to feel like they appear racist." It was the perfect way for the majority-white population of California, and later Michigan, whose Prop 2 emulated Prop 209, to codify inequity into college admissions. The measures prevented universities, particularly top public universities like the University of California at Berkeley and the University of Michigan, from using race as one criteria for admission.[22]

Syndicated columnist Leonard Pitts Jr. asked, "Who isn't fascinated at the sight of a hen campaigning for the foxes." He went on to say that

Connerly was "a confused Negro who should know better than to allow his skin color to be used as moral cover by those whose truest goals have little to do with liberty and justice for all."[23]

Social commentator Jean Hardisty wrote in her book, *Mobilizing Resentment: Conservative Resurgence from the John Birch Society to the Promise Keepers,* "When the early architects of affirmative action developed it as a policy to benefit African Americans, who had mounted a strong civil rights movement to demand an end to racial discrimination, the right reacted almost immediately. Later, when other people of color and white women began to benefit from affirmative action, many white people continued to see affirmative action as a program to benefit African Americans. The right often frames the issue to reinforce that perception, perhaps because, in the United States, African Americans are the principal target of white racism, and benefits for Blacks, especially if they are cast as 'special' benefits, are politically unpopular among many white voters."[24]

It is just that framing, along with President Bill Clinton's milquetoast support of affirmative action through his "Mend it, Don't End it" statement, that allowed Proposition 209 to pass with 54 percent of the vote. The result was immediately tested, and in 1997, after the 9th U.S. Circuit Court of Appeals upheld Proposition 209, Connerly would remark, "Now the people of California can get on with the business of making the dream of equal opportunity a reality, without the use of artificial preferences that are divisive and promote the ethnic polarization of our society. We must now focus on ways of providing access for all of our children to an education that prepares them for the rigors of a competitive society."[25]

Ward Connerly's "dream" immediately turned into a nightmare for black students, and not just for undergrads. The year after Prop 209 eliminated race from consideration for admission, only 14 black students out of 792 students were admitted to UC Berkeley's law school, Boalt Hall. And none decided to enroll.[26]

Before Prop 209, the African American undergraduate population at the University of California at Berkeley was 8 percent, roughly the same percentage as the African American population of the state of California. The next year, in 1997, black freshmen only made up 4 percent of the freshmen admitted, and from 2006 to 2010, the black student population at the state's flagship university hovered around 3.6 percent, with many of the black students on scholarship for athletics.[27]

So it's been twenty years since the passage of Proposition 209. How are things at UC Berkeley for black students? Well, in 2013 UC Berkeley conducted a survey of the campus, sort of a finger in the air to see which way the wind was blowing for the student body, administration, and faculty. One thing in the study was very clear. According to the report, "Underrepresented minority respondents and multi-minority respondents were less comfortable than white respondents and other people of color respondents with the overall climate and the workplace climate. White respondents were more comfortable with the climate in their classes than other racial groups." So in short, if you were a white Cal student, things were hunky-dory. But if you were black, or another minority, things weren't so sunny.

The decimation of the African American student population on the Berkeley campus also had a residual effect on the decisions of the qualified African American students who *were* admitted to the university. What the university found was that these students had better options than to go to a university devoid of black students. If they could get into Berkeley, then it was pretty certain that they could get into pretty much any other top academic school in the country, schools like Columbia, Northwestern, and Cal's arch rival to the south, Stanford, so why not choose based on the racial diversity of the campus, the very thing Prop 209 prevented California public universities from doing? In all, between 2006 and 2010, there were 1,539 African American students admitted to Berkeley, yet 885 black students enrolled elsewhere.[28]

"I have friends that are extremely successful, that were extremely bright, and a lot of them went to Yale and Harvard and Columbia and Stanford," said Nile Taylor of Oakland, in an interview with the *East Bay Express* in 2013. Taylor is a 2005 UC Berkeley graduate in political science, legal studies, and theater. "You have some top universities that are competing with Berkeley that these students have the option of attending. So why would you choose to come to Berkeley in a semi-hostile environment when you can go to a campus like Stanford who says, 'Come on! We love you! We want you here!' and that offers them added support as an African-American student?"[29]

"On the campus website, more often than not, you'll often find a black face representing some program or other," a senior and American Studies major, Salih Muhammad of Oakland, said to the *East Bay Express* in 2013. Muhammad is the former chair of Berkeley's Black Student Union and currently chair of the statewide UC African-American Coalition. "But when it comes to walking around the campus, those black faces are few and far between. Or, you'll see the 'I Support Berkeley' banners on campus, with all these black faces on them, but there are more black faces on the banners than there are in many of the classes."[30]

And it was increasingly clear that the black students at Cal had had enough. Like the students at the University of Oklahoma, they were tired of being ignored, unseen, and unheard. Ward Connerly had made them invisible. But one day in 2015, the biggest PR day of the year, they decided that it was time to make the Cal community realize they were there.

Cal Day 2015.

There's a Cal Day–style event at every university in the United States. It's a showcase day on which the university throws open the campus to thousands of prospective students, nervous parents, newly admitted students, and just about anyone else who'd like to see what life at Cal is like. Hundreds of balloons, tables on Sproul Plaza advertising clubs devoted to subjects ranging from Botany to Esperanto. University officials hope for a chamber of commerce blue-sky day, when the bright sun shines down on the Cal students to make them look extra handsome, pretty, and intelligent, when each and every guest will be impressed by this elaborate Open House.

At Cal Day 2015, you could check out the "famous and amazing flying dance group Bandaloop" performing over at Sather Gate. Want to hear from *Moneyball* author Michael Lewis? He was going to have a conversation with UC Berkeley chancellor Nicholas Dirks over at Zellerbach Hall, the main performing arts auditorium on campus. Want to hear the Cal Band perform? You could do that! Skeptical about human evolution? A professor could talk to you about that! You could listen to a lecture titled *Making Things: The Search for Content and the Development of Process.* And if that was too deep, an author was lecturing about his work, *In Search of Richard Pryor: A Biographer's Tale,* which sounded intriguing.[31]

It was organized chaos, but having attended Cal myself, I know that Berkeley always expects a bit of chaos. It's part of our DNA. From the early days of the Free Speech Movement in the 1960s, to the anti–Vietnam War protests, to the wooden shantytowns built on Sproul Plaza where students demanded that Berkeley divest from apartheid South Africa in the 1980s, on any random day, there is something being protested, as protests are as natural to Cal as hippies wandering around Telegraph Avenue. Cal students may major in hundreds of different subjects, but all students minor in protest.

However, despite its reputation as a liberal bastion, Cal is essentially like every other university in America. Inherently conservative, and wanting to put its best face forward, Cal sees itself as being a pretty perfect place for any intellectually curious student. But the black students at Cal didn't see a perfect place. They saw a hostile space.

A month earlier, the Black Student Union at Cal had met with Chancellor Dirks and handed him a list of ten demands. The demands included a space for black students and the hiring of two black psychologists who understood "the racially hostile campus climate" at the University of California at Berkeley. But what the press release latched onto was their demand that the chancellor change the name of the ethnic studies building, Barrow Hall, to Assata Shakur Hall, after the former Black Panther who is now exiled in Cuba.

"Black people have been oppressed at this university since its creation," declared Black Student Union member Alana Banks. "The fact that we have to come up with demands for support that has been long overdue to us is a testament to our condition. Regardless, I believe that we will win; and they believe that we will win too."

For his part, Dirks didn't respond to the demands, but he did say that he recognized that Cal was a hostile environment for black students. "Too many Black students have told us about being ignored during class discussions, verbally harassed at parties . . . and feeling isolated and invisible. This is something we deplore."[32]

Something he deplores, but does nothing about. And that brings us back to Cal Day 2015.

As I've mentioned before, Sproul Plaza is the main quad at the University of California at Berkeley. Overlooked by the stately Sproul Hall, whose grand Grecian columns and majestic steps serve as a natural platform and backdrop for protest, it serves as a communal space for all students. Football pep rallies, dancers, and black fraternities' and sororities' step routines, are all set at Sproul Plaza. Flanking Sproul Plaza is Sather Gate, the original entrance to the university—a beautiful bronze and steel structure that serves as a bridge between Sproul Plaza and the main campus, one through which most students flow.

And it was the hub for Cal Day 2015.

The students gave Dirks two different deadlines to respond to their demands, each of which passed without a response. So the Black Student Union decided that it wanted everyone at the Cal Day to know that just beneath the surface of the compelling classes, the talent-driven musical offerings, and the lectures by best-selling authors things were a tad rotten. But you had to look. The Black Student Union was going to make people look.

Dressed all in black, holding banners that read "WE DEMAND" and listed the demands, black Cal students made themselves seen and heard. The uncle of Oscar Grant, who was famously killed on a Bay Area Rapid Transit subway platform by a BART police officer while bystanders shot video, spoke about institutional racism and violence. And standing on the Sproul Hall steps, the black students held a giant black #BlackLivesMatter banner. Several groups declined to perform because black students would have been protesting in the background, including one non–African American dance troupe . . . who later had no problem dancing to African American hip-hop artist 50 Cent's hit "Up in the Club."[33]

But the coup de grace was when the black students moved their protest to the Sather Gate main entrance and refused to let people pass unless they were elderly or physically disabled. Flanking the sides of Sather Gate are two smaller openings that were left open for all, but with the main entrance blocked, everyone had a choice: Do you recognize the black students and their right to protest, or do you force your way through?

The disruptions made the news, and social media chronicled how this small group of black students had made the comfortable uncomfortable. And ironically, one prospective black Cal student had watched the protest, uploaded a picture to Instagram, and proclaimed that this was the type of campus she wanted to go to, one where black students stood up for themselves.

But these weren't the first post–Proposition 209 African American students to protest the conditions at Cal. Various generations of black Cal students had protested about the devastation of the black community under various iterations. First there was the Represent, where post–Prop 209 black Cal students of the mid-1990s demanded proper representation on campus. In 2004, 100 black students stopped traffic as part of a "Blackout" demonstration, which created a bottleneck at Sproul Plaza. Then there was the hashtag social media campaign #Can-YouHearUsNow, organized as part of the broader #BlackLivesMatter movement.[34]

"I learned about Prop 209 during my freshman year. There were a group of black students who came together as a group called the Affirmation, and I got engaged in that space," said Destiny Iwuoma, a black senior and an activist on campus. "It was a collective of students, not just black students, and I saw the multicultural unity was able to form. I saw people coming together and asserting their presence, created their own power."[35]

But under any name, these black Cal students are following a long tradition of student activism, demanding that Cal fit their needs as African Americans. They protested because Black Lives *do* Matter, and they wanted Cal to know it. But the problem is that Cal wasn't and isn't listening. And one parent, with a name that's as close to Cal royalty as one can get, regrets persuading her kids to attend her alma mater under these conditions.

"I feel like I was a liar," said Amy Nickerson.

I've known Amy and Hardy Nickerson since our days at Berkeley, and they are true college sweethearts, having met on the Cal campus back in the mid-1980s. Amy, who grew up just a few miles away from the UC Berkeley campus in Richmond, California, would get her bachelor's and master's degrees from Cal, while Hardy would get his bachelor's in 1989. But that's just the start of their relationship with Cal. Hardy made the Nickerson name golden on the Cal campus because he was a beast linebacker on the Cal football team during the mid-1980s.

Nicknamed Hardware, Hardy was one of the greatest Cal linebackers in history, ranking second overall in Cal football for tackles. He went on to the NFL, where he played for 16 seasons, most as the bulwark of the Tampa Bay Buccaneers' defense. A five-time Pro Bowl selection, a four time All Pro, Hardy was named to the NFL's 1990s All Decade Team and is a member of the Cal Athletic Hall of Fame.[36]

For the past thirty years, both Amy and Hardy have been great ambassadors for the university. Despite living across the country, in North Carolina, these two Cal alumni persuaded their three kids— Hardy Jr., a linebacker just like his dad and now a stalwart on the Cal football team, Haleigh (Hardy's twin sister), and their older sister Ashleigh—to become Golden Bears. And yet, despite their parents' status as Cal alumni, the Nickerson name did nothing to prevent Amy and Hardy's kids from experiencing the same racial microaggressions that black students around the country are facing. In fact, Amy feels that sending her children to Cal may have been one of her worst decisions ever.

"I feel like we're not even thought about," said Amy, her frustration growing when thinking about the black community. "And I know for a fact that Cal knows what's going on because I raised hell every time something crazy happened to the black students."[37]

The first of the Nickerson kids to attend Cal was Ashleigh. Ashleigh and her siblings had attended a private high school in North Carolina, where they were used to being among the handful of black students in a predominately white school, but Cal was a totally different beast.

"I remember that when I first got to campus, a lot of people thought I was on a sports team," Ashleigh remembered. "They'd ask for no reason, 'What sport do you play?,' and I was offended. But then, I was extremely surprised that it seemed like most of the black people *were* on sports teams."[38]

Soon, Ashleigh began noticing that she was often the only black face in class.

"It was really hard for me, especially in [freshman] weed-out classes. I had some classes where there were six hundred students, and I was either the only black girl, or there were only two or three of us. But when you split into labs, which are smaller, I was always the only black girl in my lab, and no one wanted to work with me. I'd go around asking if I could join a study group, and they'd say they were full. I just felt that people automatically assumed that I wasn't intelligent enough to be in their group, or that I wasn't on top of my stuff. But I was on top of my stuff. I went to class every day, but it was hard to find people who'd let me in. I was doing all the work on my own, getting B's, and wondering how are these people getting 100 percent on these labs. How were they outperforming me? Then I asked one student and I found out that half the class had been in a study group. All this affected my academics."

Haleigh, who came to Cal at the same time as her twin brother, Hardy, didn't find things much different.

"I felt very out of place," she said. "And it seemed like there were less black people than they said [in Cal's official figures] because everyone was so spread out. We were never all together at once. But sometimes during the semester, all of the black students would come together, and I'd laugh because it still didn't look like a lot of people."[39]

Like Ashleigh, Haleigh felt that being one of the few black students in her class meant that she was socially isolated from the rest of the campus. "Nobody would want to sit next to me in physics or astronomy. In discussions, people would look at you like you were stupid. I don't know if they were actually doing that, but I felt that way."

Of course the irony is that Ward Connerly, in arguing against affirmative action, said that the elimination of "racial preferences" would create a situation in which African American students would feel *better* about themselves, not worse. That their self-esteem would be *raised*, not lowered, because the "burden" of being labeled an affirmative action admit would disappear. If Ashleigh and Haleigh's experiences are any indication, his experiment failed abysmally.

But that wasn't all. Beyond the racial microaggressions that come from being part of a tiny minority on campus, both Ashleigh and Haleigh had to deal with racist incidents, particularly involving white fraternities and sororities. Among many occurrences, from a white sorority member calling the police on a black football player, falsely accusing him of carrying a gun, even though he was just walking down the street minding his own business, to random white fraternity members yelling "Nigger!" at them, there was one that stuck out in Ashleigh's mind as being the most overtly racist.

"When I was a junior in spring 2012, I was with some football players, and we were a mixed race crowd. We were trying to go into a DKE party [Delta Kappa Epsilon fraternity]," Ashleigh remembered. "DKE has a three story building, and you enter from the bottom. We were like, 'Hey, can we come in?' And they were like, no. Then someone from the third level opened up a window and started calling us niggers.

"Nigger, nigger, nigger!" Ashleigh said the DKE member yelled. "Of course, our guys were like, 'You better shut up.' And then, a white guy on the third floor of the frat house chucks a toilet seat down at us, and it hit one of the black guys in the head and cracked his head open."

That black guy was a cousin of Kameron Jackson, then the starting cornerback on the Cal football team, and he was knocked unconscious.

"I was there," remembered Gabe King, a former Cal football player. "At first, there was a line of people to get into the party, and they were mostly white people. Once the line went down, there were mostly black people trying to get into the party. My girlfriend was standing in back of Kam's cousin, and she said that there was a [fifth of liquor] bottle [that] came out first. And then a toilet seat literally comes out from the top level and crushes him right in the face. He's busted wide open, he falls, and my girl catches him as he's falling. Total concussion."[40]

"He fell and threw up three times while he was unconscious," Ashleigh continued. "We all ducked for cover, and I immediately knew that he needed medical attention. There was a big brawl, and the frat called the cops, so the [football] guys had to flee. I couldn't believe it."

The situation was so bad for Ashleigh and Haleigh that Amy began sending emails to then chancellor Robert Birgeneau, telling him that "I am fed up with how African American students at Cal are being treated, how they feel, and at the abysmal numbers." She also detailed how in 1988, when she was an undergrad and working in the chancellor's office, Asian students were unsatisfied with the atmosphere on campus and their representation there, which was about 25 percent at the time; in response, Chancellor Ira Heyman made changes. The Asian population began to rise from that point forward, Amy recalled.

"All I want to know is whether or not the powers that be can do the same for our abysmal 3 percent and dropping African American students?" Amy asked in her letter. "A case can be made for African American Cal students' possible extinction . . . are we waiting for 2 percent or 1 percent?"[41]

"I never got a response," Amy recalled. "I'm on the Cal Parents Board, and I got no response there. It's always committees, then meetings, and then we adjourn. Then it's more weeks, then more committees, then more meetings, and you see, it's death by meetings. I kept asking, 'Can you get a group of these black kids together? Can you interview them and listen to them? Can you have hearings?' And they never wanted to deal with it. They claim that they're looking into it, and that they've got to do a report. It's all designed for black parents to get tired and say, 'Forget it.'"

Ashleigh graduated; Haleigh had had enough, to the point of deciding to graduate in three years instead of four. She did not celebrate her graduation so much as hurry to escape Cal.

"It was rough, but I didn't think twice about the decision," Haleigh said about her decision to leave early. "I told my parents that for my sanity and health, I needed to be done and get out as soon as possible. The racial environment, not feeling part of anywhere, I was sick of being the outsider because of being a minority. I had to get out. I got really depressed, and getting out was the only thing I could think of doing."

For Haleigh, one of the most depressing aspects was the apathy among the non-black Cal students.

"I think some of the white people tried to understand, but I don't even think others think about it. When you're not the ones being oppressed, you're not going, 'I feel bad for those black people,'" she chuckled. "I was talking to someone a while ago about when you go to the movies, college is always [shown] as the best time of your life. And we were like, 'That's right for white people!' I had the worst time in college."

• • •

That's always been a dilemma for African American students at predominately white colleges and universities. Are these schools particularly hostile to African American students, and if so, even given the schools' resources, is the experience worth it? Or are these schools merely a slice of the real world, with college just an early primer where you learn how to deal? And if so, why do you as an African American have to tolerate that environment? Don't you have a right to a college experience without those added obstacles?

On a higher level, predominately white colleges have often been at the forefront of society's efforts to create a more integrated America, but as we'll see, whether because of state anti–affirmative action policies or peer-to-peer interactions, success has often been elusive. Lastly, what can African Americans do to make predominately white colleges and universities work for *them,* instead of being used as diversity window dressing on campuses?

With his Proposition 209 success, Connerly formed the American Civil Rights Institute, through which he started a crusade to replicate his work in other states. Soon he and others were leading anti–affirmative action efforts in Washington, Florida, Michigan, Nebraska, Arizona, New Hampshire, Colorado, and Oklahoma. They failed in Colorado but succeeded everywhere else. And with that success came the sharp reduction of black student populations at the flagship schools in the anti–affirmative action states.

Initiative 200, which prohibits racial and gender preferences by Washington State government, passed with 58 percent of the vote in November 1998. After its passage, the number of black students admitted to the University of Washington plummeted, but it has since grown slightly. In 2014 there were about 1,000 black undergraduates on the Seattle campus, out of an undergraduate enrollment of nearly 30,000, or a little over 3 percent of all students. The state's black population is 4 percent, according to the U.S. Census. The city of Seattle's black population is nearly 8 percent.[42]

African American students have always attended predominately white colleges and universities with their eyes wide open. One of the reasons most often cited by black students for attending predominately white institutions instead of historically black colleges is that they want to experience the "real world." That the diversity of the campus is more valuable than the comfort of a school where professors nurture you as part of their mission. It's a trade-off, one that every black student should have the right to make. But many are finding out that there's a steeper price than they realized. And no one pays more of a price than black students at flagship schools under anti–affirmative action laws.

UC Berkeley, UCLA, University of Michigan, University of Oklahoma, University of New Hampshire, University of Washington, Florida State, University of Florida, University of Arizona, Arizona State, and the University of Nebraska all saw their black student populations plummet after affirmative action prohibitions.

Depopulating these elite universities of black students had the effect of creating a separate-but-equal situation in state university systems, where white and Asian students dominated the flagship schools while black and Latino students were funneled to lesser-ranked schools. And by reducing black numbers at the flagship campuses, you could effectively create a hostile environment for black students that would do a number of things. For one, if a black student was admitted to the University of California at Berkeley, it's most likely that they were also admitted to top universities around the country, increasing the likelihood that they'd choose another school that fostered diversity, thereby reducing the black student numbers even more. Secondly, if the black student populations were reduced beyond a critical mass, then you could separate them and prevent them from being a cultural force on campus.

If you're an anti–affirmative action proponent like Ward Connerly, who believes that assimilation into white America and the dissolution of black identity and culture is a good thing, then you *want* black kids to get lost in a sea of white students. Each step away from blackness by these students is a positive in the eyes of Connerlyites. And if you're a white opponent of affirmative action, it's more than likely that you don't think black students should have an identity on campus in the first place, so there's no great loss.

This is not to say that the African American student can't be a successful adult by attending a school with a lesser reputation. But graduating from a flagship school means that you're able to leverage the brand for jobs and graduate school. Again, it doesn't mean that attending the lesser-ranked school prevents you from succeeding, but as with all things American, the "right" school—like the right name, the right brand, the right anything—makes it just that much easier.

One thing that affirmative action opponents stated they wanted to do was to help African American students get from under the so-called stigma of affirmative action. Black conservatives like Shelby Steele at Stanford were the face of this. Steele believes in and propagates the idea of "victimhood" when talking about African Americans and affirmative action, seeming to feel that African Americans are somehow psychologically predisposed to focus on being "victims" of racism and that that focus, not the presence of actual racism, is the reason for their lack of achievement.

It's a convenient argument, and one that gives comfort to the comfortable. In Shelby Steele's view, racism is simply a nuisance that is no longer a factor in today's society. Or if it is, it's so irrelevant that all black people need to do in order to overcome it is to buck up, pull themselves up by their racial Horatio Alger bootstraps, and get on with it.

Princeton sociology professor Douglas Massey did a study on affirmative action and found "that affirmative action exacerbates the psychological burdens that minority students must carry on campuses. Those who feel they are representing their race every time they are called on to perform academically will have a heightened sense of responsibility."[43]

However, what the report also finds is that the stigma felt by minority students was mitigated when affirmative action was couched as a way to increase diversity, instead of a way for minorities with lower test scores to be admitted to schools.

And like the Bowen study, the report also found a difference in how two other groups who were special admits, athletes and legacies, were treated. "If minority students were welcomed and supported at selective institutions in the same way that star athletes and legacy students routinely are, the grade performance of black and Latino students might improve markedly," the report read. "But, if anything, elite colleges and universities now seem to be doing the opposite of wisely intervening in support of minority students."[44]

UC Berkeley professor Claude Steele, the twin brother of Shelby Steele, is diametrically opposed to his brother and supports affirmative action. And one of the theories he has proposed is that African American students aren't seeing themselves as victims, but are always under a societal pressure called the "stereotype threat."

"Stereotype threat constitutes the existence of widely held negative beliefs about the cognitive abilities of a particular group of people with real-life, everyday consequences. In the case of high-stakes, performance-based assessments, whether or not a person in the stigmatized group actually shares those beliefs, stereotype threat can adversely affect their test performance. Students consciously or subconsciously do not want to confirm the stereotype, thereby putting too much pressure on themselves while taking high-stakes tests; they then underperform relative to their full capabilities."[45]

But the stereotype threat may have nothing to do with affirmative action. Massey found that "the receipt of an affirmative action benefit by minorities and other preferred groups does not exacerbate the internalization of stereotypes to heighten stigma and produce disidentification with academic achievement."[46]

A team of researchers at the University of Waterloo and Stanford University, led by Christine Logel and Gregory Walton, demonstrated in a paper that appeared in *Educational Psychology* in 2012 that when black students have the opportunity to be in a stereotype-safe environment, they outperform white students with comparable test scores upon admission.[47]

But conservatives insisted that black students who were admitted to colleges under affirmative action were unfairly burdened with that stigma. That if we just got rid of affirmative action, then non-black students would know that the black students got in on their own merit.

Au contraire.

In Florida, former governor Jeb Bush eliminated affirmative action in 2000 via a program called One Florida. One Florida guaranteed admission to at least one of the ten state universities for high school students who graduate in the top 20 percent of their classes. But the policy essentially segregated the state universities in Florida, with blacks all but excluded from the top schools, the University of Florida and Florida State, and funneled instead into lesser-ranked universities.[48]

This means that the oldest African American students at the University of Florida were in the first grade the last time affirmative action was policy, yet they still deal with the same things conservatives said would be eliminated once affirmative action was gone. For these black students, the reality is much different.

"It's funny they say Jeb Bush ended affirmative action," said Dashari Kearse, a twenty-year-old linguistics major at the University of Florida. "People still think I got in because I'm a minority."[49]

So what does this mean for African American students, not just on campuses where affirmative action has been banned, but on all predominately white campuses? It means there's a conscious effort to limit educational resources for African Americans students, and as a result, universities passively and overtly help propagate hostile campuses. Because the lack of a critical mass of black students means that they're always marginalized among the majority student body.

As the *Los Angeles Times* reported, "The law says that universities can't consider race, even though race has an enormous effect on the lives of applicants. California's best high schools offer so many A.P. and honors classes—which confer bonus points on a student's G.P.A.—that the average G.P.A. of white and Asian freshmen at U.C.L.A. is now 4.2. At many of the largely black high schools around Los Angeles, it is sometimes impossible to do much better than a 4.0, because of the relative lack of A.P. classes."[50]

U.S. congressman Chaka Fattah once said, "African American children can't be educationally disadvantaged for twelve years and then experience a miracle cure when it comes time for admission into college," and yet that is the operating model for many flagship universities, and the public policy behind anti–affirmative action laws.

"Academic achievement is No. 1, but we look at other things to get a well-rounded student body. The only thing we can't consider is race, and that seems to me wrong. We're still not seeing enrollment numbers for the African American population that we should. We need to be focused on outreach, working to increase those," said Janet Napolitano, president of the University of California.[51]

For predominately white universities, the rhetoric of wanting diversity hasn't changed. Soft affirmative action, through which one concentrates on getting those African American students who qualify for admission into flagship schools to actually enroll, has replaced hard affirmative action, which acknowledges the racial disparities in K–12 education and thus gives African American students of all stripes a chance to succeed at top schools. And soft affirmative action has been much less effective.

Highly sought-after African American students who get into the Michigans, Berkeleys, and University of Floridas of the world are looking at the paltry African American student populations of these flagship schools and thinking, "Why bother?" So they're headed to smaller private schools and historically black colleges that aren't governed by anti–affirmative action laws.

And so the cycle starts: low numbers of African American students are accepted, so there's a tiny African American student population on campus. The university goes with an outreach strategy of soft affirmative action, usually employing their black alumni association to encourage students to attend. New black students look at the tiny numbers, and decide to go elsewhere. But what of those who *do* decide to attend these predominately white schools? How are they feeling about the experience?

Not good.

In 2013 a group of black UCLA male students dubbed the Black Bruins created a YouTube video, decrying their situation on campus. Organized by Sy Stokes, cousin of UCLA alumnus and tennis legend Arthur Ashe, the YouTube video went viral. In it, the Black Bruins stood in UCLA sweatshirts and talked about their sense of isolation on campus and how UCLA's diversity efforts weren't enough.

In an interview with the *Daily Bruin,* Stokes commented, "We have more [athletic] championships (109) than black male freshmen (48)." He said that this sends a message that black students are there to "improve your winning percentage." UCLA is very good at "talk" about diversity, but this "fraudulent reputation" needs to be exposed, he says. "We are not asking for a handout. We are asking for a level playing field."[52]

According to UCLA enrollment figures, African Americans make up 3.8 percent of the student population. In the video, Stokes points out that black males make up 3.3 percent of the male student population, and that 65 percent of those black males are undergraduate athletes. Of the incoming men in the freshmen class, only 1.9 percent were black.[53]

UCLA disputed that 65 percent of the school's African American males are athletes, putting the figure closer to 19 percent. Still, even they had to come out with a statement acknowledging the claims of the students, as the video went viral.

"We certainly recognize that the low numbers of African Americans and other underrepresented students on campus does lead to a sense of isolation and invisibility," Montero said in her email statement. "It is difficult to eliminate this painful imbalance without considering race in the admissions process."[54]

"Being the cousin of Arthur Ashe, I feel as though it is my responsibility to uphold the strong voices of the Black Bruin community," Stokes said. "This school has experienced unacceptable instances of injustice recently, and many people are not aware of what is happening at this university."[55]

Just as at UCLA, black enrollment at the University of Michigan has fallen precipitously over the past decade, largely due to Proposal 2, an amendment to the state constitution that was passed by Michigan voters in 2006 and that bans affirmative action policies. The proposal, formally named the Michigan Civil Rights Initiative, bars the university from considering race in its admissions process.

According to the *Michigan Daily,* immediately after the passage of the proposal, university president Mary Sue Coleman gave a dramatic address on the Diag, promising to maintain the school's commitment to diversity. However, the institution has been unable to stanch the decline in minority enrollment through alternative outreach policies in the wake of the affirmative action ban.

In the fall of 2006 black students made up around 7 percent of the undergraduate population. In the fall of 2013 the University of Michigan reported that black undergraduate enrollment had fallen to 4.65 percent. Hispanic enrollment as a percentage of the overall undergraduate body also declined over the same period.[56]

Often overwhelmed, underfunded, and understaffed, university student affairs offices *try* to foster a campus that's inclusive and understanding and whose students are respectful of each other by creating activities that take all students into account. Often, they'll try to cobble together programming in conjunction with *other* underfunded, underutilized university departments, like the African American studies department or the Equal Opportunities Program, to provide some semblance of a cohesive campus society that is at least more welcoming to black students than it would be without their efforts. But despite those efforts, it's too little, and nothing close to a real solution.

As someone who's lectured at predominately white schools as part of these efforts, I've seen these professionals struggle to get their students, black and white, to attend, and more importantly, to interact with each other so that at least a conversation could get started. But the fact is that these students, despite their individual good natures or goodwill, are intentionally put in a campus society that works *against* diversity and encourages separation. So it's easy to see why black students would be apathetic about participating in university efforts. As soon as they walk on campus, they quickly realize that these schools are not there for them, but for others.

When universities are as stratified as they are racially, particularly at an anti–affirmative action flagship school, the logical reaction from both black and white students is to remain in their various silos. African American and white students, by and large, arrive on these campuses from hyper-segregated schools and neighborhoods and duplicate their earlier experiences.

According to the Civil Rights Project at UCLA, 40 percent of black students attended schools that were 90 percent minority, while in contrast, the average white student attends a school that's 73 percent white. Congressman Bobby Scott noted that "70 percent of African American children attend schools that are predominately African American, about the same level as in 1968 when Dr. King died."[57]

So when black and white students arrive on these predominately white college campuses, these spaces aren't predominately white, they're overwhelmingly white, even whiter than the segregated communities where white students have grown up. Black students form an ignorable presence on campus, statistically insignificant. For many black students, to quote Gertrude Stein, there is no there there, when it comes to their college campus. And they certainly aren't there in enough numbers to be seen.

So to protect themselves, black students group together, which is the direct opposite of what assimilationists like Ward Connerly envisioned. Connerly's vision was that in a so-called color-blind campus society, the black students would somehow ignore their race and harmoniously blend in with the rest of the student body, with seemingly no ramifications. In fact, if Connerly's policies were successful, it would pretty much guarantee that African American students would disappear as an identity from college campuses.

Back in 2003 Connerly tried to introduce a new initiative, the Racial Privacy Initiative. The initiative would have prohibited California state colleges and universities from collecting statistics about the racial composition of their students or faculty members. So the numbers cited by the Black Bruins as proof of the paucity of black students on campus wouldn't, no, couldn't, have been compiled, thus keeping the race problem hidden. Also under Connerly's initiative, colleges and universities wouldn't have been able to create policies or plans based on, or influenced by, the racial count of faculty, students, or employees, which would have effectively ended the *soft* affirmative action of outreach. All diversity efforts would have been ended.

The initiative was given the designation Proposition 54, but unlike Proposition 209, it encountered broad opposition. A coalition of groups, including the American Medical Association, Planned Parenthood, all of the major teachers' unions, and the University of California Regents, all came out against Proposition 54. But more importantly, the opposition put skin in the game and outspent Connerly by overwhelming margins, nearly $4 million to $250,000, and Proposition 54 lost in a landslide, 64 percent to 36 percent.[58]

"The perception of linked fate and that feeling of being always on the spot as a representative of the race, at least in mixed company, are features of African American life that predate affirmative action and arise outside of its presence,"[59] said Randall Kennedy, the esteemed Harvard Law professor.

Just being black in America makes one an outlier, and the social prejudices baked into the American DNA are inescapable. Historically, what made up the strength of black folks was the ability to come together in the presence of white supremacy and triumph. The civil rights movement is a clear example of that. It seems like Connerly's ultimate goal is to erase those links and eradicate the black presence from these campuses. To erase blackness from the college experience.

Malcolm X once said that America preaches integration and practices segregation, and anti–affirmative action policies end up being arms of white supremacist, segregationist public policy.[60] And yes, that can even happen when the faces promoting that policy are black. Black surrogates as fronts for policies that hurt African Americans aren't unusual or even new. But what such policies do practically is create universities that are hostile environments for black students . . . and white students, for that matter. Hostile for white students in that these hyper-segregated white colleges and universities hard-wire the societal racism they've benefitted from into a lifelong point of view and encourages them to perpetuate it. If there are no African American students at your college or university, then how will you understand a worldview that's different from your own white, segregated point of view? You can't, and as a result, the white racism is transmitted from generation to generation.

A long view of history points to the inevitability that Ward Connerly's anti–affirmative action policies will end up, as the College Republican conservative hero Ronald Reagan once said about communism, in the "ash heap of history." America's saving grace is that we as a country tend to reevaluate policies once the damage has reached critical levels. So Prop 209, and all of the other anti–affirmative action laws, will eventually join other discredited laws like *Plessy vs. Ferguson*. Long after Connerly's dead and forgotten, people will wonder, as they try to rectify the damage, how Americans could have created such discriminatory policies against minorities. But in the meantime, generations of black students will be locked out of campuses that their tax dollars help support, while the black students who do attend these schools will find them daily hells, and there's not much being done about it.

God only knows how much the cake costs when that variable is baked into it.

Former South Carolina governor and U.S. Senator Ben "Pitchfork" Tillman, who helped found Clemson University in South Carolina. Tillman's name is on numerous buildings at Clemson and Winthrop University, even though he was a white supremacist who took part in the Hamburg Massacre, which killed scores of African Americans. (Courtesy: Billy Hathorn [State of South Carolina, 1940 Ben Tillman statue] via Wikimedia Commons)

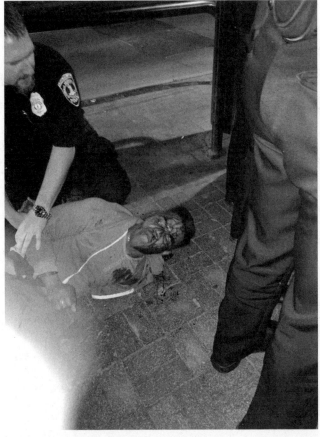

University of Virginia student Martese Johnson after being tackled by Virginia state Alcohol Beverage Control officers after presenting his ID at a local bar. All charges against Johnson, including resisting arrest, obstructing justice without threats of force, and profane swearing or intoxication in public, were dropped. (Courtesy: Bryan Beaubrun)

University of Alabama Student Government Association president Elliot Spillers was able to defeat the Machine, a formidable political entity for both on campus and off campus politics. (Courtesy: Elliot Spillers)

Patricia Hamilton Gyi, who in the early 1960s was invited to join Delta Gamma sorority at Beloit College in Wisconsin, but was rejected by Delta Gamma's national organization, causing the chapter to close. (Courtesy: Melinda Gyi White)

African American students at the University of California protest during Cal Days 2015, blocking Sather Gate. Their protests tapped into the #BlackLivesMatter movement, as they demonstrated against the low numbers of black Cal students and the hostile atmosphere against blacks on campus. (Courtesy: Rachel Garner/The Daily Californian)

In an act of civil disobedience, "Black Lives Matters" was spray-painted on a controversial statue of Confederate president Jefferson Davis on the University of Texas campus. Black students throughout the country are confronting statues and buildings named after white supremacists and Confederate icons. (Courtesy: Jesus Nazario/The Daily Texan)

Byrd Stadium, football home of the University of Maryland and named after long time university president, Harry "Curley" Byrd. Byrd was a noted segregationist who fought to keep African American students from attending the University of Maryland. (Courtesy: Antonio D. Jordan)

Kappa Sigma fraternity jug for the University of Vermont annual "Kake Walk" celebration. (Courtesy: Special Collections, University of Vermont Libraries)

At Stetson University student wears blackface to a fraternity party in 1950. (Courtesy: University Archives, Stetson University)

Kappa Alpha Fraternity at the University of Maryland holding up a Confederate Battle Flag and the Star Spangled Banner in 1976. (Courtesy: University of Maryland, College Park)

The members of Delta Zeta sorority at the University of Louisville in their "Good Pickin's Tonight" homecoming float in 1948. This float won first place in the "Best Decorated Sorority Float." (Courtesy: University of Louisville Digital Archives)

5

THE JOKE'S ON YOU, BLACK

"If you as parents cut corners, your children will too. If you lie, they will too. If you spend all your money on yourselves and tithe no portion of it for charities, colleges, churches, synagogues, and civic causes, your children won't either. And if parents snicker at racial and gender jokes, another generation will pass on the poison adults still have not had the courage to snuff out."

—Marian Wright Edelman

ON SEPTEMBER 15, 1963, JUST A MONTH AFTER MARTIN LUTHER King Jr.'s iconic "I Have a Dream" speech, four young black girls, fourteen-year-old Addie Mae Collins, Cynthia Wesley, and Carole Robertson and eleven-year-old Denise McNair, were murdered by white supremacists who bombed the 16th Street Baptist Church in Birmingham, Alabama. The bombing was one of three in eleven days, causing the world to nickname the city "Bombingham," and came as a result of the federal courts' mandate that the state of Alabama had to integrate its school system.

A month later, 2,000 miles away on the campus of Cal State Long Beach, members of Tau Kappa Epsilon fraternity, the one white fraternity without a racial clause in its constitution, were suspended for singing a song titled "Bye, Bye, Black Man" at a fraternity rush party.

"Bye, bye, black man, you'd better play it cool. Else we'll bomb your Sunday School."[1]

Sound familiar?

The tradition of predominately white colleges and universities being actively hostile spaces for African American students not only goes back decades, but can be traced nearly to the presence of the first African American college students. But it's only been within the last half century, as the numbers of African American students have risen, that we've seen a combination of racial microaggressions and overtly racist acts become normalized behavior on college campuses. As noted above, these hostile spaces aren't just in the South, as we tend to think, but all over the country. From California to New Hampshire, from Wisconsin to Mississippi, students on predominately white campuses are assaulted with ridicule, disparagement, and sometimes outright violence, simply because their bodies are black.

For the most part, colleges and universities are reactive and not *proactive* to the racism on their campuses, with a ready-made, pro forma statement designed to reassure the public that they are indeed just as shocked as you about what just happened on their campus, and how those racist actions don't fit with their mission or goals. But in reality, if university chancellors were given sodium pentothal, we'd find that dealing with racial issues is far down on their list of priorities, right behind deciding whether the band travels to away football games or whether to change the school mascot from a lion to a tiger.

This is not to say that university officials don't care about their black students. That would be unfair. But too often, schools reluctantly set up African American Studies offices, Multicultural Affairs departments, and Greek life offices that are woefully understaffed and underfunded, and then give the overworked administrators of these departments the thankless task of making sure students don't do anything racist. It's a hopeless mission, because no matter how many educational classes you force them to attend, white students see through the façade of concern. After all, if the university chancellor is concerned mainly about keeping State U out of the newspapers, then they're not really concerned about the fundamental issue of making the campus a hostility-free zone for African Americans. At the end of the day, racist acts on campus are the costs of doing business for most universities, and white students know that getting suspended, along with the temporary shaming of the toothless public reprimand, is the price of doing *their* business. The racism must go on, no matter what.

The 2014 indie film *Dear White People* beautifully illustrates the racial microaggressions that black students feel and the toll they can take. The film is set on the fictitious Ivy League campus of Winchester University, a typical predominately white university that's filled with class, gender, and racial conflict. We follow Samantha White, a biracial student whose controversial radio show, *Dear White People,* skillfully skewers the racial tropes that white students on campus embrace, while she and the other black characters also deal with their own internal conflicts.

Written by Justin Simien, the film ably uses satire to talk about the real-life racial microaggressions black students suffer on these campuses. Whether it's a lack of safe spaces like African American–themed dorms, or the lack of support from college administrations who are more interested in keeping up appearances for their donors than dealing with their racial problems, *Dear White People* is almost documentary-like in its accuracy.

With blacks always outnumbered, their voices otherwise unheard, the Samantha character cleverly uses the radio show platform to shoot down the uninformed views of white students, including one who describes her show as being racist for talking about the realities of racism.

"Black people can't be racist," responds Samantha. "Prejudiced, yes, but not racist. Racism describes a system of disadvantage based on race. Black people can't be racist since we don't stand to benefit from such a system."[2]

"I think that was so smart," said Lena Waithe, one of the producers of *Dear White People,* about how Simien wrote the film, "because it said something very poignant. It said something about how racism affected millennials specifically. What he was saying was so honest and real . . . and he wasn't pulling any punches."[3]

Predominately white universities tend to have systems of hostility on their campuses, beginning with racial microaggressions against black students and extending to overtly racist acts, which are designed to threaten, humiliate, and intimidate black students until they leave. These systems are designed to make the African American student feel like the exotic, the other, that is not part of the white normative student population.

Racial microaggressions are defined as being "brief and commonplace daily verbal, behavioral, or environmental indignities, whether intentional or unintentional, that communicate hostile, derogatory, or negative racial slights and insults towards people of color."[4]

"Can I touch your hair?"

"How did *you* get into this school?"

"Are you from the ghetto?"

"You only got in this school because of affirmative action."

"Why do all of the blacks sit together?"

"You're pretty . . . for a black girl."

Typically, non–African Americans write these racial microaggressions off as being inconsequential, not worthy of noting, and things that black students should "get over." By the way, there seems to be an inexhaustible list of items black students should "get over" when white students get tired of hearing about racial issues. But I digress.

Racial microaggressions stem from ignorance of the *other,* which is exacerbated by the segregation that white students experience growing up in their overly white communities and the lack of a critical mass of black students on college campuses. There's nothing inherently exotic about blackness, but the racial prejudices about African Americans are passed from generation to generation in white America because of a systemic isolation of white America from African America.

The conservative Reagan era of the 1980s seemed to open a Pandora's box of racist behavior on college campuses, all designed to denigrate African Americans.

In 1988 PBS' documentary program *Frontline* broadcast a special called "Racism 101." The segment detailed incidents of college racism, ranging from racial epithets being spray-painted at Smith College to a newsletter with racial slurs being seen at Harvard Business School. There was even a racial brawl at Columbia University.[5]

And back on the University of Alabama's Greek Row, a cross was burned on the lawn of a house where a black sorority, Alpha Kappa Alpha, planned to move. "I was pretty upset and frustrated," AKA member Deidre Chestang recounted in 1987.[6] "There had never been a black sorority house on sorority row, and when the university gave us the opportunity to move into the house, things started getting tough . . . race relations are worse now than when I was a freshman."[7]

In 1990, right after the Reagan era, the National Institute Against Prejudice and Violence reported that as many as one million college students were victims of racial attacks ranging from verbal slurs to physical assaults. That figure amounted to one-in-five minority students, and the report partially blamed the conservative policies of Reagan for the aggressions.

"If we had an incidence of disease at 20 percent, the surgeon general would have declared a public health crisis," Howard J. Ehrlich, research director for the group, said at a news conference. The report, "Campus

Ethnoviolence and Policy Options," said that minority students at predominately white campuses suffer almost constant pressure because of their ethnic backgrounds.[8]

"It seems to me that the mood of the country, as orchestrated in Washington, D.C., has said to a lot of people that all things we were once concerned about in terms of promoting equal opportunity don't matter anymore," said Barry Beckham in 1987. Beckham was the author of the *Black Student's Guide to Colleges* and an English professor at Brown University.[9]

Ehrlich went on to note that many of the white students came of "political age" during the Reagan era when "civil rights were being devalued in this society." A Reagan spokesman, for his part, called the report "cheap political finger pointing."[10]

But it wasn't cheap, it wasn't finger pointing, and the problem still hasn't been solved twenty-five years later. These racial microaggressions can be a daily occurrence for black students, often unseen and unrecognized by university administrations, and even when they are recognized, the efforts to fix them tend to be ineffectual. Universities sometimes address the circumstances of minority students on their campuses by focusing their efforts on new students through one-day diversity programs that emphasize tolerance and sensitivity; unfortunately, though, most campuses are reactive in their approach to managing racial crises.

"There's no question about it," Reginald Wilson, then head of the office of minority concern of the American Council on Education, said back in 1987, "not only were colleges slow to react, but I suspect that a number of things are happening on campus that would tend to give students the idea that minority interests are of diminishing value . . . I don't think there's been a great deal of leadership on the part of university presidents."[11]

All through the 1980s, there were scores of racial incidents at campuses throughout the country. The University of Pennsylvania would kick Kappa Sigma fraternity off campus after a series of racist incidents, including one in which black students complained about Kappa Sigma fraternity members' using bed sheets to mimic the Ku Klux Klan at a Halloween party at their fraternity house.[12]

In 1982 at Willamette University, in Oregon, the Sigma Alpha Epsilon fraternity chapter held a "ghetto party" where students dressed as pimps, prostitutes, and alcoholics, with two of the "ghetto girls" appearing in blackface makeup. The year before, an SAE chapter at the University of Cincinnati had been suspended for sponsoring a "Second Annual Martin Luther King Trash Party."[13]

Back in 1986 someone copied fliers of a coiled white snake with the words "Don't Tread on Me, Blackie" and spread them throughout the campus. In addition, black students complained about receiving anonymous racist phone calls.[14]

Over at Purdue University in 1987, a cross was burned in front of the Black Cultural Center, and two weeks later the words "Death Nigger" were found carved into the door of a black counselor.[15]

Also in 1987 at Wellesley College, a trustee was forced to resign after remarking that black employees at her firm preferred selling drugs to working.[16]

At the University of Colorado at Boulder in 1987, the Sigma Chi chapter created a fraternity rush party flyer that featured an obese, nude black woman with the caption, "Hey, Big Boy, Come Play With Me! Bad Mama Jama says rush Sigma Chi." The rush party was to be held on Martin Luther King Day.[17]

At Louisiana State University at New Orleans in 1988, a white fraternity displayed a Confederate rebel flag during a Martin Luther King Day parade.[18]

In 1986, over at the University of Mississippi, Trent Lott's alma mater, arsonists torched what was supposed to be the future home of Phi Beta Sigma, the first black fraternity on the all-white Greek Row. At the time, a member of Phi Kappa Psi, which was right next to the destroyed Phi Beta Sigma house, didn't think the fire was motivated by race.

"I just don't think it [the black fraternity's move] was that big a deal here," John Gleason said. "I think most people took it in stride. If the fire was the work of arsonists, it was probably set by someone off campus."[19]

Eventually, donations would help Phi Beta Sigma get a house on Greek Row, but the arsonists were never found.

And in surveys at college campuses around the country in 1987, black students at the University of Virginia and the Massachusetts Institute of Technology said that the racial climate was poor, while Smith College appointed an outside national commission to evaluate its race problem after a racial slur was found on a campus building.[20]

On campuses throughout the country, writing racial slurs on campus property was a trend in the 1980s. At Stanford in 1988, the word "nigger" was scrawled across a black fraternity poster, while a poster of German composer Ludwig van Beethoven was altered so he appeared to be black.[21] And at DePauw, in Indiana, Alpha Tau Omega fraternity held a "ghetto party" where they decorated their house with racist graffiti, including disparaging remarks about blacks, the Reverend Jesse Jackson, and South Africa. In addition, some partygoers wore blackface and dressed as pimps and prostitutes.[22]

A string of incidents at the University of Michigan in 1988 ranged from fliers announcing that it was "open season" on blacks to a student disc jockey broadcasting racist jokes. And in 1985, at the Citadel, the military academy in South Carolina, five white students dressed up as Ku Klux Klan members and broke into a black freshman cadet's room, shouting obscenities and burning a paper cross.[23]

One of the 1980s' hotbeds of racial incidents was the University of Wisconsin. First, in 1988, Phi Gamma Delta fraternity, better known as Fiji, was involved in scuffles with minority students after using a black caricature as a yard sign to advertise their tropical party.[24]

During the same year, Zeta Beta Tau fraternity members conducted a "slave auction," where the fraternity pledges "wore blackface makeup and Afro wigs and performed impersonations of Oprah Winfrey and the Jackson Five on stage."

"People in the Greek system are saying the incident was no big deal, but other students are outraged," one fraternity member said at the time. Amy Miller, then a Wisconsin senior, said that the frat "probably didn't have bad intentions," but that its actions were "really stupid." When asked, some University of Wisconsin students said, "The racial character of the ZBT auction was highly unusual."[25]

They were wrong.

That year, the University of Wisconsin conducted a poll of African American students, asking "How would you describe race relations among students?" Only 15 percent of the respondents said, "Good," with 85 percent saying either fair or poor. Not one said, "Excellent."[26]

There's a notion that today's white millennials are somehow immune from campus racism because of a generational shift toward greater racial tolerance.

That is inaccurate.

These white millennials were taught by their white Gen X parents, who, for the most part, engaged in the same behavior, just as *their* Baby Boomer parents did. If the white Greek system is filled with legacies, meaning the sons and daughters of white fraternity and sorority members, it's not hard to surmise that they're learning *all* the traditions, including the racist ones. So the Tau Kappa Epsilon racist song of 1963 is connected to the Sigma Alpha Epsilon racist song of 2015. The ghetto parties of the 1980s would be the same ghetto parties of the 2000s.

If you believe that every generation gets "better" on race, then you expect a progression in which the volume of incidents goes down based on a greater understanding of race, racism, and the impact that these racial microaggressions have on black students. The fact, based only on reported incidents (and we must recognize that most racial microaggressions and overtly racist incidents may go under reported), is that these incidents don't show any sign of slowing down.

And because these incidents often happen under the radar, they can make African American students feel isolated and disconnected from the college community, just like Ashleigh and Haleigh Nickerson at Cal. It's as though black students are under constant assault, but no one is protecting them. Not reacting after the fact (and universities aren't even doing a great job at that), but *protecting* them. And that feeling of a lack of protection can occur even when the administrators, and the deans, are black. African American students often feel a sense of conflict between their needs and the black administrator's need to receive a check on the first and fifteenth. But what's even worse is when universities treat these slights as being insignificant.

So to the question, "Where did all of these racist incidents come from?," the answer has to be, "They never, ever stopped in the first place." From the beginnings of white fraternities and sororities, there have been racist parties that denigrate blacks. At Dartmouth College, Kappa Kappa Kappa fraternity held a blackface party in 1916, which was a reaction to the growing number of black students on campus.[27]

Even a cursory analysis of white fraternities and sororities quickly shows that racist incidents aren't aberrations or isolated incidents, but longstanding traditions, like kegs at homecoming and the word "bro." There are spikes during various polarizing political eras, like the Reagan and Obama presidencies, but the racist incidents themselves are omnipresent. And part of this can be blamed on the nearly all-white Greek Rows themselves and how they function on college campuses, while another part can be blamed on society itself.

I talked earlier about how the typical white student on a college campus grew up in a white community, but when we look at the composition of Greek Rows across the country, well, we don't know what the racial composition is, mainly because the governing bodies don't keep statistics about race. This in itself is disturbing, because how can you solve a problem if you don't identify the problem?

But even anecdotally, it's quite easy to see that most Greek Rows are at least 70 to 90 percent white, with the black population inside these organizations being either nonexistent or negligible. For example, Princeton's demographic study of its Greek system shows that white and higher-income students are much more likely to join fraternities and sororities—77 percent of sorority members and 73 percent of fraternity members were white, compared with only 47 percent of the student body. And since most black fraternity and sorority houses are not on these Greek Rows, the diversity levels tend to be even more minuscule.[28]

"This history of segregation in the Greek system is incredibly harmful because it's not just 40 years and then it's done," said U.S. Attorney Joyce Vance, who was monitoring Greek life at the University of Alabama. "It's really shaped many of the business and social relationships that survived long past college, so it's in many ways a generational issue."[29]

Over the past forty years, as African American college attendance has spiked in schools previously closed to them, there's been a consistent and predictable counterreaction from white fraternities and sororities. Part of it is bred from fear of the other; part comes from an ignorance of the other. But by having these areas of hyper-whiteness on campus, universities create the fertile environment not just for racist acts, but racist acts that are almost casual in their nature.

Dr. Walter Kimbrough, president of Dillard University, in New Orleans, and the author of *Black Greek 101,* recalled entering the University of Georgia in 1985 as a freshman and being interested in joining a fraternity. But "since I attended an overwhelmingly black high school, the thought of joining a white fraternity never seriously entered my mind. Any black freshman at UGA abruptly learned that segregation and racism still existed in the mid-1980s. In fact, my naiveté quickly ended during an intramural game of football as my residence hall floor team beat a white team, and one of the losers (in retrospect, in more ways than one) called us 'niggers.' I had never been called that to my face, and fully expected that we were about to come to blows . . ."[30]

It can be argued that white privilege is an inherent and inevitable manifestation of white supremacy, and on college campuses, it thrives in environments where whiteness goes unchallenged. White fraternities and sororities, through their housing system and extensive alumni associations, don't have the same transitory relationship with their schools as most students. Most students of all ethnicities arrive on campus to get their degrees and leave without any particular affection for the physical campus itself. You may remember great times in a dorm, but the dorm itself isn't created to make you feel as though it's *your* dorm. It's simply a dorm for you, and a few hundred strange and disconnected students, until it's time for you to move out and bring in the next batch of students.

It's different with the fraternity and sorority house. There's permanence to their relationships, both for individuals and the university, which includes passing down the same views from generation to generation. The power of fraternal tradition, which includes taking pride in the idea of continuation rather than progression, means that the current, millennial white fraternity or sorority member emulates the actions of their Gen X fraternity alumni mentor. So there's a continuous view of white racism as acceptable, without any effective internal resistance to change, mainly because to fight against white privilege and white supremacy would be to fight against one's own interests.

It's the main reason why white fraternity and sorority houses are different from any other entity on the college campus. You're joining a fraternity or sorority, or, in fact, you're joining a *house,* and that house itself represents a mindset for the people inside, just as the principles and ideals of the fraternal organization represent a reason to gather in the first place. The house itself is the embodiment of tradition, the idea that things may change at the university, but not too much. The people who live at the fraternity or sorority house are invested in making sure that the experiences are not just deep for them while they're there, but also correlate to the experiences of fraternity and sorority members who came before. It's why homecoming at the frat house is so popular. Hours and hours of reminiscing, telling stories, and reaffirming traditions is a function of codifying behavior. And that behavior is frequently racist in nature. So when you are a breeding ground for racist behavior, you're an integral part of creating a hostile campus for African American students, students you don't know, interact with, or care about.

According to the Century Foundation, "one-in-eight college students live in a Greek house." This is a problem, as the houses themselves keep white fraternity and sorority members from integrating with the rest of the campus.[31]

Those interested in creating a false equivalency would point to the fact that African American fraternities and sororities are overwhelmingly black, which is true, so one would certainly expect to see the same racist dynamic going on within these groups. Is there an anti-white point of view that colors their actions, and isn't that racist?

The answer is quite simply . . . no.

African American fraternities and sororities, and other African American campus groups for that matter, don't exist to exclude white students. Culturally, their focus is on a world that has an African American point of view, but that seems strange only when you're not privy to the idea that black students live in a duality, both in a white-dominated society and within a separate racial group with its own culture and traditions. But where the culture and traditions of white fraternities and sororities often exalt symbolism that has inherently racist overtones, like Confederate iconography, and disingenuously explain it away via convoluted logic like pointing to "tradition" and "heritage," it's also true that African American organizations don't inherently, and intentionally, create a hostile environment for white students on college campuses via their presence. There is no privilege in these black student groups that would cause them to think they had the power to affect the lives of white students, and as a result, there are no "Irish Potato Famine" parties sponsored by black fraternities and sororities on St. Patrick's Day as a "joke." Or "Malibu Barbie Days" on which black students wear whiteface as a way to ridicule white, blonde women. Instead, racial intimidation of white students by black fraternities and sororities is rare to nonexistent.

But racist-themed parties, racial incidents, and exclusion based on race are essential parts of white fraternity and sorority life. It's as if the white fraternity or sorority member doesn't have to apologize for using the symbolism of white supremacy, like Confederate flags, uniforms, and the like, since the black student is the outsider. Any protests against these racist incidents are denigrated, as are the *others* trying to impede *your* freedom of expression. And to add insult to injury, they'll accuse those who protest of not having a sense of humor, or taking things too seriously. White privilege also mandates that ignoring black voices of objection is a right, and that only you, as the white actor in this racial play, get to determine the boundaries of what can be explained away and what cannot. This means black and white students are in constant conflict, as black students don't, and never will, get the joke of how denigrating their race is a tradition worth carrying on. But while blacks are without power on those college campuses, the status quo will remain the status quo.

For example, Kappa Alpha Order, a fraternity founded in 1865 at Washington and Lee, continues to embrace its Confederate past by lauding Confederate general Robert E. Lee as its spiritual founder. The school is known for conspicuous displays of the Confederate battle flag, a symbol used throughout the civil rights movement by segregationists as a sign of their resistance to integration that is highly offensive to African Americans.

Kappa Alpha Order also regularly holds "Old South" parties designed to "celebrate and to perpetuate the social attributes of courtesy, graciousness, and open hospitality, which are the values of the Old

South, and were prominent in Virginia when our Order was founded in 1865 . . . the event must be conducted with restraint and dignity and without display of trappings and symbols which might be misinterpreted and objectionable to the general public . . ."[32]

But as schools began to integrate, Kappa Alpha Order began to encounter resistance to its neo-Confederate traditions. Frequently, Kappa Alpha Order chapters would dress up in Confederate uniforms and parade through African American neighborhoods that adjoined the campus, akin to how Unionist Protestant orders parade near or through Catholic areas of Northern Ireland. But over the past thirty years, black students have fought back, and Kappa Alpha Order has adjusted.

Auburn University's chapter ended its 1992 Old South parade after black Auburn students confronted Kappa Alpha Order members holding Confederate flags. Kappa Alphas at Centenary College, in Shreveport, Louisiana, moved their Old South events off campus in 2002, after drawing protests from the Black Student Alliance and others over their Confederate uniforms. The University of Georgia chapter canceled its parade in 2006 after complaints by residents of a black neighborhood.[33]

And in 2009, at the University of Alabama, in Tuscaloosa, members of Alpha Kappa Alpha, the first African American sorority ever founded, complained after a Kappa Alpha parade stopped in front of its house on campus. KA members were dressed in the gray uniforms of Confederate officers, while young women wore antebellum hoop skirts.[34]

As a result, Kappa Alpha Order's national organization sent out directives to its chapters saying that they could no longer wear Confederate uniforms during Old South parties, and the Confederate battle flag was banned, although some chapters still hung it from their fraternity houses.[35]

Yet when it comes to fostering a racially hostile environment, Kappa Alpha Order is by no means alone with its symbolism. The *Journal of Blacks in Higher Education* magazine has chronicled hundreds of racist social events springing from the white fraternity and sorority ranks in just the past 30 years.

"Racial hatred may be more hidden today than a generation ago, but it remains prevalent throughout society, even on the campuses of our most progressive colleges and universities," said *Journal of Blacks in Higher Education* managing editor Robert Bruce Slater. "Americans on college campuses and elsewhere in society have become more politically correct about open displays of racism, but when no one is looking or when whites are sure they are alone amongst themselves, the racial slurs come out."[36]

In fact, these racial slurs have become so common and popular that one white fraternity website even came up with a satirical name for them: racist ragers.

The popular fraternity website TotalFratMove.com is a part-satirical, part-realistic look at the inner world of white fraternities. Full of irreverent "bro humor," it's also a place that filters fraternal news through its own eyes, and those eyes speak their own truths.

In 2013 the website wrote a tongue-in-cheek article titled "A Guide to the Racist Rager," advising fraternities to follow some important steps "if you really want to throw a racist rager the right way."

Among the various pieces of advice was to avoid using blacks as party subjects, which is too racist, but also avoid bashing the Irish, because it's not "racist enough." The guide also advises, "If there's one party the entire campus needs to know about, it's the one where you and all your brothers will be dressing up as formerly/currently oppressed minorities." Dressing up in "outrageous costumes," creating "ridiculous house decorations," and then posting to social media, "because the people who didn't get a chance to see your invitation depicting some stereotypes doing stereotype stuff need to see what they missed" is a pretty accurate description of standard operating procedure for most racist ragers, along with the inevitable "apology" that the guide says comes after the party. Unfortunately, most fraternities don't follow the guide's last bit of advice, which is to "just celebrate America" instead of hosting these parties. And the frequency of racist ragers shows no sign of slowing down.[37]

A university shouldn't have to go to Total Frat Move to know that the racist parties on its own campus, hosted by white fraternities and sororities, aren't unusual or new. The racist parties have always been there; it's just the students who change every four to five years. And despite the protestations by the fraternity and sorority members that these racist ragers have no connection with race, for some reason, these parties tend to involve racially offensive imagery around Halloween—focusing on Kwanzaa, the Martin Luther King Jr. holiday, and Black History Month. And usually, blackface plays a starring role.

Auburn University saw a huge uproar in 2001 when Halloween pictures from a party hosted by two white fraternities, Beta Theta Pi and Delta Sigma Phi, were exposed. The photos included members of Beta dressed as members of Omega Psi Phi, an African American fraternity, with another man wearing overalls and a straw hat; each man had his face and body painted black. Photographs from the Delta Sig function included one of a member dressed in Klan attire and another member clothed in mock FUBU—a popular line of clothing, especially among black Americans—with a noose around his neck. Various members of the fraternity posed holding rifles on the costumed student, and a mock hanging was performed for the camera.

Sanford Johnson, president of the Black Student Union at the time of the incident, said he was not surprised that university officials allowed the fraternity to return to campus. He noted that Auburn's "bigger problem" is achieving racial diversity on campus.

"Keeping Beta off campus would not have solved the problem," he says. "What they did was offensive, but it's small compared to the bigger problem Auburn has to face, and that's finding a way to establish an environment that would allow every group, regardless of race, to feel like part of the Auburn family."[38]

This is a constant theme for the black students. They want to feel part of the university family. It's the same thing that the black OU Unheard students were saying. They wanted to become part of the Sooner family. And yet, the racism they felt made it quite clear that they were outsiders to the university community, temporary interlopers who were to be denigrated as eternal outsiders. And university administrations typically, particularly when it came to white fraternities and sororities, bent over backwards to accommodate the racists over their black students.

But Auburn wasn't alone in 2001. Within just weeks of the Auburn incident, Alpha Tau Omega fraternity members at the University of Mississippi dressed up as KKK members and pointed a gun at a frat brother who was in blackface . . . kneeling and picking cotton. ATO couldn't explain that away as being nonracist. Over at the University of Wisconsin Whitewater, on the same day, a member of Tau Kappa Epsilon fraternity used blackface in a homecoming skit. He said that he was portraying Charles Barkley. Not to be outdone, some members of another TKE chapter, at the University of Louisville, decided to wear blackface and had a *black member* dress as a Klansman, which shows you how white supremacy doesn't require white people to make it work.[39]

What's sad is that all of these incidents happened within weeks of one of the most traumatic events in American history, the terrorist attack of September 11, a transformational event that is thought to have brought all Americans together. But to Cynthia Tucker, a syndicated columnist and Auburn alumna, the Halloween parties represented why black students were often reluctant to attend predominately white universities.

"The incident is also a striking reminder of the reasons why traditionally white universities have a hard time recruiting African American students. It's not that black kids are too dumb to get in, as many critics of campus diversity efforts seem to think.

"Instead, black students show a healthy skepticism toward attending college on a campus where they have to endure overt racism of the sort displayed by the dolts of Delta Sigma Phi and Beta Theta Pi. And many parents are understandably reluctant to pay tens of thousands of dollars to subject their children to such humiliation. What is funny about lynching?"[40]

So what makes wearing blackface offensive and racist? Well, blackface is one of the oldest American pop cultural traditions, going back to the mid-nineteenth century, when a character actor named Thomas Dartmouth Rice, nicknamed Daddy Rice, decided to dress in shabby clothes, put burnt cork on his face, and create a comedic caricature of African Americans.[41] It was one of white America's first appropriations of the black identity and has consistently represented some of the worst stereotyped depictions of African Americans as being ignorant, lazy, unintelligent, and criminal.

More importantly, it shows a conscious effort to denigrate black people. Too often, university officials have placed the use of blackface, ghetto parties, and the like under the rubric of "a lack of understanding" about race, while protecting the white students by letting them use convoluted and implausible explanations for clearly racist behavior. But these white students, as isolated as they may have been from African Americans while growing up, are not dumb. Nor are they ignorant about the shock factor of using blackface to mock black people. They simply don't care. And white fraternity and sorority members show no signs that they're done perpetuating these blackface depictions; it's almost turned into a rite of passage.

In 2011 six Phi Mu sorority members at the University of Southern Mississippi, in Hattiesburg, were placed on probation by their sorority for putting on blackface to attend an off campus party. The students' costumes were meant to depict them as members of the Huxtable family from the 1980s television sitcom *The Cosby Show*.

The students weren't disciplined by the university. Dean of Students Eddie Holloway stated, "Though it is clear that these women had no ill intent, it was also clear that they had little cultural awareness or competency, and did not understand the historical implication of costuming in blackface."[42]

Syracuse University placed the Sigma Alpha Epsilon fraternity on interim suspension after one of its members went to a campus bar wearing blackface as part of a costume. The fraternity issued a statement explaining that the incident occurred during the fraternity's annual bar-golf tour, where the student, Aaron Levine, came dressed as golfer Tiger Woods.

"Unfortunately, this year's golf tournament was scarred by our insensitivity toward the African American community. Our Brotherhood did not intend to cause any harm to anyone," the SAE statement read. "We should have recognized how the Tiger Woods costume could be offensive and cruel."

Syracuse chancellor Kenneth Shaw's apology, "I offer my apologies to students of color and to all members of the university community that a Syracuse University student could have progressed to this point in his academic career and not understood the hurtful consequences of his actions," drew a lukewarm response from black students.[43]

Imitating African American celebrities in blackface is fairly popular during Halloween, and not just among white fraternity and sorority members. In 2013 Lambda Theta Delta, an Asian American fraternity at the University of California at Irvine, came under fire after a video was posted on the fraternity's YouTube page that featured a member in blackface. The video was meant to introduce the fraternity to new members. Some members are shown lip-syncing to a Justin Timberlake song; then another member appears in blackface, supposedly playing hip-hop mogul Jay-Z.

The fraternity president released a statement that read, "We sincerely apologize if we offended anyone whatsoever. On behalf of my

brothers who were involved in the video, we know that it was unintentional. But unintentional or not, we do know that it was wrong."[44]

Over at Washington University in St. Louis, the Sigma Alpha Epsilon chapter was suspended when it had pledges recite a Dr. Dre song
to black students while using the word "nigger."[45] And at the University
of Florida, two members of Beta Theta Pi fraternity posted images of
themselves on Instagram showing them in blackface, complete with fat
gold chains and baseball caps.[46]

In fact, the "gangster" theme has been popular in white fraternities and sororities since the spread of so-called gangster rap in hip-hop.
The white generation that embraced the black musical art form of hip-
hop, so that it eventually became one of the most dominant genres in
the world, is also the generation that uses it as a weapon against black
students.

Theta Xi fraternity at the University of Michigan faced disciplinary
procedures for issuing a racially insensitive invitation to a campus party.
The event was billed as "World Star Hip Hop Presents: Hood Ratchet
Thursday." The invite was directed at "bad bitches, White girls, basketball players, thugs, and gangsters."

A headline on the invitation read, "We goin back to da hood
again!!" A picture included on the invitation showed a black man holding cash and warned those invited that "hood IDs would be checked."
The party was canceled.[47]

So-called hood parties, or ghetto parties, tend to be preferred by
many white fraternities and sororities for their plausible, but ultimately
very implausible, deniability when it comes to their obvious racial overtones. The argument made by the white fraternities and sororities is that
the word "ghetto" isn't automatically "African American" but can refer
to any group of people. Or that the black paint on the faces of the partygoers isn't about blackness, but just gangs in general. Yes, it's ridiculous,
but is it any more ridiculous than how the word "thug" has become a
euphemism in American society for "nigger?"

To "celebrate" Black History Month in 2010, some members of the University of California, San Diego, chapter of Pi Kappa Alpha threw a "Compton Cookout," advertising the off campus party with a flyer that depicted an African American with a bucket of Kentucky Fried Chicken. Students were encouraged to dress up as "ghetto chicks" and gangsters.

"It's insulting, it's degrading, it's derogatory," said UCSD sophomore Elize Diop. "We're being made fun of, we're being made a mockery of, and we're not being taken seriously. It's hard enough that we have less than 2 percent on this campus. We have it hard. These are the people who are insulted. These are your black friends on campus."[48]

Back to Tau Kappa Epsilon: its chapter at Arizona State University in Tempe was suspended after it held a "Martin Luther King Black Party." Pictures posted online from the event showed partygoers dressed in basketball jerseys, flashing gang signs, and drinking from cups made from watermelons. And to make sure that everyone saw them, they posted those pictures on social media under the hashtags #Ihaveadream and #blackoutforMLK.[49]

Following pressure from local African American civil rights leaders, including a threatened boycott of the construction of the Arizona State football stadium, the university permanently revoked the fraternity's charter.

A Halloween party with the theme "Rockers and Rappers" was held at an off campus fraternity house near the University of Florida. Photographs were posted on the Internet the next day showing two white students at the party in blackface wearing sagging pants, gold chains, and baseball caps.

The students who wore the costumes, the president of the local fraternity, and the national fraternity all issued apologies, admitting that the act was "a very ignorant and poor decision." They claimed that they did not know the racist history of blackface minstrelsy. In their statement, the students said, "At no point in time were we ever trying to negatively portray African American stereotypes. We have since learned about the history of blackface and fully understand how our actions were insulting to the African American community."[50]

At Dartmouth in 2013 Alpha Delta fraternity hosted with Delta Delta Delta sorority, the same sorority whose members were on the bus when the SAE song video was shot at the University of Oklahoma, a Bloods and Crips Party. The local chapter of the NAACP found out about the party and reported that "individuals mingled for hours while dressed as Bloods or Crips while using racialized language, speech and dress. Over 200 individuals attended this event."[51]

So what did the good brothers of Alpha Delta have to say for themselves? The apology tip from the Total Frat Move guide to racist ragers was followed to the letter.

"The idea was never meant to be derogatory to any group, and was intended to introduce a costume theme to the party," the fraternity said in a statement. "While there was never any ill intent in the party's theme, the brothers of Alpha Delta now realize that it was insensitive and thoughtless to make light of a very serious issue that affects many people nationwide, particularly young people. Gang violence is obviously an incredibly serious problem across America, and while we as a house failed to preemptively recognize the offensive nature of the party's theme, the gravity of our oversight is now apparent to us."[52]

Now this wasn't the first "ghetto party" at Dartmouth. In 1998, when most millennials were just being born, Chi Gamma Epsilon and Alpha Xi Delta fraternities hosted a party where white students showed up in fake Afro wigs and carried toy guns.[53] As always, it was up to the African American students, in this case Rahsaan Sales, to set up meetings where students could talk about why a party like this wasn't a good idea.

"Everyone came together to discuss an environment that could allow these things to happen, an environment where people sometimes don't feel safe."

Fifteen years after Sales was on campus, the party was replicated there, with the students again claiming ignorance of its ramifications. Nothing had changed.[54]

And at Clemson, just a few months before their SAE fraternity brothers at Oklahoma would make national news, the Sigma Alpha Epsilon chapter hosted a Christmas party called "Clemson Cripsmas," where social media showed partygoers dressed up as gang members. As always, SAE spokesman Brandon Weghorst localized the issue, saying that only a "few brothers" were responsible for the party, and that "their behavior in no way reflects the values and creed of the fraternity, and we apologize to [the] campus and local community for their actions."[55]

But as we've seen with Sigma Alpha Epsilon and the great majority of predominately white fraternities and sororities, these parties *do* reflect the values and creed of their organizations. If not, why are they so ubiquitous in white fraternal life?

The problem of white fraternities and sororities wearing blackface, or mocking Latinos and Asians with stereotypically racist costumes, is so bad that before each Halloween, a social media campaign, "We're a Culture, Not a Costume," is directed toward universities across the country, warning white students not to mock other cultures, ethnicities, and races. The program, started at Ohio University by the campus organization Students Teaching about Racism in Society, features posters of African Americans, Latinos, Native Americans, and Asian students standing next to white students in blackface, sombreros, Japanese costumes, and other ethnic apparel.[56] But despite the genuine good efforts of We're a Culture, Not a Costume, the beat goes on.

What I find amazing is the almost insatiable need for white fraternities and sororities to host these racist parties. It's not like they keep doing so because they're limited by theme. Or like they couldn't quite easily mock things that have nothing to do with race. You're young, you want to shock, I get it. But right now, it's as though racism is some sort of rite of passage, with the goal of imitating some ethnic minority in a grotesque way. And the racist parties against blacks are only the tip of the iceberg, as white fraternities and sororities have been equal opportunity offenders when it comes to other minorities.

For example, Phi Gamma Delta, better known as Fijis, hosted a "Run for the Border" party at the University of Texas, where some fraternity members dressed as border patrol, while others dressed as "Mexican" construction workers with "jefe" and "Pablo Sanchez" written on construction hard hats. Yet, the Fiji president, Andrew Campbell, protested the characterization of this party as being about Mexicans and border agents, saying instead that it was an "Old West" party.

"We notified our chapter prior to the party via email that the theme was Western—not south of the border or anything Mexican related. It was our intention to monitor and enforce this policy to the best of our ability . . . If any individual or cultural groups were offended, Texas Fiji apologizes for any insensitivity that our guests or members may have portrayed. It is never Texas Fiji's intent to alienate or demean any ethnic group."[57]

Not Mexican-related, even though fraternity members wore ponchos and wide-brimmed sombreros, and there was a wooden cutout of a man and a woman in traditional Mexican clothing, where partygoers could stick their heads into the open holes and "be" those Mexicans. Nope, not Mexican-related at all. Oh, and ignore that huge silver bar that had "Patron. Tequila 100% De Agave."

It's as though white fraternity and sorority members think the public is as ignorant as they are when it comes to racism. More importantly, I'm amazed at the amount of room universities give these organizations to be this dumb over and over again. It's not as though the University of Texas hadn't had *other* race-themed parties. In 2012 Alpha Tau Omega fraternity had to cancel its own "A Border to Cross" party.[58]

Campus racism doesn't begin and end with parties when it comes to white fraternities and sororities. Often, the clash between white fraternity and sorority members and black students gets even more threatening, and more ominous, as verbal and symbolic violence toward blacks can be a surrogate for actual violence.

In 2015 black students at the University of Washington alleged that members of the Sigma Alpha Epsilon fraternity had made obscene gestures and referred to black students participating in a Black Lives Matter protest as "you apes." Again, Sigma Alpha Epsilon, the same fraternity whose University of Oklahoma chapter members sang about lynching "niggers."

"There's this kind of culture where a lot of people are intimidated into keeping silent, and I think this is why this behavior continues," Black Student Union member Sarra Tekola said.[59]

The Chi Omega sorority at the University of Alabama in Tuscaloosa expelled a sorority member who used a racial slur on the Internet. The student allegedly shared a Snapchat photo showing a university event with the caption "Off probation, niggers!"

Deborah Lane, associate vice president for university relations at the University of Alabama, told the student newspaper, "The University of Alabama is extremely disappointed when any student uses language that is disrespectful or offensive to any segment of the UA community. Behavior, actions and choices that disparage other students are particularly reprehensible and do not represent the values or meet the expectations of our University community."[60]

But as we know, that's not true. The University of Alabama, through all of its reforms, *is* represented by the values of its white fraternities and sororities. There are too many incidents on its campus that tell the world that when you go to the University of Alabama, you'll be entering a world where the white fraternity and sorority row *will* have racist parties, *will* have racist social media postings, and *will* discriminate against black participants at rush. And if that wasn't enough, and you're thinking about making substantive change, then the Machine will make sure to institutionalize the racism. These are exactly the values of the University of Alabama, and the realities for black students on campus. The fact that the university doesn't come to grips with that reality means that it allows its racist culture to flourish.

But again, the University of Alabama isn't the only campus where racist behavior happens on Greek Row. Members of the Delta Gamma sorority at the University of Maryland, as Patricia Hamilton Gyi noted earlier, presented a birthday cake to a young white woman who was celebrating her twenty-first birthday. Written on the cake's stand was the phrase, "Suck A Nigga Dick," referring to a song by hip-hop group Three Six Mafia.

Photographs of the cake were posted on Instagram and subsequently removed. Before the image was removed, however, it was allowed to receive seventy-seven "likes," just as Total Frat Move satirically advised.[61]

In 2013 an African American mail carrier was asked to bring seventy-nine packaging boxes to "Reggin Toggaf" at a fraternity at the University of Chicago. The carrier made six or seven trips up the stairs to the fraternity carrying the boxes. After he had made the deliveries, one of the frat members told him it was a practical joke, and another suggested that he read the name backwards. When spelled backwards, the nonexistent recipient's name read, "Faggot Nigger."

The fraternity said it was the victim of a prank on the part of another fraternity. The University of Chicago investigated the incident along with Chicago city police. There was no evidence that members of the fraternity where the prank took place had anything to do with the incident.[62]

The problem with all of these incidents is that it's not as if predominately white fraternity and sorority members aren't aware that these parties are, at best, racially insensitive, and, at worst, racist. Most, if not all, of their national organizations have evolved to the point of at least putting up the appearance of being tolerant. Organizations like the Association of Fraternal Leadership Values and the Association of Fraternity/Sorority Advisors have conferences filled with speakers who preach to young impressionable minds about the need to stop having racist parties.

And still, most white fraternity and sorority members don't care. Because if they did, we'd see a dramatic drop in the number of those incidents.

At least the University of Texas is being proactive, and it recognizes that campus racism is a real problem when it comes to their students. When it comes to their buildings, that's something else, which I'll talk about later. But in 2011 the university administration created the University of Texas Campus Climate Response Team so they could monitor, and then react to, campus racist incidents. They noted that in 2013–14 alone, there were at least four race- or ethnically themed parties on the campus.[63]

But while these racist parties are offensive, and help create a hostile campus, African American students are often under the threat of real violence on predominately white campuses through the use of racist symbolism. Racially charged graffiti denigrating African Americans has been seen on campuses nationwide. Just in the past five years, we've seen:

After Williams College students found the phrase "All Niggers Must Die" scrawled on the hallway wall of a campus dorm in 2011, the college canceled classes and held a day of programming centered around diversity. Over 1,000 students, staff, and faculty participated.[64]

At the University of Southern Illinois at Carbondale in 2012, "Kill Niggers" was scrawled on the walls of the campus greenhouse. This caused one black student, Kwalee Kemp, the coordinator for the Black Affairs Council at SIU, to claim that black students at SIU "experienced more pure, unadulterated racism in one semester" than in recent years combined. "Both the university and city," she told the *Southern Illinoisan* newspaper, "simply don't make black students feel welcome in Carbondale, and the word is starting to spread."[65]

At Mercer University in Georgia, anonymous fliers were distributed in campus dorms declaring November and December as "White

History Months." The flier noted, "There are African American societies, black student organizations, and Indian heritage associations; however, there is not one white society of engineers, white student organization, or Caucasian heritage association. Why? Because if there are, various individuals will say this is racism."[66]

A series of incidents in 2013 included vandals' writing racial slurs on book covers, walls, and desks in the African American studies section of the library at the University of North Carolina at Greensboro. Two white men were seen on surveillance video leaving the area where the vandalism occurred. A white male freshman at the university was later arrested and charged with ethnic intimidation in connection with the incident.

The *Journal of Blacks in Higher Education* reported that the word "nigger" was written in chalk on the sidewalk near the Nebraska Union building on the campus of the University of Nebraska at Lincoln. A member of the student senate was also chastised for using the same racial epithet during a speech before the student government group.[67]

At Emory University, *The Dooley Show,* a satirical campus television show like Comedy Central's fake news show *The Daily Show,* had its anchor tell his audience, "Now that the Supreme Court has effectively ended affirmative action as we know it, we at the *Dooley Show* are making a call to all 83 of our loyal followers. It's up to you to find those kids who shouldn't be here, and are only at this school because of affirmative action. Proven methods here at the *Dooley Show* include lynching, tar and feathering, and cross burning."[68] The students were made to apologize for their bad joke.

And also in 2013, an African American student, Charity Lyons, at the University of California at Irvine, found a racist note in her backpack while she was in the science library on campus. The note read, "Go back 2 Africa, slave." Charity's mother, Stephanie Lyons, told the *OC Weekly,* "If they were brave enough to put that note there, who knows what extent they'll go to next time?"[69]

At the University of Virginia, the Beta Bridge, a campus bridge UVA students use as a place to celebrate events and announce parties, was vandalized by students with racial graffiti.[70] This wasn't the first time the bridge was marred with racial content, as the FBI was called in to investigate a similar event in 2005, when members of the African American fraternity Kappa Alpha Psi saw their party fliers defaced. In fact, in just a few weeks during the 2005 school year, there were at least nine different racial incidents at the University of Virginia, including racial slurs written on message boards.[71]

Joy Omenyi was the president of the Black Student Alliance at the University of Virginia in 2013 when the latest defacing incident occurred.

"We saw that, took a picture of it, and then spread it through social media. We heard from the president of the university, and she said that it was an isolated incident, and not representative of the culture at the university, or the community of trust. The community of trust is a big thing here. We, of course, knew that wasn't the case. The following year, someone wrote 'UVA Hates Blacks' on a student health sign. And again, the rhetoric was that this was an isolated incident."[72]

President Obama, as the first African American president, also seems to have become a catalyst for violence on campus, often acting as a surrogate for the black student community.

In a scene reminiscent of a lynch mob, the 2012 reelection of President Obama caused over forty Hampden Sydney students to angrily gather in front of the school's Minority Services Union to shoot off fireworks, break bottles, and yell racial epithets at the black residents.

Christopher B. Howard, the college's first African American president, wrote at the time, "I am terribly disappointed with the students who participated in this harmful, senseless episode including those men who stood idly by and watched it happen. There is no place for bigotry or racism on this campus."[73]

But the occurrence at Hampden Sydney paled in comparison with the post-election reaction at the University of Mississippi. Over five hundred students gathered and burned an Obama/Biden poster, while the crowd shouted racial epithets. One person was arrested for public intoxication, and another for failure to comply with police orders. University of Mississippi chancellor Dan Jones said in a statement that he was disappointed in the "immature and uncivil approach" the students used to protest.[74]

Two years later, the University of Mississippi offered a $25,000 reward for information leading to the arrest of two individuals who were seen defacing the statue of James Meredith on campus. The statue honors Meredith's efforts to racially integrate the university in 1962. A noose and an old Georgia state flag emblazoned with the Confederate Stars and Bars was placed over the statue. The two perpetrators were heard yelling racial slurs. The statue was erected in 2006; this is the first time it has been vandalized. The Federal Bureau of Investigation joined local police on the case, and later three members of Sigma Phi Epsilon were suspected of being responsible for the noose.[75]

And a week after *this* incident, *The Journal of Blacks in Higher Education* reported, "A black senior at the University of Mississippi says that she was attacked as she returned to a housing complex about a mile from campus that is populated almost entirely by Ole Miss students. The woman says she was doused with an alcoholic beverage by a group of men in a truck yelling racial slurs. One of the occupants of the truck allegedly called her a 'Black nigger' during the incident."[76]

Even President Obama, speaking at a memorial for the Sandy Hook tragedy in Newtown, Connecticut, where twenty-year-old Adam Lanza murdered twenty school children and six staff members, brought out the ire of white racist college students. When NBC preempted its coverage of an NFL game to report on the memorial, Bradley Patterson, a North Alabama football player, took to Twitter to tweet, "Take that nigger off the tv. We wanna watch football." Patterson was later kicked off the team.[77]

Sometimes, just walking through Greek Row while black causes problems for black students. At the University of Florida in 2013, a member of the Alpha Tau Omega fraternity yelled racial slurs and inappropriate sexual remarks from the fraternity house porch as a black female student was walking home one evening. Several fraternity members were present, but only one member voiced objection to the behavior, according to the UF dean of students. The fraternity issued a statement apologizing for the incident, but the university couldn't sanction the student because doing so would have violated his First Amendment rights.[78]

In 2012 a group of black students at Cornell University were taunted as they walked past the Sigma Pi fraternity house. After they asked the men to stop, one individual yelled, "Come up here, Trayvon," referring to Trayvon Martin, the African American boy who was killed by George Zimmerman in Sanford, Florida, on his way home.

"Cornell prides itself on its diverse environment," Black Students United, a campus advocacy group, said in a statement, "yet as students of color, we are not always safe—not even on our own campus."

Cornell would eventually place Sigma Pi on "interim suspension status" while it investigated the incident.[79]

Speaking of Trayvon Martin, the *Daily Texan,* the University of Texas' student newspaper, ran an editorial cartoon related to Martin's killing. The cartoon shows a woman on a chair that is labeled "The Media." She is reading a book to a child with the title, *Trayvon Martin and the Case of Yellow Journalism.* The woman is quoted as reading, "And then, the big bad white man killed the handsome, sweet, innocent, colored boy." After protests by students, the cartoonist, Stephanie Eisner, left the newspaper, which promised to hold a campus forum on race.[80]

And in an incident that resembled the toilet-seat assault at Cal, two black female students at the University of Wisconsin reported that partying members of Delta Upsilon fraternity yelled racial slurs at them as they walked across the fraternity's property, with someone hurling two glass bottles at them. The previous summer, members of Delta Upsilon had hung a dark, life-sized Spider-Man doll outside their fraternity house, which caused racial tensions on campus to rise.[81]

But one of the most disturbing acts of campus racism came not from the ranks of white fraternities and sororities but from alcohol beverage control officers at the University of Virginia and ordinary white students at San Jose State.

The photo was iconic. There was Martese Johnson, a black University of Virginia student, whose bloodied face was pressed onto the jagged brick sidewalk outside a club, after three white Virginia alcohol beverage control officers had tackled him and thrown him to the ground. Why? All because he'd shown a club owner the wrong ID.

Johnson, who's from the South Side of Chicago, was doing what a lot of UVA students were doing on St. Patrick's Day in 2015: attempting to join his friends at a local Irish pub. But when he presented his ID to the club owner at the door, he answered a question about the Chicago zip code on the card incorrectly, and the club owner wouldn't let him in.

"I had lost my driver's license about two weeks before, so I had new ID, but I forgot, and handed him my old ID. When he asked for the zip code, I gave him the zip code for my new driver's license, but it didn't match. So he said, 'Sorry, the zip codes don't match, I can't let you in.'"[82]

After that, with both Johnson and the club owner being from Chicago, they had a casual conversation, maybe twenty seconds or so, about Chicago. Then he was handed back his ID, and Johnson started to leave the entrance of the pub, only to be grabbed from behind, and he pulled back.

"Naturally you'll pull back if someone is grabbing you from behind, if you don't know them," Johnson said. "Then I looked back to see who was grabbing me, and that's when I noticed the badge, and it was an ABC officer. He continued to grab me and pull me to the curb. He started asking me the standard questions about whether I was twenty-one, and then he said that I'd presented a fake ID at the door. And when he said that, I immediately said that my ID wasn't fake, and I explained to him how there was a discrepancy. As I reached for my ID to show him, another officer grabbed me and pulled my other arm. At this point, they put my arms behind my back, and I can't show them my ID. Then a third officer approached us . . . and grabs me, and they slam me to the ground.

"My face is bleeding everywhere, my peers are watching and screaming, and the only thing I can scream is 'How can this happen to me?' and 'This is racist.'"

Johnson was then arrested, put in both handcuffs and leg shackles, put in an ambulance, and taken to the hospital, where he required ten stitches for the gash on his head.

The scary part is that when we hear about these types of incidents, we automatically turn our attention to the character of the victim. Is he a good guy, or is he a guy who had problems in the past? We do so as if the answers matter. Still, in the case of Martese Johnson, you couldn't have dreamed up a better ambassador for the university.

Johnson, upon arriving at the University of Virginia, had the same type of initial experience that a lot of black students face on predominately white campuses.

"I was uncomfortable. It was clearly a university that catered to upper–middle class white culture, where every student I see is wearing khakis, Sperrys and ties to football games," Johnson, twenty, said in an interview with the *Washington Post*. "Freshman year, I was the only black male in my entire dorm building. It was one of the first times I had to endure being in a place where I was the absolute minority."[83]

Still, Johnson would go on to join the African American fraternity Kappa Alpha Psi and then be elected to the University of Virginia Honor Committee. The second-oldest honor committee in the country, it's responsible for adjudicating any alleged honor code violations by students, usually centering on accusations of lying, cheating, or stealing. The accused student is brought before an honor trial and, if convicted, is asked to leave the University of Virginia. What made Johnson run for a seat on the Honor Committee in the first place?

"I got interested in the Honor Committee during my second year, when I learned about a phenomenon called disproportionate reporting," Johnson said.

Disproportionate reporting refers to the fact that when it came to honor violations being reported, minority students and athletes were being targeted and accused far out of proportion to their numbers on campus. Taken at face value, the accusations would have created the impression that either white students were inherently honest, or minorities and athletes were inherently dishonest. In other words, racism, and the negative perception of minorities and black athletes on campus, was driving this disproportionate response, in the same manner that in some communities in the United States, police are called with disproportionate frequency by white residents to investigate their law-abiding black neighbors for being "suspicious."

"This has been happening for decades at the university, but in my second year at the university, there were zero black students on the honor committee," Johnson recalled. "It made no sense that there was no black representation to change the culture, so this problem could not be a problem anymore."

It was here that Johnson received his first push back on race. "I got a lot of white students saying that it [disproportionate reporting] wasn't an issue, I was playing the race card, and I was just an ignorant black person," Johnson remembered. But despite that opposition, Johnson was able to gather a coalition of black and minority communities.

"Black and minority communities tend to not vote," said Johnson, "because they don't feel that their voices are heard, so they cannot effect change in the system. So when they finally saw a black candidate on the ballot, they had a reason to be invested. And I proved to them that I would serve those communities, as well as serve the larger community, but make them a priority for once. So they came out and voted."

That was in 2013–14 school year, and Johnson was reelected in 2015, his senior year. But none of this prevented Johnson from having his face slammed to the sidewalk that St. Patrick's Day in Charlottesville. Nor did it prevent him from being handcuffed and having his legs shackled as he was taken to jail.

All over a *mistaken* ID.

Johnson's arrest caused the black University of Virginia student community to take action. But in reality, they'd been taking action all year, only the UVA administration hadn't been paying attention.

"This school year, even before the Martese incident," said Joy Omenyi, president of the UVA Black Student Alliance, "across the nation with the Mike Brown and Eric Garner incidents, here at UVA, we also had our demonstrations as well . . . and when we were doing our demonstrations, we never heard from the administration. We'd had a candlelight vigil for Tamir Rice, and Emmanuel Brown, a black employee who passed away, and Eric Garner."[84]

What upset the black UVA students at the time was that UVA president Teresa Sullivan typically sent students an email whenever a student, faculty member, or staff died, yet Emmanuel Brown, a maintenance worker for three decades at UVA, received no recognition when he passed away while cleaning a university bathroom.

"Whenever there's a disaster, or something that can affect UVA students," Omenyi said, "the president will send out an email saying that our thoughts are with those students or professors.

"The only contact we had with the administration was an email that told us to not use real candles during our vigil, and don't block traffic," recalled Omenyi. "But the very next day, when they announced no indictments for Eric Garner, students ended up taking over the libraries, and other buildings. And they also stormed the president's house. It was at that time that students began to chant, 'Where's our email?' referring to the lack of an email for Emmanuel Brown."

Omenyi said that only when a rumor spread that the black students would disrupt a campus event did President Sullivan send an email mentioning Eric Garner, along with an invitation to come to the campus event. According to the students, she also promised a future meeting with the black students, which never happened.

But the Johnson incident further galvanized the black students. Omenyi worked with the president of the UVA campus NAACP to take action.

Immediately, they called students, and the Charlottesville police, in order to find out where Martese was. In the morning they picked him up from jail and began a plan of action. Images of Martese's bloody face were emailed to students and administrators. Within minutes, Martese was on national media.

"As soon as that happened, the administration made us meet with all of the black deans on campus," Omenyi laughed. "The vice president of diversity and equity, along with three or four deans of African American affairs. I knew that was going to happen because I work in that office, and when something happens to black students, they get called first. And before we went into the meeting, I told Martese to not reveal anything. Just because they're black doesn't mean that they don't work for the university. They're protecting the interest of their paycheck."

After the meeting, the BSA decided that they wanted to have a space for healing, so they called a meeting at one small room on campus, only to find out that more than 500 students had shown up. So the meeting was moved to a larger space, and instead of focusing on a space for healing, it became a vigil for Martese Johnson, which isn't what the black students wanted to happen.

"We just wanted it to just be black students coming together, and we weren't able to do that. Somehow, someway, it got co-opted by the university."

The meeting took three hours, as UVA students began talking about their own experiences with racism at the university and in the community. But the university suddenly wanted to hear from the black students. The media glare was getting hot, especially since UVA had been the center of a controversial *Rolling Stone* article, later retracted, that alleged that a sexual assault had occurred at a fraternity house on campus. This was *not* the type of publicity the university wanted or needed.

"The only time they wanted to listen to us was after the Johnson incident. Of course, the media was there. CNN, ABC, and other national media were in Charlottesville, and were willing to give microphones and cameras to black students so they could say what they felt, that's when President Sullivan dove in and said she wanted to sit down and talk."

The students soon hit the streets of Charlottesville, protesting Johnson's treatment. Months later, the courts dropped the charges of public intoxication and obstructing justice. But the dismissal of the case didn't mean that there wasn't a cost. Because his case became national news, Johnson lost out on an internship with a private wealth management firm. Still, he understood the bigger picture.

"It is a tremendous opportunity for me to have a second chance at not having charges and being free," Johnson said. "But I think that in many instances, minorities are not allowed this privilege. It shouldn't just be the honors student who goes to the University of Virginia and has some great academic record who has the opportunity to have his charges dropped for something that happened so unjustly. This should be an opportunity for every minority in the country to be able to experience. This should be something that isn't a privilege to those who have certain accolades, have a certain image that makes them passable in a way.

"So for the rest of my life, I hope to work to serve the minority community and also society by shedding light on what is injustice and serving those who are overlooked and mistreated throughout our county."[85]

• • •

Over at San Jose State in 2013, Donald Williams Jr., an African American freshman, was assigned to live with seven young white roommates in a four-bedroom campus suite. According to police reports, the white students began taunting Williams by calling him "Three-fifths," as in the way the United States counted slaves (each was deemed three-fifths of a person) when calculating southern populations prior to the Civil War. Once Williams protested, the white students decided to simply call him "Fraction."[86]

It gets worse.

According to a later civil lawsuit, the students hung a Confederate flag over a cardboard cutout of Elvis Presley in their dorm. They wrote the word "nigger" on a dry erase board in the living room. Williams' parents saw it and complained to campus officials; two of the roommates were immediately transferred, but the harassment continued. White students locked Williams out of his room. On another occasion they wrestled Williams to the ground, fastened a metal bicycle lock around his neck, and told him they'd lost the key . . . and then tried to do it again weeks later.[87]

Based on the civil lawsuit, when investigators searched the suite, they found a picture of Adolf Hitler, swastikas, and the SS lightning bolt symbol. After Williams' father spoke to the roommates and reported the incidents, the white students, who called themselves "The Residents," wrote a sarcastic "apology letter" that the police said referenced "the Beloved Reverend Doctor Martin Luther King Jr." and urged the freshman to let bygones be bygones.

Four of the white students were arrested and charged with hate crimes, with their trial scheduled for October 2015. They were subsequently expelled from San Jose State and banned for life from any campus on the Cal State University system. A fourth student was placed on permanent probation.[88]

This is only a very small sampling of the continuous assault on African American students over the years. What we learn is that while the Reagan and Obama eras may have brought slight spikes in the number of incidents, the racist behavior is consistent and universal. It happens mostly with white fraternities and sororities, but it spreads beyond these groups. And what's clear is that despite the forums, the white paper studies, and the work of Greek life offices, multicultural affairs offices, and diversity offices no one has been able to figure out how to stop it.

So that means that African American students continue to take it.

6

HONORING THE DISHONORABLE

"Who could look on these monuments without reflecting on the vanity of mortals in thus offering up testimonials of their respect for persons of whose very names posterity is ignorant?"

—Marguerite Gardiner

IMAGINE A WORLD WHERE JEWISH COLLEGE STUDENTS IN THE United States had to walk into campus buildings bearing the name of a Nazi who not only advocated for the mass slaughter of Jews, but also participated in their killing. Or perhaps they were taught in a building named after a German who helped pass the Racial Purity Act of 1924, an act that would drive Jews from schools, and place many into institutions where they'd be forcibly sterilized. Or maybe there was a school where Jews and Aryans weren't allowed to date. And another school where Jewish students were taught history in a building that honored a local Nazi gauleiter.

The world would be rightly repelled.

Now replace "Jew" with "African American," and you've entered the reality of thousands of African American college students throughout the United States. A reality where African American students not only deal with the legacy of white supremacy on a daily basis, but also are told that things can't change, so just deal with it. And these legacies, these overt manifestations of a white racist past, help create the hostile campus environment of racial microaggressions and stereotypes that plague colleges and universities today.

African Americans are asked to deal with the microaggressions of race, the little reminders of degradation that we're supposed to simply transcend under the rubric of seeing the bigger picture. Millions of African American elementary and high school students attend schools named after slaveholders like George Washington and Thomas Jefferson, and despite the fact that these men owned human beings, we're taught that you can't judge their greatness by the standards of today. Their great contribution to the American ideal supposedly transcends their ownership of black students' ancestors in the system of chattel slavery.

And perhaps that's true. Perhaps African Americans can't escape the fact that nation building is messy, full of imperfect people who can't be judged by modern standards of morality, even though we consistently point toward them as examples of American exceptionalism.

So these are the Founding Fathers, we'll give them a pass.

But what isn't justifiable is the fact that millions of African American students also attend schools that glorify the treasonous *Confederate* slaveholders who tore this country apart in order to *maintain* an economic system of chattel slavery. The naming of the Jefferson Davis and Robert E. Lee high schools is justified under the Lost Clause myth that the Civil War wasn't about slavery but, rather, about some more noble principle like states' rights. And that these men, these treacherous men who fought and killed to keep black people in bondage, should continue to be looked upon as honorable men and women is perverse.

And the perversity doesn't end with Confederates' being honored. On college campuses throughout the country, there are hundreds of buildings, plazas, flags, and plaques honoring the contributions of white supremacists and racists. But more and more schools are recognizing that it's intolerable to have such icons on campus, mostly justified under the tag of "tradition," while on the other hand, preaching tolerance to students.

But those colleges and universities that resist changing the names of buildings honoring long-dead, long-disgraced white supremacists speak to the idea that African American college students aren't *really* important members of the campus community, but mere visitors. Transitory members of a college community who come and go without having ownership of the place where they get their education, even if they are tax-paying members of the state. If these blacks were considered full-fledged students, then the insults on college buildings wouldn't be debated. They'd be eradicated. But in an echo of Supreme Court Justice Roger Tandy's statement in the infamous *Dred Scott* decision, when he argued that the ex-slave had "no rights that the white man was bound to respect," instantly turning Scott into nothingness, black college students often feel as though they are nothing on these campuses, where the icons of white supremacy feel permanent, justified by the university administration and alumni under the idea of upholding "tradition."[1]

Take, for example, the University of Maryland. Colin Byrd is a student there, "a second-generation Terrapin," as he likes to say, as his father also attended the school in the early 1970s, and he's proud of the university. But there is one thing associated with the University of Maryland that does not make him proud . . . the name Byrd.

"It's ironic that the name on the football stadium is Byrd Stadium," Colin chuckles. He grew up close to the campus, and the family took many trips to football games where they'd see the signs leading to Byrd Stadium. "My Dad used to joke that the stadium was named after him, but to be honest, I'm not sure if he knew anything about who the stadium was named after."[2]

The answer to that mystery is Harry Clifton "Curley" Byrd, former University of Maryland football player and coach, who became the longest-serving president of the University of Maryland, holding the post from 1935 to 1954. Byrd, also a Sigma Alpha Epsilon fraternity member, was so interlinked with the University of Maryland that he even successfully changed the university's nickname from the Old Liners to the Terrapins.[3]

The controversy around Byrd stems from his segregationist political views. A staunch supporter of separate-but-equal Jim Crow policies, like most southern universities, the University of Maryland had a tortured history with race. In a cynical bid to prevent the University of Maryland from being integrated by black students, Byrd would often support funding for historically black colleges in Maryland.[4]

In 1935 Alpha Phi Alpha, the oldest African American fraternity, initiated a successful lawsuit that would see Donald Gaines Murray, an African American law student, admitted as the first black student at the University of Maryland Law School.[5] But only after a court order would the University of Maryland have its first black undergraduate in 1951. Meanwhile, an earlier incident that occurred on Byrd's watch had shown his true colors when it came to race.

The year was 1937, two years after Byrd had become president of the university, and Syracuse was scheduled to visit Maryland for a football game. And one of the stars of the Syracuse team was a "Hindu" (the common term at the time for people of Indian origin) named Wilmeth Sidat-Singh.

Sidat-Singh was a two-sport star at Syracuse, excelling at both basketball and football. As a halfback, he was so good that the legendary sportswriter Grantland Rice wrote a poem about his exploits. At the time, the University of Maryland, like a lot of southern universities, had a rule against playing football games against teams with black players, but no rules prevented their all-white teams from taking the field against players of different ethnic origins. The *Washington Post* described

Sidat-Singh as "the only Hindu basketball player in the United States." There was only one problem.[6]

He wasn't an Indian.

Legendary black sportswriter Sam Lacy of the *Washington Tribune,* an African American newspaper, scooped the sports world when he found out that Sidat-Singh's original name was Wilmeth Webb, and that he was an African American. As it turned out, Webb's mother had married an Indian doctor, and the doctor had adopted Webb and changed his name to Sidat-Singh.[7]

The *Washington Tribune* ran a banner headline, "NEGRO TO PLAY U. OF MARYLAND," along with the subhead, "THEY CALL HIM A HINDU," a day before the game, and it caused a sensation.

Sam Lacy and the *Washington Tribune* reveled in the hypocrisy of the University of Maryland and the conundrum it faced under Jim Crow.

"Sophisticated Maryland University's tradition stands to be knocked into a crooked hat Saturday," Lacy wrote. "For behind the scenes stands a Negro. He's been exploited by local dailies as a Hindu, obviously for the purpose of explaining the presence of the dark skinned footballer in the visiting backfield . . . And now—oh, horrors—[Maryland] must match wit and brawn, shoulder to shoulder, with a colored person. What ironical tricks are played on the poor unsuspecting Nordics!"[8]

Now that they had found out that their team would be playing not a "Hindu" (acceptable), but an African American (not acceptable), Byrd and the athletic director, Geary Eppley, demanded that either Sidat-Singh be benched or the game canceled. Eventually, Syracuse agreed to sit Sidat-Singh, and Maryland beat Syracuse. As for Eppley, the University of Maryland would go on to name its recreation center after him. There have been calls to change the name of that facility too.

Recently, the University of Maryland decided to try to make amends by honoring Sidat-Singh at the 2013 Syracuse vs. Maryland game—played inside Byrd Stadium, named after the very man who'd discriminated against him in the first place.[9]

Byrd would eventually leave the University of Maryland to challenge Republican incumbent Theodore Roosevelt McKeldin as the Democratic candidate for governor. One of Byrd's supporters, state senator George W. Della Sr., enthusiastically backed Byrd by urging voters to vote Democratic "so that we may come back and have white supremacy again in our schools." Byrd went on to lose decisively to McKeldin.[10]

"When I got to the university," said Colin, "I was exposed to the Nyumburu Cultural Center on campus, the black cultural center, and they do a lot of programming where they teach you about black history. But specifically, they try to localize the black history to give you a sense of what life was like for black people at the University of Maryland. That's when I heard that Byrd was a staunch segregationist. I thought to myself, 'What if [the stadium] could be renamed?' In the past, there hasn't been that much strategy that went into the efforts to rename the stadium . . . Frederick Douglass once said that power concedes nothing without a demand, and in the past, the students hadn't really given the administration a straight up demand regarding this."

And Colin has been making demands. As a member of the campus NAACP and other organizations, he's seen as a leader in the black student community. He sent Wallace Loh, the president of the University of Maryland, a letter demanding a response to the idea of changing the name. Colin was blunt in his assessment of race relations at the university.

"I would say that the state of race relations at the University of Maryland is terrible, and I think the university attempts to do a masterful job of concealing that by putting on a lot of fluffy events devoted to diversity and inclusion in order to perpetuate an image of a 21st Century campus that's moved past Jim Crow, but when you look below the surface, you see an institution that hasn't gotten rid of its institutional racist roots. The issue of Byrd Stadium is just one of many."

But before Colin could get a response to his letter, a couple of racial incidents exploded on campus.

First was the "Suck A Nigga Dick" cake that I mentioned before. But the second incident, which prompted a town hall meeting on campus hosted by the Student Government Association and the Office of Multicultural Involvement & Community Advocacy and attended by President Loh, was the discovery of a viral email sent out by a member of Kappa Sigma fraternity. Originally sent in January 2014, the email surfaced right after the SAE video.

"Regardless of the rush shirt let's get rachet [*sic*] as fuck during rush week. My dick will be sucked and fucked in compound basement whether you guys like it or not. Don't invite any nigger gals or curry monsters or slanted eye chinks, unless they're hot. Ziggy you're [*sic*] girl can come she's cool. Remember my niggas, erect, assert, and insert, and above all else, fuck consent . . . dicks untouched."[11]

"Just within that email," Colin said, "you saw racism, sexism, and sexual misconduct references."

With the email surfacing so soon after the Oklahoma SAE incident, someone wrote "Racist Frats" in chalk in front of a campus library. So when a campus town hall meeting was held in response, the tension was palpable.[12]

Colin stepped to the microphone and asked President Loh whether he'd work to change the name of Byrd Stadium. After President Loh explained to the packed audience the process of name changing, noting that the proposal would have to go through various committees before he could make a recommendation to the Board of Regents, he then said, "Curly Byrd, I believe, was the longest serving president, for about twenty years. If I recollect correctly, he began his presidency in 1935. He ended his presidency before *Brown v. The Board of Education* was announced in March 1954 that declared segregated schools are unlawful. As an official of the state, in the 1930s and 1940s, he was living in a state that was segregated. The University of Maryland was segregated. All the other institutions were segregated. I'm not saying it's right, but you're raising the question, and yes, he was a racist, he was a segregationist, and should we today change the name? It's a valid question, and you have a First Amendment right to ask that question, and to probe very deeply. I will set up a process where different groups will discuss this issue, and make a recommendation to me, just as they would on any other issue."[13]

But after President Loh had given that noncommittal answer, Colin pressed him about his own opinion regarding the name change.

"My personal opinion is the final opinion sent to the Board of Regents," President Loh said very carefully. "It would be an insult to these committees if I were to stand here and say, 'This is my opinion,' before they'd even gathered together to discuss this. But I will say this. Last month was the 50th anniversary of the Selma march. They crossed that bridge in March of 1963 or so, where they were bludgeoned and bloodied. The name of that bridge is the Edmund Pettus Bridge. No one in Selma wants the name of that bridge changed, even though he was the head of the Ku Klux Klan of Alabama. Why? Because that is part of our history. We do not condone that history, but we don't want to forget it."[14]

Unfortunately for President Loh's argument, his statement about Selma is only partly true. While there *is* a debate in Selma among the residents about changing the name of the bridge, a group of Alabama students, Students UNITE, not only gathered 180,000 signatures in support of changing the name of the bridge, but also convinced the Alabama Senate to vote in favor of changing the name to the Journey to Freedom Bridge.[15]

After the meeting, the president finally responded to Colin's letter, writing a short note reaffirming the process the university would have to go through in order to change the name.

"We are not inclined to ignore or try to erase the past of our University, or the past of our state for that matter," the note read. "However, in accordance with our shared governance practice, this matter has been sent to the University's Facilities Naming Committee for further review."[16]

Colin admits that for some black students, the name change wasn't number one on their agenda, and some students were apathetic. But he was successful in tying the Byrd issue to the plight of the Nyumburu Cultural Center, the one space on campus that every black student cared about. And to Colin, that center always seemed to be a target for possible fiscal cuts.

"Even though technically it's very symbolic in nature, when you have the renaming of a stadium or a facility that was named after someone who was a racist, or a segregationist, I think what it does is ignite a conversation about race relations on a campus that expands far beyond that.

"Everyone on campus has a clear and practical interest in the work of Nyumburu Cultural Center, and it always seemed to be on the chopping block for funding, so I tied those two things together. Everyone looks at it as a home away from home. Nyumburu means 'freedom' in Swahili, and that's what we want at the University of Maryland."

• • •

The university sent the request to the naming committee, which scheduled a meeting for the summer of 2015, a decision Colin thinks was made to avoid any disturbances that would occur if the committee decided to not change the name. But he didn't stop his own work. Colin continued to agitate by writing an open letter, bearing the hashtag #TerpPrejudice, to black high school athletes who'd received scholarship offers from the University of Maryland. Colin mentioned several topics that he said the prospective student athletes should raise with the University of Maryland football and basketball coaches, including lower graduation rates for black students and, of course, the Byrd stadium issue. "You can run. You can shoot. And you can tackle. But you can't have the dignity of not having to play the sports you love within the symbolic shadows of someone who would have hated you."[17]

The Byrd stadium issue is still unsettled, but the University of Maryland is not the only institution of higher learning with buildings, facilities, and statues named for white racists and segregationists. In fact, it's actually quite common to find them. And when you dig into the backgrounds of the honored, it's no surprise that African American students nationwide are demanding that universities remove names from buildings along with the statues of some really reprehensible people.

Clemson University, in South Carolina, has been at the forefront of black students' efforts to rename buildings still bearing the legacies of white supremacists. Clemson was founded by one of the most murderous and virulently racist white men in American history, Ben "Pitchfork" Tillman.

The son of South Carolina slaveholders, Ben Tillman made his post–Civil War fortune as a farmer, one who used innovations like crop diversification to maximize the productivity of his fields, while still whipping his freed black workers like an antebellum overseer. In 1865 Tillman worked on the South Carolina state constitution, making sure that the newly freed slaves would be disenfranchised.[18]

Tillman later joined the Red Shirts, a terrorist organization designed to murder white and black opponents of white supremacy in South Carolina. In 1876 he and a mob of Red Shirts confronted an African American militia, and at least seven African Americans were killed. Tillman later described that incident, termed the Hamburg Massacre, as one of his proudest moments. Tillman recalled that "the leading white men of Edgefield" had decided "to seize the first opportunity that the Negroes might offer them to provoke a riot and teach the Negroes a lesson" by "having the whites demonstrate their superiority by killing as many of them as was justifiable."[19]

Later, in 1909, Tillman addressed his Red Shirt brothers during a reunion, saying, "The purpose of our visit to Hamburg was to strike terror, and the next morning [Sunday] when the negroes who had fled to the swamp returned to the town [some of them never did return, but kept going] the ghastly sight which met their gaze of seven dead negroes lying stark and stiff, certainly had its effect . . . It was now after midnight, and the moon high in the heavens looked down peacefully on the deserted town and dead negroes, whose lives had been offered up as a sacrifice to the fanatical teachings and fiendish hate of those who sought to substitute the rule of the African for that of the Caucasian in South Carolina."[20]

But this wasn't all. As governor of South Carolina, Tillman discouraged northern benefactors from sending aid to African Americans after the 1893 hurricane that devastated the Sea Islands, saying that "it would result in lazy, idle crowds [wanting to] draw rations, as in the days of the Freedmen's Bureau . . . They cannot be treated as we would white people."[21]

Tillman's official position on race relations was that blacks should be either dominated or exterminated, and only the potential loss of white life prevented him from actively advocating for the mass murder of blacks. And when Booker T. Washington became the first African American to dine at the White House, at the invitation of President Theodore Roosevelt, Tillman said that "the action of President Roosevelt in entertaining that nigger will necessitate our killing a thousand niggers in the South before they learn their place again."[22]

And yet, Tillman is still honored with a building at both Clemson University, a school he helped found for white agricultural students, and Winthrop College, a school he helped build for the education of white women. When black Clemson students, and others, protested that a murdering racist shouldn't continue to be honored, the Board of Trustees at Clemson found nothing wrong with continuing to honor Tillman.

"While we respect the many differing opinions of our graduates, our students, our faculty and staff regarding this matter, the Clemson

University Board does not intend to change the names of buildings on campus, including Tillman Hall," said board chairman David Wilkins in a statement to *The Greenville News* in early 2015.[23]

Of course, Wilkins went on to reiterate his commitment to "diversity," but he said that there were other, more substantial changes that Clemson could make instead of the "symbolic gesture" of renaming a building.

"It is time to put this issue behind us and move on," Wilkins continued in his statement. "Every great institution is built by imperfect craftsmen. Stone by stone they add to the foundation so that over many, many generations, we get a variety of stones. And so it is with Clemson. Some of our historical stones are rough and even unpleasant to look at. But they are ours and denying them as part of our history does not make them any less so.

"For that reason, we will not change the name of our historical buildings," Wilkins said. "Part of knowledge is to know and understand history so you learn from it. Clemson is a strong, diverse university in which all of us can be proud. That is today's and tomorrow's reality and that is where all our energy is focused."[24]

In other words, Tillman's violent, racist white supremacy was just part of his being an imperfect person who just happened to hate and murder blacks in his spare time. Definitely not enough reason to remove his name from campus buildings nearly a century after his death.

Does Wilkins truly think that more African Americans will want to attend a university that believes that removing the name of a racist who advocated genocide on black people is a bridge too far? To his credit, Wilkins said the board recognizes Clemson has more work to do in its outreach to black students, and with that purpose in mind, they've increased opportunities for minority students through scholarship programs like Emerging Scholars and Call Me Mister. Now, no one will ever criticize efforts to increase diversity on college campuses. But what price dignity? Is the amount of money Clemson is going to spend on these two programs enough to stomach the daily insult of having a racist honored on campus? If not, what is that cost, and how do you calculate it?

This goes back to the earlier notion that universities can mitigate an injustice by maintaining that injustice while simply taking small steps in the other direction. So in essence, "We're not going to change the injustice, but we think if we balance it out with something just, that's enough of a compromise."

That is abhorrent.

Just as they are expected to understand that the Founding Fathers were imperfect men who created a Land of Opportunity, African American college students are expected to take the indignities of racism and microaggressions as being part of student life that can't be changed. And the fact that Clemson, and Winthrop University for that matter, won't change the changeable, and continue to defend the indefensible, is a canary in a coal mine. If they can't make this change, how can African American students trust them to have their best interests in mind in other matters involving race?

At Washington and Lee University, top administrators are considering whether to take action after law students called for civil disobedience if the college did not ban "neo-Confederates" from marching on campus with Confederate flags and remove those flags from a campus chapel. The flags in Lee Chapel are "designed for historical and educational purposes," President Ken Ruscio said in a statement.[25]

What many colleges don't realize is that when they continue to elevate the racists of the past, they denigrate the black students who currently walk on their campuses. Fortunately, other schools have recognized that symbols matter and, as a result, have made changes to buildings and policies as a matter of principle.

North Carolina governor Charles Aycock was an avowed segregationist who once said, "Indeed it has become the fashion among Republicans and Populists to assert the unfitness of the negro to rule, but when they use the word rule, they confine it to holding office. When we say that the negro is unfit to rule we carry it one step further and convey the correct idea when we declare that he is unfit to vote. To do this we must disfranchise the negro. This movement comes from the people. Politicians have been afraid of it and have hesitated, but the great mass of white men in the State are now demanding and have demanded that the matter be settled once and for all. To do so is both desirable and necessary—desirable because it sets the white man free to move along faster than he can go when retarded by the slower movement of the negro." Aycock's name was removed from buildings at both Duke and East Carolina University, and is being protested at the University of Carolina.[26]

"This is our role, to create this kind of discussion and make students look at their campus with fresh eyes so they can see things they didn't see before," said UNC senior Stéphanie Najjar. "We want to recover from historical amnesia."[27]

Acclaimed musician and racial theorist John Powell, who helped draft the Racial Purity Laws of 1924, which established the one-drop rule for determining race, was also the founder of racist Anglo-Saxon Clubs during the 1920s. Powell was also an ally of an infamous Virginia state registrar of vital statistics and eugenics advocate, Walter Plecker.[28]

Using the new laws as justification, Plecker worked diligently to reclassify all members of Virginia Indian tribes as "colored" to exclude them, as well as blacks, from public schools and other institutions. "Some of these mongrels, finding that they have been able to sneak in their birth certificates unchallenged as Indians, are now making a rush to register as white," Plecker was quoted as saying at the time.[29]

Under the state's eugenics policies, thousands of people deemed unfit to reproduce, including many poor whites, were committed to institutions such as the Virginia Colony for Epileptics and Feebleminded near Lynchburg. There, many of them were surgically sterilized, and then put to work for pittance wages for the state or in private homes.

Researchers estimate that about 60,000 people across the United States were forcibly sterilized in the first fifty years of the twentieth century. Some of them were elementary school–aged children.

It is said that Adolf Hitler used Virginia's legal framework for eugenics as a model for the Nazi sterilization law and efforts to purge Jews and other "undesirables" from German society. Hundreds of thousands were sterilized in the years leading up to the Holocaust.[30]

In 2005, when a history professor at Radford University, in Virginia, informed the school about the racist history of its Arts and Music building's namesake, the Board of Trustees unanimously agree to take Powell's name off the university building. It still took them five years to finally remove his name.[31]

At the University of Virginia, the School of Medicine building is named Jordan Hall, after Dr. Harvey E. Jordan, a past dean of the medical school. Dr. Jordan, an enthusiastic eugenicist who influenced the Virginia Eugenical Sterilization Act, wrote in an essay for a 1912 edition of *Science* magazine, "The negro is a primitive type of man, as indicated by numerous anatomic marks (e.g., relative length of arms and legs, male external genitalia, shape of nose) . . . he apparently stands much closer in the evolutionary scale to the anthropoid apes, with pigmented faces." Jordan's name remains on the building at UVA.[32]

At the University of North Carolina, black students urged the university to remove William Saunders' name from Saunders Hall and rename the building after noted Harlem Renaissance author Zora Neale Hurston, who was the first black student to take classes at the school. William Saunders was a Confederate colonel in the Civil War, UNC trustee, and a chief organizer for the Ku Klux Klan. Over fifty students of color rallied on campus with the support of UNC geography professor Altha Cravey, who made their rally the subject of an essay assignment.

"I remember an incident when two faculty members who worked in Saunders Hall were describing how they enjoyed intimidating a black student," Cravey recalled. "They were casually laughing about it over lunch with me. Having that name on the building facilitates that kind of behavior."[33]

W. Lowry Caudill, chair of the Board of Trustees, initially wrote in a statement that the board was listening to students' concerns but would abide by the "policy on renaming campus facilities."

The standards are hazy: while a building can be renamed if the honoree's "reputation changes substantially so that the continued use of that name may compromise the public trust," the policy also states that "namings should not be altered simply because later observers would have made different judgments."[34]

Still, the students succeeded in late May 2015 in getting the university to remove Saunders' name from the building. But as a way to show that they weren't conceding to the black students, the board renamed the building Carolina Hall instead of using the opportunity to honor Zora Neale Hurston. I suppose they chose Carolina Hall only because Acme Hall, or Building Hall, was already taken from the list of nondescript names. Right after the change, Sam Schaefer, the summer editor for the University of North Carolina newspaper, *The Daily Tar Heel*, told reporter Richard Prince in an email:

> We think the choice of "Carolina Hall" (besides being hopelessly milquetoast) is a slap in the face of activists because activists have proposed their choice of Hurston Hall as a way of highlighting the voices of people of color, and "Carolina Hall" seems to be a way of whitewashing an issue that is very explicitly about race.
>
> The "contextualized" plaque that will accompany the new name on the hall is so vague as to be very near meaningless. Even if the board found the evidence of Hurston's connection to UNC to be tenuous, there are many other people of color in the University's history who would have made for excellent choices for the hall, and at the very least, they could have opened up the process for further

public input and deliberation. Shallow "unity" rings false when the divides on campus are very real—the board's decisions may have just deepened them.[35]

And this isn't just an American phenomenon, as black South African students at the University of Cape Town successfully demanded the removal of a Cecil Rhodes statue on campus. Rhodes was an English imperialist who subjugated Africans throughout southern Africa.[36]

African American college students are just expected, like blacks in American society in general, to grin and bear the indignities. When universities don't change the names of the buildings, they're making a tacit admission that the repulsive views of the racists trump the humanity of the African American students on their campus. No university would honor a rapist with a building on campus and then expect women to attend classes there. Women would rightly be insulted.

But Clemson doesn't stop with Tillman. There's the Strom Thurmond Institute and Thurmond Lake, both named after former U.S. senator Strom Thurmond, who represented South Carolina for forty-eight years. Thurmond was most famous for having conducted the longest filibuster ever held by a lone senator—twenty-four hours and eighteen minutes—in opposition to the Civil Rights Act of 1957.[37]

Richard Russell Jr., who served as the governor of Georgia from 1931 to 1933 and as a U.S. senator from 1933 to 1971, was staunchly in favor of segregation and supported the ideals of white supremacy. Russell once stated, "It was an insult to the people of Georgia . . . to even insinuate that I stand for political and social equality with the negro."[38]

Yet at the University of Georgia, there's Russell Hall, a dormitory for first-year students, where black students sleep in a place named for a man who thought them to be inferior. Oh, but you say you're not affected by Russell Hall because you don't live there? Don't worry! The University of Georgia dedicated the Richard B. Russell Building Special Collections Libraries in 2012.

Wade Hampton Hall at the University of South Carolina is named after Wade Hampton III, a Confederate general and South Carolina governor. An ally of Ben Tillman and a fellow member of the Red Shirts, Hampton worked to suppress the black vote through violence and intimidation.[39]

At Oklahoma State University, Murray Hall is named after Oklahoma governor William "Alfalfa Bill" Murray, who in the early twentieth century campaigned for governor under a slogan that railed against what he called the "Three C's: Corporations, Carpetbaggers, and Coons."

Murray once said, "Blacks were inferior to whites in all ways, and must be fenced from society like quarantined hogs."[40] Murray also described what he thought was the ideal black in his state. "I appreciate the old-time ex-slave, the old darky—and they are the salt of their race—who comes to me talking softly in that humble spirit which should characterize their actions and dealings with the white man, and when they thus come they can get any favor from me. When a Negro says to me: 'Set 'em up,' or taps me on the shoulder as would an equal friend I would want to land on his shins."[41]

When addressing the 1906 Constitution Convention to transform Oklahoma from an Indian Territory to a state, he said, "As a rule they [African Americans] are failures as lawyers, doctors and in other professions. He must be taught in the line of his own sphere, as porters, bootblacks and barbers and many lines of agriculture, horticulture and mechanics in which he is an adept, but it is an entirely false notion that the negro can rise to the equal of a white man in the professions or become an equal citizen to grapple with public questions. The more they are taught in the line of industry the less will be the number of dope fiends, crap shooters and irresponsible hordes of worthless Negroes around our cities and towns."[42]

Oklahoma, home to numerous all-black towns like Boley, Langston, and Tullahassee, was often marketed as a place where African Americans could live in relative freedom from the oppression of whites.

However, this was a myth. In 1921 the white race riots in Tulsa saw thousands of African Americans murdered and the segregated section of town, nicknamed "Black Wall Street," burned to the ground.

Murray represented the racist reality of Oklahoma, and when blacks tried to hold an Emancipation Day parade in a park in Oklahoma City, the governor imposed martial law on the city and ordered his National Guard troops to shut them down. In Murray's eyes blacks were supposed to be invisible in his state, quietly working the land or manning factory stations.[43]

And yet not one but two buildings, Murray Hall and North Murray Hall, honor him on the Oklahoma State campus, despite protests and Change.org petitions detailing Murray's racist ideology and past.

They're still there.

The University of Mississippi honors former Mississippi governor and U.S. senator James K. Vardaman, who once described the education of African Americans as "a positive unkindness that renders him unfit for the work which the white man has prescribed him and which he will be forced to perform." Known as the "Great White Chief," Vardaman wasn't satisfied with keeping African Americans uneducated; he went a step further. Vardaman was perfectly fine with mass murder of black Mississippians, if needed: "If it is necessary every Negro in the state will be lynched; it will be done to maintain white supremacy."[44]

And yet his name stays on the building at the University of Mississippi.

In 2012 the University of Mississippi chancellor Dan Jones ordered the formation of a committee, the Extended Sensitivity and Respect Committee, to study the racial climate on the campus. This came after the reelection of President Obama led to numerous racially motivated disturbances on campus. Among the committee's twelve recommendations was that Vardaman Hall, along with the Paul B. Johnson Ballroom, named after the segregationist former Mississippi governor, be renamed. Along with that, the committee recommended that various

Confederate and Jim Crow segregationist symbols be eradicated from the campus.

"Campus symbols, particularly those that became associated with the university during Jim Crow segregation and the resistance to civil rights (e.g., the Confederate monument, Rebels, Colonel Rebel/Colonel Reb and Dixie) are a source of contention among different members of the university community," the report states. "UM should strive to support symbols that represent all on our campus."[45]

A year later Chancellor Jones announced various changes, including renaming Confederate Drive as Chapel Lane and honoring the University of Mississippi football player Chucky Mullins, an African American who died tragically after being paralyzed during a game, as a commitment to diversity. But among the things that were *not* going to change were the names on Vardaman Hall and the Paul B. Johnson Ballroom. Instead, plaques will be placed to put those names, said Chancellor Jones, in "historical context and perspective."[46]

What keeps white powerbrokers from changing the names on the buildings isn't some fidelity to the racists themselves. Instead, it's the psychological leap required to break away from white racism and acknowledge the humanity of African Americans. For some, any such acknowledgment is a bridge too far. The excuses given typically center around ideas of "tradition" or "bigger issues," or there are superficial concessions designed to mollify African Americans, so that, as with a "to those I may have offended" apology, there's really no resolution to the dispute, and white supremacy remains intact and unchallenged.

But some schools are changing.

Dixie State, a university in St. George, Utah, was founded by Mormons from the South. In 2012 the university removed a statue called "The Rebels" from campus and placed it in storage. The statue depicted Confederate soldiers and a horse. One of the soldiers carried a Confederate battle flag. At that time, then Dixie State president Stephen

Nadauld said, "It's a beautiful piece of art. We are nervous something might happen to the statue. It might be vandalized."

Now the university has returned the statue to the artist, eighty-year-old Jerry Anderson. In return, Anderson will create another (less controversial) work that will find a permanent home on the Dixie State campus. Anderson told the *Salt Lake Tribune,* "I think it's a bunch of baloney, but it had to happen. I think America is too politically correct."[47]

Proponents of maintaining the status quo often like to say that the men and women honored on campus are both people of their times and typical, flawed human beings who shouldn't be judged by the standards of today. It's a red herring. It's also ahistorical, as these racist men and women *were* judged often by the men and women of their own age as being racist, and yet universities are choosing to ignore those voices as being insignificant. Tillman, even in an age of overt racism, was judged to be a racist.

• • •

However, when black students, like those at the University of California at Berkeley, attempted to name a building after their *own* flawed hero, Assata Shakur, a political prisoner living in exile in Cuba for the past thirty years, their choice was subjected to a fine-toothed comb, and every possible argument against honoring that person is brought to the fore.

And at Marquette, where the historically black Alpha Kappa Alpha sorority hung a mural of Shakur inside the Gender and Sexuality Resource Center, they were made to apologize for the mural, and the university took it down. So why the controversy with honoring Shakur?

In 1973 Assata Shakur, a Black Panther and Black Liberation Army member and an activist at the Borough of Manhattan Community College and the City College of New York, was accused of murdering New

Jersey state trooper Werner Foester during a shoot-out on the New Jersey turnpike, where another member of the Black Liberation Army was also killed. Shakur herself was shot and lay shackled to her hospital bed as she was charged with murder. After a heated trial, where evidence suggested that there was no gunpowder residue on her fingers and that none of her fingerprints were found on any of the guns at the scene, Shakur was convicted of first-degree murder in 1977.[48]

Shakur's record prior to the shoot-out included six arrests on charges of alleged kidnapping, bank robbery, and attempted murder, but all cases had resulted in either acquittals or dismissals for lack of evidence. This was also during the time that the FBI was infiltrating various black nationalist groups like the Black Panther Party through COINTEL-PRO (Counterintelligence Program). FBI head J. Edgar Hoover had directed his agents to "expose, disrupt, misdirect, discredit, neutralize or otherwise eliminate" the activities of these groups and their leaders. And in a missive to FBI offices across the country in 1967, Hoover had told his agents that "no opportunity should be missed to exploit through counterintelligence techniques the organizational and personal conflicts of the leaderships of the groups and where possible an effort should be made to capitalize upon existing conflicts between competing black nationalist organizations."[49]

Shakur spent six years in prison, becoming the first woman ever confined in a men's prison in New Jersey. Placed under twenty-four-hour surveillance, she later escaped, fleeing in 1984 to Cuba, where she was given political asylum. In 2013 the FBI placed Shakur on its Most Wanted Terrorist List, along with members of the Taliban and Hezbollah.[50]

"No person, no matter what his or her political or moral convictions are, is above the law. Joanne Chesimard [Shakur's married name] is a domestic terrorist who murdered a law enforcement officer execution style," said former FBI special agent Aaron Ford in 2013. Until 2015, Ford was the head of the FBI's Newark division.[51]

Over the decades Shakur has turned into a cause célèbre, particularly among African American college students, with the publication of her autobiography, *Assata*. Those students see Shakur as a symbol of resistance against oppression, rather than merely an escaped fugitive, and they look upon the university as a representation of that oppression. But it was her unflinching resolve to fight systemic and institutional racism that attracted their support.

"I advocate self-determination for my people and for all oppressed people inside the United States. I advocate an end to capitalist exploitation, the abolition of racist policies, the eradication of sexism and the elimination of political oppression. If that is a crime, then I am totally guilty."[52]

Through the years, various black student groups have advocated for the naming of buildings and rooms in her honor. At Shakur's alma mater, CCNY, the Guillermo Morales/Assata Shakur Student and Community Center had served as a safe space for African American, gay and lesbian, and other marginalized students on campus. But in 2013, under pressure from outside critics, the university suddenly boxed up the contents of the space and locked out protesting students. The university's official response was that it was creating an annex for the career service center, two floors above. But once the defiant black fist on the door was painted over, it was clear to the students why the center was closed.

"I think that the CUNY administration is really scared of a lot of the organizing and community-building coming out of the building," Alyssia Osorio, director of the Morales/Shakur Center, told the *New York Times*. "We provide so many services for the community—know-your-rights training, a farm share that provides healthy food, we've run a soup kitchen, we have provided baby-sitting services for people in the community."[53]

When the black students at UC Berkeley demanded that a building on campus, Barrows Hall, be named after Shakur, the right-wing media had a meltdown.

"Berkeley Students Outrage Police with Demand to Honor Cop Killer," screamed the *San Diego Union-Tribune* newspaper, whose article was complete with a Most Wanted Terrorist poster.[54]

The UK's *Daily Mail* went with a somewhat longer, unwieldy headline, apparently wanting to make sure its readers understood who a building could be named after: "UC Berkeley Students Want to Rename a Campus Building after a Notorious Cop Killer Who Was the First Woman on the FBI's Most Wanted Terrorists List."[55]

To be fair, when the *Daily Mail* reported on the removal of the Cecil Rhodes statue, it did give white supporters of the noted racist just as long a headline: "Furious White Groups Say South African University's Decision to Remove Statue of British Colonialist Cecil Rhodes Following Black Student Protests Is 'Racism in Disguise.'"[56]

And the *Fox News* headline, considering that it came from *Fox News,* was relatively subtle: "College Students Want to Name a Building after a Convicted Cop Killer." Although they did add the word "outrageous" to the column.[57]

As for the black students at Cal, they picked Shakur for one reason.

"We want the renaming for someone—Assata Shakur—who we feel . . . represents us as black students," Cori McGowens, spokesman for the school's Black Student Union, said. "We're at a crisis on campus."[58]

And while the Berkeley administration has yet to answer the demand that it change the name of Barrows Hall, over at Marquette University, the administration *has* moved to block Shakur from being honored.

In March 2015, as mentioned above, the Alpha Kappa Alpha chapter at Marquette sponsored a mural of Assata Shakur. It hung mostly unnoticed by the university for two months, until John McAdams, a disgruntled conservative Marquette professor, demanded it be taken down.

"A professor can hang something on their door, or office, and that's just their space," McAdams said. "But if it's a mural on a wall of a

Marquette office then that is Marquette University's official action. And that's what's so odd, so strange about this . . . What in the world were they thinking?"[59]

On his blog, *Marquette Warrior,* McAdams described the decision to hang the mural as "yet another case of the extreme leftist agenda of the organization." ("Warrior" is the previous name of Marquette's sports teams, which was changed to the Golden Eagles following pressure from Native Americans who objected to being seen as mascots.)

The mural included two quotes from Shakur about education:

No one is going to give you the education you need to overthrow them. Nobody is going to teach you your true history, teach you your true heroes if they know that knowledge will help set you free.

Before going back to college, I knew that I didn't want to be an intellectual, spending my life in books and libraries without knowing what the hell is going on in the streets. Theory without practice is just as incomplete as practice without theory. The two have to go together.[60]

These ideas about learning didn't fit what Marquette wanted for its students' Jesuit education.

"This is extremely disappointing as the mural does not reflect the Guiding Values of Marquette University," a Marquette official said in a statement. "It was removed immediately. We are reviewing the circumstances surrounding the mural and will take appropriate action."[61]

In a curious move, Alpha Kappa Alpha sorority national headquarters issued a statement that expressed regret that its campus chapter had sponsored the mural in the first place. "In March 2015, the MU Beta chapter of Alpha Kappa Alpha Sorority, Inc. at Marquette University hosted a series of scheduled campus based service projects and activities for Marquette University students. As part of these activities, MU Beta members proposed a mural theme, which was approved by Marquette University, to be painted at the university's Gender and Sexuality Resource Center . . . The chapter, along with other university staff and students painted a mural that featured an image and quote by Assata Shakur to promote student thinking about their educations and history. Unfortunately, Ms. Shakur's entire history and background was not fully researched. If that process had occurred, she would not have been featured in the mural."[62]

In other words, Alpha Kappa Alpha sorority wasn't backing their campus chapter on its decision to choose Assata Shakur for the mural.

Ironically, the person who complained the loudest, McAdams, hadn't actually *seen* the mural. He'd been banned from the Marquette campus after writing an October 2014 blog post that Marquette administrators eventually characterized as "inaccurate and irresponsible."[63]

The blog post stemmed from an interaction between a philosophy teacher's assistant, Cheryl Abbate, and a student over the issue of a classroom discussion of gay marriage. The student, who surreptitiously recorded the conversation, accused the TA of shutting down conversation because the student held conservative beliefs. After the conversation, the student played the recording to McAdams, which caused McAdams to write a blog post that said, among other things, that Abbate was "using a tactic typical among liberals," in which opinions they disagree with "are not merely wrong, and are not to be argued against on their merits, but are deemed 'offensive' and need to be shut up."[64]

The Marquette administration, particularly Dean Richard C. Holz came down hard on McAdams, accusing him of distorting the facts and using his tenure to "carelessly and arrogantly intimidate and silence the less powerful and then raise the shields of academic freedom and free expression against all attempts to stop such abuse."

In a letter to McAdams, Holz didn't mince words.

"As a result of your unilateral, dishonorable and irresponsible decision to publicize the name of our graduate student, and your decision to publish information that was false and materially misleading about her and your university colleagues, that student received a series of hate-filled and despicable e-mails, including one suggesting that she had committed 'treason and sedition' and as a result faced penalties such as 'drawing, hanging, beheading, and quartering.'"[65]

In response, McAdams said on the *Marquette Warrior,* "We will indeed fight this. We have excellent legal counsel, and most certainly will not go quietly."

Ironically, McAdams ends his blog post by defending free speech and ideas. "In *real* universities, administrators understand (or more likely grudgingly accept) that faculty will say controversial things, will criticize them and each other, and that people will complain about it. They understand that putting up with the complaints is part of the job, and assuaging those who complain the loudest is not the best policy."[66]

Using McAdams' logic, you'd think that he would not object to the Shakur mural but would fight to defend it, as he'd previously said that he was against the idea of opinions' being "deemed 'offensive'" and needing "to be shut up." But he didn't. He had the loudest voice, and the Marquette administration listened to it.

But whatever side of the Assata Shakur debate you fall on, we have to agree that it's exceedingly hypocritical to point to Shakur as being a no-go zone when it comes to African Americans' picking their own heroes for buildings, when America's campuses are overwhelmingly littered with the names of white supremacists, Confederate traitors, and other repulsive human beings on the fronts of halls, administrative buildings, and dorms. You can't stand on a soapbox and say you're repulsed by Assata Shakur, and yet justify the name of Ben Tillman being honored at two South Carolina universities.

Or maybe you're at the University of Texas, where a statue of Confederate president Jefferson Davis stands, supported by the Sons of Confederate Veterans of Texas, who say that the statue represents history that is "not a matter of opinion."[67] And as with all racist iconography on college campuses, you have to follow the money. At the University of Texas, that money stops at an early donor named George Washington Littlefield.

Littlefield, a former slaveholder and major in the Confederate army, would dedicate his life to making the University of Texas his personal tribute to the South's myth of the Lost Cause, donating thousands of dollars so that his name could be on a myriad of buildings and monuments, including the Littlefield dorm, the Littlefield House, and the Littlefield fountain. On a wall next to the fountain is the inscription: "To the men and women of the Confederacy, who fought with valor and suffered with fortitude that states' rights be maintained and who, not dismayed by defeat nor discouraged by misrule, builded from the ruins of a devastating war a greater South and to the men and women of the nation who gave of their possessions and of their lives [so] that free government be made secure to the peoples of the earth this memorial is dedicated."

And what about slavery? Apparently, the Confederacy didn't have a position on that.[68]

Eventually, Littlefield would sprinkle the UT campus with six statues of Confederate heroes, along with noted Confederate sympathizers like U.S. president Woodrow Wilson and Governor James Stephen Hogg.

The president of the student government at the University of Texas has come out in favor of removing the Jeff Davis statue, but in regards to the other offensive statues, the administration has passed the buck until a new UT president comes into office, who will probably do what other UT administrators have done—pass the buck.

"In previous decades, there have been proposals to remove the statue," UT director of media relations Gary Susswein said in a statement. "The university administration chose at those times to leave it in place but also to emphasize the university's values by adding prominently placed statues of such leaders as Martin Luther King and Barbara Jordan."[69]

So according to the University of Texas' logic, the presence of Confederate statues, monuments to men who fought to continue the enslavement and degradation of African Americans, can be mitigated by two true American heroes who happen to be black. It's the same logic Clemson uses: "We do this for you blacks, so shut up about things that repulse you."

This will not end well for the University of Texas.

Twice in 2015, anonymous antiracist protesters have spray-painted the Davis monument with the messages "Davis must fail" and "Emancipate UT."[70]

I'd offer that unlike the racist graffiti that assaults black spaces on campus, this act of political defiance and destruction is completely righteous. There is absolutely no value in a monument to a person who advocated for the continued enslavement of your ancestors. It is an affront to all modern Americans, and the University of Texas' resistance to removing it makes it a moral imperative for those who want it gone to take action to degrade it as much as it degrades them.

Malcolm X, during a 1963 lecture at the University of California, noted that blacks should have the right to defend themselves against physical brutalization by white bigots. Today, the continued existence of racist iconography on college campuses, be it names on buildings, Confederate flags being flown, or statues honoring the dishonorable, represents a continued psychological brutalization of the black student on behalf of the university.

Malcolm X concluded by saying, "If someone sics a dog on you, then kill that dog."[71] And today, in the same way, if a university refuses to remove a statue of a racist, then black students on that campus have a right to kill that statue. If a racist Confederate flag is raised anywhere on campus, black students have a right to burn that flag. If a racist is honored on a building, black students have a moral right to erase that name wherever they see it on campus.

Black students have a right to demand that the degrading iconography of the past be eradicated from their college campuses, in the same way that all through the Soviet Union the statues honoring Lenin were destroyed. Or the way Saddam Hussein statues in Iraq were taken down during the Iraq War. And in fact, it is their *duty* to do so. And doing so will force the university to decide between the hateful racist they're honoring and the black student they're educating.

It has only been in the past decade that university administrations have begun to understand that these buildings' names are not only offensive to African American students, but should be offensive to the entire student body. And keeping these building names, statues, and monuments on campus also tells African American students that they don't matter enough to change them, and that their views are unimportant. But when most colleges and universities refuse to engage in self-analysis and think about how each and every item either does or doesn't represent their commitment to diversity, inclusion, and a pluralistic society, then they're complicit in institutionalizing and normalizing white racism in American society.

Or in the words of Assata Shakur, "People get used to anything. The less you think about your oppression, the more your tolerance for it grows. After a while, people just think oppression is the normal state of things. But to become free, you have to be acutely aware of being a slave."[72]

The same goes for the names on the buildings that grace college campuses.

7

WE'RE MAD AS HELL . . . AND WE'RE TAKING OVER THE BUILDING

"There's a time when the operation of the machine becomes so odious—makes you so sick at heart—that you can't take part. You can't even passively take part. And you've got to put your bodies upon the gears and upon the wheels, upon the levers, upon all the apparatus, and you've got to make it stop. And you've got to indicate to the people who run it, to the people who own it that unless you're free, the machine will be prevented from working at all."

—Mario Savio

IN 2014, AT COLGATE UNIVERSITY, OVER THREE HUNDRED BLACK students staged a three-day sit-in of the Hurwitz Office of Admissions building. The reason? Anonymous racist postings on Yik Yak, a popular social media app for college students. Organized by the Colgate University Association of Critical Collegians, the students were upset after reading Yik Yak posts from white Colgate students, including, "White people won life, Africa lost, sorry we were so much better than you that we were literally able to enslave you to our will," "I don't want Blacks at this school," and "Niggers be complaining."

"In order to obtain a complete liberal arts education, one must learn and be aware of different identity politics," the group stated. "Colgate University, at this moment, has insufficient methods to address equity and inclusivity."[1]

The black Colgate student activists organized using the social media hashtags #CanYouHearUsNow and #ThisIsColgate. The group also posted student video testimonials on YouTube as well as photographs of students sharing their stories with handmade signs on Instagram.[2]

Jeffrey Herbst, Colgate's president, like university presidents everywhere after racist incidents happen on their campuses, said all of the right things.

"Bias incidents and racism, while not unique to Colgate, are unacceptable and will not be tolerated. They have no place on a college campus, and they have no place at Colgate. We have heard you, and we will join you in the common goal of creating a campus environment that is welcoming and supportive of all of our students."[3]

But because George Santayana's theory about history continues to ring true, this wasn't the first time that Colgate faced a sit-in over racial microaggressions. Back in 2001 more than seventy black students occupied the same admissions office over "a series of racially insensitive events, including an email message from a political science professor to a student saying that many minority students took soft courses where they could discuss their feelings and might get 'undeservedly high grades.'" Also, three black men were accosted by a white man on campus and taunted with a racial epithet.[4]

"You can look at this as problems to be solved," said John Dovidio, the interim faculty dean at the time. "We see them as symptoms of larger issues Colgate needs to address to become even better than it is, that will move us ahead and not simply put Band-Aids on a series of temporary problems."[5]

And yet it's clear that the problem hasn't been solved at Colgate, just as it hasn't been solved at other schools. American University had to deal with racist Yik Yak posts like: "I really don't like 99 percent of the Black people I meet"; "Their entire culture just isn't conducive to a life of success: The outfits. The attitudes. The behavior"; "Tell your people to dress cleanly. No hootin and a hollerin in public"; "At my work, EVERY single case of theft and fraud has been committed by a Black person."[6]

The common response by non–African Americans to the concept of racial microaggressions is to see them as individualized experiences and not part of a larger picture. Where only the white individuals themselves are responsible for the actions, and aren't tied to any systemic racism that's assaulting black students as a whole on a daily basis. As a result, African American students are then told to get thicker skins about the insensitivity that assails them, even though their skins are already thick by the time they get to college.

By dismissing these racial microaggressions, we build a tinderbox among black students that is bound to erupt. And with the election, and reelection, of the first African American president, Americans continue to be seduced, and deluded, by the idea that we're now in a new state of racial being, a postracial world where race is insignificant. But on today's campuses, the racial hostility is as prevalent as ever, and it's a ticking time bomb.

"We're clearly not postracial," said Tiya A. Miles, chairwoman of the University of Michigan's Department of Afro-American and African Studies. "Sometimes I wonder if having a black president lets people feel like that gives them cover. It absolves people of being prejudiced."[7]

David J. Leonard, a professor in the Department of Critical Culture, Gender and Race Studies at Washington State University, said young people often view racism as being associated with extremist groups like the Ku Klux Klan. "People who don't see themselves like this think: 'We can poke fun. We can engage in stereotypes,'" Dr. Leonard said. "Racism gets reduced to intent, as if intent is all that matters."[8]

But the fact of the matter is that white students at colleges and universities *have* been acting like they're members of the KKK. Over the past twenty years, *The Journal of Blacks in Higher Education* has documented hundreds of incidents in which white college students have assaulted black students with a volume of withering racist aggressions that would make the Ku Klux Klan proud. And as a result, there's been an awakening of black activism on these campuses.

At the University of Michigan, black students started a twitter hashtag, #BBUM, or Being Black at the University of Michigan, and Twitter timelines were flooded with over 10,000 tweets about the isolation and microaggressions that come from being among few black students on the school's campus: "That first class when black culture becomes the topic and you suddenly become the voice of all black people #BBUM"; "#BBUM is my mom calling me worried about my safety because I wrote an opinion piece about my identity"; "Assuming that because I'm black I don't deserve to be here and am a result of affirmative action, which is not even in place right now #BBUM"; "When every room you stand in on campus 9x out of 10 your the only one that is black #BBUM."[9]

The concerns ranged from being the only black student in classes, to being subjected to white students who are racially insensitive if not hostile, like those at the aforementioned Theta Xi fraternity "Hood Ratchet Thursday" party. And of course, ironically, one of the main complaints was that despite the demise of affirmative action, white students assumed that black students were only admitted *because* of affirmative action. This demonstrates that the racial stereotypes white students held about black students were independent of the facts and were much more destructive than any self-esteem issues arising for black students who were *indeed* admitted via affirmative action. Black students were damned if they were, and damned if they weren't, at least in the minds of white students, so the conservative argument that affirmative action needed to go for the benefit of the black student was fraudulent.

As for the campaign itself, Black Student Union president Tyrell Collier said, "I don't think this is a problem specific to the University, I think it's an experience that Black students at predominantly White universities across the nation are facing."[10]

Again, the university expressed support for the students—"Thanks for engaging in this conversation. We're listening, and will be sure all of your voices are heard. #BBUM"—but was essentially impotent when it came to addressing the students' concerns. Typically, universities left the burden of dealing with these social issues on the backs of their student affairs offices.

Inspired by the #BBUM campaign, black students at the University of New Hampshire created their own hashtag, #BAMUNH, for Being African American at the University of New Hampshire, to recount their own experiences: "#BAMUNH realizing that the things you have experienced aren't rare and happen many times to students on this campus"; "When a whole table of white students try to justify saying 'nigger' . . . 'it's only offensive if black people take offense to it' Right #BAMUNH"; "When people stare at you anytime the topic of race, ethnicity, and skin color comes up. #BAMUNH"; "When professors assume your either on the basketball team or the football team. #BAMUNH"; "#BAMUNH talking about race causes havoc with those it doesn't effect on a daily basis"; "1998 UNH promises 300 Black students by 2004. 2013 and we still aren't there. #BAMUNH."[11]

Just over the past two years, we've witnessed the following incidents:

- In 2015 Bucknell University, in Lewisburg, Pennsylvania, expelled three students who were said to have made racist comments during a broadcast on WVBU-FM, the student radio

station. According to Bucknell president John Bravman, the
following discussion occurred on the broadcast:

> Student #1: "Niggers."
> Student #2: "Black people should be dead."
> Student #3: "Lynch 'em!"[12]

- On October 21, 2014, racist messages were scrawled on
  dormitory room doors at the University of Massachusetts at
  Amherst. One of the messages read, "Kill these Niggers!!" Nearly
  200 students attended a meeting at the Student Union building
  to discuss the incident. Chancellor Kumble Subbaswamy also
  attended the meeting, telling the students, "We are doing
  everything we can to find the perpetrators. I wish I could tell you
  this will never happen again, but I can't."[13]
- In 2014 the Office for Civil Rights at the U.S. Department
  of Education launched an investigation into whether Lehigh
  University, in Bethlehem, Pennsylvania, had properly addressed
  racial bias incidents on campus. The investigation began after a
  Lehigh alumna, Susan Magaziner, notified the Office of Civil
  Rights that the Umoja House, a multicultural residence on
  campus, had been vandalized in 2013 with eggs and graffiti
  that included the word "nigger" on both the building and the
  sidewalk. Years before, the skinned head of a deer had been left
  in front of the house.[14]
- The stakes were high for Lehigh, as the university's counsel
  had warned their students. If the Office of Civil Rights found
  that the school had violated federal laws, then the school could
  lose federal funding and be forced to close. But in 2014 Lehigh
  avoided that fate. A voluntary agreement, by which Lehigh
  would create a new racial harassment policy and chronicle racial

incidents, was agreed upon with the Office of Civil Rights. And with this, the investigation ended.[15]

Black student activism has a long tradition on both white and black college campuses, as students struggle to make the campus space reflective of their wants and needs. Activism among black college students typically reflects the ever-changing mindset of African America, the shifting political, cultural, and social philosophies as black people strive for self-determination, both on college campuses and in larger society. Every generation of black students has an activist awakening, based on the realization that the status quo is no longer satisfactory, and that it's now their turn to throw their bodies upon the gears of the machine, whether that machine be on a black or white campus. In essence, each generation of black college students is determined to make the college campus their own, by any means necessary.

The tradition of black student activism goes back to the early nineteenth century, when John Newton Templeton, an ex-slave, pro-Africa colonizer, and the first black Ohio University graduate, spoke at his alma mater in 1828. He noted in his talk, "Claims of Liberia," that "slavery is one of the greatest evils existing in our day, and for the abolishing of which, was the object in forming the Colonization Society; it is an evil which has long existed, its decline must therefore be gradual, in order that its total overthrow be permanent. You will, therefore, hear me while I urge upon your patronage and liberality the claims of Liberia."[16]

And the establishment of black colleges, and the flood of new black students entering these schools during the post–Civil War Reconstruction era, did nothing to dull their activism. In fact, these black college students, eager to use education as a way to transcend the ravages of racial and economic degradation, heightened their activism. In a world where all colleges treated their students paternalistically, regardless of color, students at these newly created black colleges saw themselves as being equal partners with the school. And that meant confronting school administrators about how they expected to be educated, along with consistently demanding respect.

Hiram Revels, the first black U.S. senator, resigned his seat to become the president of Alcorn State, a black college, where he quickly learned that his propensity for ingratiating himself with white racists didn't go over well with the student body. In 1874 angry Alcorn State students held a crippling strike, filed complaints with school officials, and triggered a mass exodus from the school.[17]

Black student activism on black campuses shouldn't be surprising, mainly because for much of the twentieth century, many black colleges were still led by white presidents and staffed by white teachers, who pursued the paternalistic educational objectives of white philanthropists and lawmakers. These white administrators were more interested in creating a black workforce geared toward keeping the status quo in the South than in teaching blacks to challenge it. For those reasons, a black campus was sometimes as hostile a space as a white campus, without the sense of isolation.

Booker T. Washington, with his Tuskegee Institute in Alabama, created the initial road map for a successful black college during the early twentieth century. His emphasis on self-reliance and practical vocational skills attracted white northern philanthropists like George Eastman, founder of Kodak, and Julius Rosenwald, part-owner of Sears & Roebuck. Rosenwald would establish the Julius Rosenwald Fund to educate African Americans in the South and provide grants to African American artists and writers like Gordon Parks, James Weldon Johnson, and W. E. B. Du Bois.

But for white Americans, part of the allure of the Washington way was the idea that black students would be, for the most part, docile and compliant. As an auxiliary to Washington's accommodationist policy, illustrated by his 1895 Atlanta Compromise speech, in which he emphasized economic security over social equality, Washington's educational model was supposed to produce black college students who followed orders and did what they were told.

Not all blacks, or whites for that matter, accepted Washington's strategy of accommodation as a fait accompli. Only a few months after Washington's Atlanta Compromise speech, a white missionary, Dr. Henry Lyman Morehouse, wrote in 1896 about an idea called the Talented Tenth. The idea? A philosophy according to which, in contrast to Washington's emphasis on industrial education, a classically college-educated African American elite would become leaders of the black community.

"In the discussion concerning Negro education we should not forget the talented tenth man. An ordinary education may answer for the nine men of mediocrity; but if this is all we offer the talented tenth man, we make a prodigious mistake . . . The tenth man, with superior natural endowments, symmetrically trained and highly developed, may become a mightier influence, a greater inspiration to others than all the other nine, or nine times nine like them."[18]

W. E. B. Du Bois, who would be the first African American to graduate from Harvard with a PhD, in history, advocated for Morehouse's concept of the Talented Tenth in his 1903 book *The Souls of Black Folks.*

"Men we shall have only as we make manhood the object of the work of the schools—intelligence, broad sympathy, knowledge of the world that was and is, and of the relation of men to it—this is the curriculum of that Higher Education which must underlie true life. On this foundation we may build bread winning, skill of hand and quickness of brain, with never a fear lest the child and man mistake the means of living for the object of life . . . The Negro race, like all races, is going to be saved by its exceptional men. The problem of education, then, among Negroes must first of all deal with the Talented Tenth; it is the problem of developing the Best of this race that they may guide the Mass away from the contamination and death of the Worst."[19]

In response to the call for a Talented Tenth, black students on black campuses were rising up to demand change that reflected their desire for greater control of their education. At Howard University in 1905 students gathered at the chapel to demand that the white president, John Gordon, resign and be replaced with a black president.[20]

According to the *New York Times,* Gordon "was hissed and jeered as he entered the chapel. The negroes charged that Dr. Gordon did not show proper respect for their race." What they hissed and yelled was, "Down with Gordon!" as they went on strike. Eventually acquiescing to their demands, Gordon would indeed resign, but another white president, Reverend Wilbur Thirkield, would take his place.[21]

Black college administrators typically used a heavy hand to keep their students obedient. But that didn't stop black students from protesting. In 1911 two hundred students at North Carolina A&T protested the imposition of Saturday classes and the entire junior and senior classes were expelled. And back at Howard University, the newly formed Delta Sigma Theta sorority joined the March 3, 1913, suffragette march on Washington, despite criticism both on and off campus.[22]

After World War I, black activism shifted into high gear, as the racial climate in the United States became deadly. The summer of 1919, called "Red Summer" by Harlem Renaissance writer James Weldon Johnson, saw hundreds of African Americans, some still in their World War I uniforms, attacked and murdered by roaming white mobs, who often had the protection and participation of the police and military. Some of the tensions came from a new attitude from African Americans, who often refused to conform to the tenets of Jim Crow. Refusal to observe social codes like getting off the sidewalk when passing a white person or simply forming a gathering, got many African Americans lynched. Roaming bands of whites rioted and burned black communities all around the country.

From mid-May to early October, from Arizona to Mississippi, upstate New York to Nebraska, small towns to big cities, African Americans were terrorized, murdered, and sometimes burned at the stake, culminating in events on October 1 in Elaine, Arkansas, where 237 people where lynched.[23]

A month after the first white riots, W. E. B. Du Bois published an essay titled "Returning Soldiers," writing: "We return from the slavery of uniform which the world's madness demanded us to don to the freedom of civil garb. We stand again to look America squarely in the face and call a spade a spade. We sing: This country of ours, despite all its better souls have done and dreamed, is yet a shameful land . . . We return . . . We return from fighting . . . We return fighting."[24]

That spirit of defiance was felt on the black college campus, as during the 1920s many black students were swept up by the ideas of the New Negro, as offered by Alain Locke, and the burgeoning Harlem Renaissance. The New Negro represented a new way of thinking. A new way of seeing the worth of African Americans, without whiteness being the standard. Add Marcus Garvey's Universal Negro Improvement Association, one of the largest black nationalist organizations the country had ever seen, and you have black student activists moving away from Booker T. Washington's accommodationist philosophy of seeking a vocational education and toward W. E. B. Du Bois' philosophy of following a classical education to full citizenship.

The post–World War I black campus rebellions began in 1922, when Florida governor Cary Hardee changed the curriculum of Florida A&M from teacher training to trade training. In 1923 the Florida A&M students went on strike, eventually burning down the mechanical arts building, Gibbs Hall, and firebombing Duval Hall. Eleven students were eventually expelled. Soon, black schools throughout the South boiled with student activism.[25]

In 1924 at Fisk University, in Nashville, Tennessee, the students demanded the resignation of the white president, Fayette McKenzie, having tired of his overly strict code of conduct, which included a restriction on men and women walking together on and off campus.

McKenzie believed that black students' inadequate level of cognitive and social development required strict and uniform standards of conduct with a minimum of deviation.[26]

The Fisk students may have been emboldened by the words of Fisk alumnus W. E. B. Du Bois, who as the 1924 commencement speaker at his alma mater told students, alumni, and President McKenzie, "For a long time a powerful section of the white South has offered to give its consent and countenance to the higher training of Negroes only on condition that the white South control and guide that education."

That was enough to inspire the students. Soon, Fisk students were chanting the name "Du Bois!" around campus, urging a boycott of classes until changes were made. One Fisk student, George W. Streator (who would later become the managing editor of the NAACP magazine *The Crisis*), led the campus activists, giving President McKenzie a list of eleven demands, which went beyond a change in the code of conduct to include the establishment of Greek lettered societies, athletic associations, and a student newspaper, which McKenzie had folded years earlier.[27]

The students' demands were ignored, as McKenzie's favorite phrase was, "If you don't like Fisk, Get Out!" As a result, in early February 1925, the students boycotted classes, with over one hundred male students smashing windows and overturning chapel seats in protest. It was a full-blown riot, which gave McKenzie the excuse needed to bring the police on campus and have the students arrested for inciting violence. Eventually, the students were expelled, but McKenzie's presidency did not survive the incident. Following an investigation into the student protests by the Board of Trustees, McKenzie submitted his resignation letter later in the year.[28]

To say that Du Bois had an immense effect on activists at black colleges would be to make an understatement. For too long, the black college had been a hostile space for the intellectual potential of the African American student, and Du Bois spoke truth to power, telling Hampton and Tuskegee to "stop running your schools as if they were primarily for the benefit of Southern whites and not for blacks."

"Say frankly to all comers . . . this school is not a sanatorium for white teachers or a restaurant and concert hall for white trustees and their friends. Those who wish to visit us are more than welcome but they must expect to be treated as we treat ourselves. Our aim is to make Negroes men—nothing less. Those who do not agree with us though they be old teachers, 'best friends' of the Negro or what not, must stand aside. We are going ahead to a full fledged college of A grade and no longer to pretend that we are simply educating farm hands and servants."[29]

On predominately white campuses, from the University of Michigan to Harvard, from New York University to the University of Kansas, black student activists were fighting the one aspect of segregation that was the linchpin of Jim Crow, the restrictions on interracial social contact. Often on predominately white campuses, regardless of their geographic location, African Americans were prevented from living in dorms and boarding houses with white students. For some predominately white universities, especially those Ivies like Harvard and Cornell, which prided themselves on their lack of race prejudice, the issue presented a conundrum.

At Harvard in 1923 there had been a scandal when African American alumnus Roscoe Conkling Bruce, a former Phi Beta Kappa, was told that his son wouldn't be able to stay in the dorms because of his color. That sparked a battle with Harvard president Abbott Lawrence Lowell, who years earlier had sought to end social class segregation at Harvard, while still maintaining racial segregation in the freshman dorms, in which all but black students were required to stay.

"The social relations of the undergraduates among themselves are quite as important as their academic lives," Lowell would remark.[30]

Through the years, one or two African American Harvard students would mistakenly be assigned to the freshman dorms, where some stayed without incident. But Bruce's case was different in that prior to his son's admission, a committee of Harvard alumni, including future writer and newspaper reporter Walter Lippmann, protested the exclusion of black students from the freshman dorms. Once Bruce's son was excluded, discrimination against black students became public knowledge.

When Bruce protested the policy, Lowell responded with incredulity that an African American would expect to live with whites.

"It seems to me that for the colored man to claim that he is entitled to have the white man compelled to live with him is a very unfortunate innovation which far from doing him good, would increase prejudice that, as you and I thoroughly agree, is most unfortunate, and probably growing . . . To maintain that compulsory residence in the Freshman Dormitories—which has proved a great benefit in breaking up the social cliques, that did much injury to the College—should not be established for 99 percent of the students because the remaining one half of one percent could not properly be included seems to me an untenable position."[31]

In other words, Lowell's fallacious solution for the scourge of segregation was to have more segregation, which sounds ominously close to the modern-day logic of Supreme Court chief justice John Roberts, who famously said about affirmative action, "The way to stop discrimination on the basis of race is to stop discriminating on the basis of race." Bruce was not amused by Lowell's logic, and responded by saying, "Of course I protest."[32]

Then all hell broke out.

The NAACP and black newspapers protested the Harvard color bar, while W. E. B. Du Bois wrote an article in *The Crisis* that tied Harvard's Jim Crow policies to southern lynching, noting that "President Lowell . . . who [was] recently asked by the NAACP to join leading Americans in denouncing lynching did not even acknowledge the letter."[33]

Even more disturbing was the support Lowell received for keeping Bruce's son out of the dorms. Albert Bushnell Hart, nicknamed the

"Grand Old Man" of American history, both a trustee of Howard University and a Harvard professor, had testified during 1921 congressional hearings on the illegal violence against blacks by the Ku Klux Klan. A self-proclaimed "friend of the negro race," he wrote a letter to Lowell that read: "I have been convinced for years . . . that the negro race, as a race, is inferior to the white, and that a mixture of the races in the South or elsewhere would mean a decline in civilization. Furthermore, I have felt and said in my book [*The Southern South*], that I felt the South was justified in using whatever means were necessary to prevent the union of the races."[34]

Eventually, Harvard and Lowell reached a compromise. In 1923 the *New York Times* published the article "Harvard Overseers Ban Discrimination in Race or Religion," stating: "All members of the freshman class shall reside and board in the freshman halls, except those who are permitted by the Dean of Harvard College to live elsewhere. In the application of this rule men of the white and colored races shall not be compelled to live and eat together, nor shall any man be excluded by reasons of his color."[35]

In other words, blacks were allowed to live in the freshman dorm, but if the rest of the white students wanted to shun them, that was none of Lowell's business. And to be sure, not even this compromise was followed, according to many African American students at Harvard, as most said that Harvard's dorms followed Jim Crow rules into the 1950s.[36]

For example, Dr. Ewert Guinier, the first African American head of Harvard's African American studies department, and the father of civil rights theorist Dr. Lani Guinier, entered Harvard in 1929, where he was "barred from the dormitories, was denied financial aid because he had failed to send his picture with his application, and was spoken to inside and outside of class by only one person."[37]

The early part of the twentieth century saw the establishment of various interracial clubs on predominately white campuses, like the Negro-Caucasian Club at the University of Michigan, with African

American student Lenoir Beatrice Smith at the head. With the goal of the "abolition of discrimination of Negroes" in the Ann Arbor area after Smith was refused service at a lunch counter, the NCC presented its grievances to UM dean John R. Eiffinger, who feigned impotence. "My grandfather owned a slave in Virginia, but you mustn't think prejudiced," he protested.[38]

And just as the members of Alpha Phi Alpha and Kappa Alpha Psi fraternities were effectively segregated from social activities when they were founded, in 1906 and 1911, respectively, the University of Michigan black students were barred from college dances and swimming pools and any other place or social activity involving physical contact.[39]

The struggle for social acceptance on predominately white campuses continued through the Great Depression and well into the 1950s, as black students asked for the basic accommodations that any student would have, including the right to associate with anyone, on and off campus, without barriers. The question of why black students should have to accept Jim Crow on campuses that publicly stated that they were nondiscriminatory transitioned to the question of why black students should have to live in a segregated America in the first place. The American college space wasn't free as long as America wasn't free. And the 1954 *Brown vs. the Board of Education* ruling would accelerate black enrollment at colleges throughout the second half of the twentieth century. Black student activists would soon demand that America recognize their humanity, both in the larger society and on campus.

The 1950s and early 1960s found African American students deeply involved in the civil rights movement. Lunch counter sit-ins by black students began in 1960, when four North Carolina A&T students, Joseph McNeil, Franklin McCain, Ezell Blair Jr., and David Richmond, attempted to desegregate the "whites only" lunch counter at the F. W. Woolworth store in Greensboro, North Carolina. When they were turned away, they recruited more students, and the movement began. Soon, black students from around the country began sitting in.

In Raleigh, forty-one African American students from St. Augustine College were arrested for trying to desegregate an F. W. Woolworth in Raleigh's Cameron Village center. Shaw University students joined the St. Augustine students, going back day after day. The sit-in strikes spread through the South, with students from historically black colleges and universities (HBCUs) taking the lead. And as in earlier times, HBCU presidents often expelled students for their off campus activities, usually under pressure from white politicians, who threatened their funding if they didn't discipline their students and discourage them from participating.[40]

The latter half of the twentieth century saw African American students embracing the civil rights movement, the black consciousness movement, and the need to make their own space on college campuses. Black colleges weren't exempt from this, as many were still without curricula that featured African American studies and history. HBCUs across the country demanded a mindset change, like at Fisk, where in 1967 members of the Student Nonviolent Coordinating Committee persuaded the school to offer African American history courses. The *Baltimore Afro American* noted, "The colored student is demanding not just black power, but a shaking, from the roots up overhaul of their college, aimed at upgrading academic standards."[41]

This was a complete mindset change, as the students were reflecting the shift in the African American community in general toward the philosophy espoused by Malcolm X. Malcolm not only challenged whites with regard to their motivations for seeking integration but also challenged blacks to define themselves apart from white society. Activists like the Howard-educated Stokely Carmichael helped to propel the idea of black power, rather than the integrationist policies of previous generations, as the ideology of the times. And as noted in the

Baltimore Afro American article, Fisk students were demanding to be called "black" instead of "Negro" as part of that mindset change.

Dr. Nathan Hare, a professor at Howard University, and later chair of San Francisco State's Black Studies department, was one of the leaders demanding that black studies be instituted at both black and predominately white colleges and that colleges create black student unions. But he was also skeptical and highly critical of putting just anyone in charge. "If all a black studies program needs is a professor with black skin to prattle about Negro subject matter, then our Negro schools would never have failed so painfully as they have."

As African American students grew more numerous on newly desegregated, predominately white campuses, so did black studies departments, with over 500 formed by the early 1970s.[42]

In her article "In Defense of Themselves: The Black Student Struggle for Success and Recognition at Predominantly White Colleges and Universities," author Joy Ann Williamson noted, "Any who were involved in the establishment and operation of Black Studies programs did not view a college education as an instrument by which to socialize young adults into the dominant culture. Instead, they saw the postsecondary experience as serving an openly political purpose and as an instrument with which oppressed peoples could learn to change society."[43]

By the late 1960s black college students were in open rebellion, as black power consciousness began asserting itself. There would be building takeovers, the familiar boycotts and sit-ins, guns, and, in some cases, death.

In 1968 law enforcement officers at South Carolina State, in what would later be called the Orangeburg Massacre, killed three students who had taken part in a protest of a segregated bowling alley. The students chanted "Black Power" and carried a banner that read, "Just Us for Justice."[44]

At Cheney State in 1968 students successfully demanded the resignation of the president, LeRoy B. Allen. During the same year at

Northeastern University, in Boston, black students presented thirteen demands, to which the university acceded. The demands included "an increase in the number of black students, increases in the number and scope of courses and cultural activities involving the black community and the black race, and the establishment of a committee of faculty, administration and black students to insure implementation of the demands."[45]

When Columbia University attempted to build a new gym in the Morningside Heights area of Manhattan in 1968, black students felt the school was discriminating against black Harlem residents, who would receive only limited access to the new building. The students called it "Gym Crow."[46]

At Voorhees College in South Carolina in 1969, thirty students took over two buildings on campus and were later arrested over the protests of the school's president Dr. John Potts. At Belmont Abbey, a nearly all-white campus in North Carolina, seven black students seized a building on campus and issued fifteen demands. After barring the doors, the ten-hour seizure was ended.[47]

In all, over 150 campuses would see black student activists either sit-in, boycott, protest, or strike. And black student activism wouldn't pause in the 1970s and '80s, as students on college campuses as diverse as Howard, Columbia, Stanford, and Berkeley led the South African divestiture movement, an important plank in the antiapartheid movement.

We're now seeing African Americans make the same type of connections between their plight on campuses and what is going on in the black community, as was seen during the New Negro period of the 1920s, the civil rights and black consciousness period of the 1960s and '70s, and the South African divestiture movement of the 1970s and '80s.

Today, black college students from around the country have galvanized around the #BlackLivesMatter theme, the black power slogan of the millennial generation, and begun making conscious efforts to connect their plight on their own campuses with what is going on in communities. And one of their spiritual leaders is Phillip Agnew.

Agnew, the leader of the Florida-based Dream Defenders, a group of black activists who famously took over the Florida state house in Tallahassee after the acquittal of George Zimmerman in the Trayvon Martin murder, got his start as an activist at Florida A&M. After graduating he engaged in community activism at Florida A&M University following the death of fourteen-year-old Martin Lee Anderson at a Florida boot camp. That tragedy led to the formation of the Dream Defenders, which has chapters on nine college campuses and "highlights racial and social economic-justice issues like prison privatization, racial profiling and 'zero tolerance' policies in schools—which many believe lead students of color straight into the prison system."[48] His vision of black student activism should serve as a guiding light for black students at predominately white institutions (PWIs):

> I want to see us move from protest to resistance to full revolution. Constructing and building our own economy and systems and schools. I want to see community control of our food and [access] to food that enhances our bodies and our minds. And to see true self-determination for every person in this country, and that does include white people. But it means balance. Right now, black people, brown people, poor people don't have any rights to their lives and their destinies. I'd like to see the government not engage in wars where we perpetuate an economic system that ruins democracy around the world. That's not a five-year goal; that's probably a lifetime goal. And I'd like to see the prison-industrial complex end. In five years, I'd like to see a good majority of states around this country closing jails, and police departments looking completely different—being governed by the people.[49]

To make change in society, we first have to make change where we already are. And for black college students at predominately white universities, campus racism is the one issue that prepares you for making revolutionary change as a college graduate. It is a reason why some African Americans go to college, not just for individual goals, but also to change the lives of other African Americans. By winning the battle of campus racism at PWIs, they'll be ready for that revolution.

ENOUGH.

Racism is icky to talk about, as everyone usually retreats to their comfortable box when dealing with it. To make folks feel good when we confront issues of campus racism, there's always a call for reaching some sort of middle ground of understanding. A place where compromise can be found, and all points of view are taken into consideration in order to reach some sort of consensus. Maybe we agree to meetings, a commission, or a white paper, all so we can pretend to create solutions, while in reality, all we're trying to do is push the ball far enough down the line so that a future administration, or another group of students, will have to deal with it. "Let's look forward, and not backward," is always the cry.

Enough.

No more conversations, town hall meetings, white paper studies, or toothless appointments of diversity officers as stopgaps for dealing with the racism on campus. The era of gradualism is over when it comes to white campus racism, and colleges and universities need to understand this. They need to take proactive and not reactive measures *now*.

Whether college administrations recognize it or not, African Americans are constantly under attack via the white racism that flows through American society. Whether it's a black Florida teen walking home, only to be murdered by a vigilante with a gun, or police targeting African American communities for overpolicing, or the slaughter of African Americans in black churches, or the predominately white college campus becoming yet another hostile space for African Americans, one that is a ticking time bomb. And to be blunt, if predominately white universities aren't proactive, instead of being reactive, that time bomb is destined to go off, and they'll be the ones watching a tragedy during the next national news cycle.

No one wants that. And it is preventable.

There are some harsh truths when it comes to white college students and their racist aggression against black students, and one is that unless universities work to decrease that behavior to levels below infinitesimal, then they're part of the problem. Not one black student on a college campus should have to spend one second dealing with the scourge of racism or its symbols. It goes beyond the idea of zero tolerance; it means creating such a level of proactive antiracism that white high school students think twice before applying to your school.

Universities need to move campus racism from the backwaters of their administrations to the forefront. They need to triple their current budgets for diversity education. The programs they create for white students should not just be a one-off during freshman orientation but a process that continues through each year of attendance.

And for students, this shouldn't just involve listening to lectures. White students on PWI campuses need to fully participate in discussions and academic classes that break down the racist beliefs, prejudices, and bias they bring to campus from their own communities. Breaking the cycle means undoing the hardwiring, the connection to white supremacy, that these white students bring to campus, and making them cognizant of the complexities of race and racism. No more "we didn't know" excuses.

Universities need to demand *radical* change within the white fraternity and sorority systems, with comprehensive antiracism plans from the national headquarters of each organization. It is obvious that the current workshops, conferences, and advising systems aren't working, and the penalties for racist acts are not strong enough to have an effect. Also, many national white fraternities and sororities are myopic with regard to patterns of racist behavior and thus empower the local chapters to continue that behavior.

Today, the penalty for racist activities on college campuses is basically the equivalent of a hand slap, when decisive action, like that taken by University of Oklahoma president David Boren, needs to be the norm. In other words, the safety of the university's black students needs to trump the pressure schools receive from alumni fraternity and sorority members, some of whom represent the powerful donor classes of their schools. If white fraternities and sororities can't deal with that, or if they see continued instances of campus racism in their chapters, then those chapters need to be shut down permanently.

Every predominately white university should do a complete audit of its physical campus and investigate the backgrounds of those who are honored with statues and buildings. Check to see if the honorees are as diverse as your student body, and if there are reprehensible characters among those honored, then remove them immediately.

Too often, black students feel like interlopers on their own campuses. All they want is to be members of the university family, and yet their needs are shuffled to the side and not prioritized. This needs to stop. Budgetary cuts should not happen at the expense of the few black spaces on PWI campuses. Black student unions, African American–themed houses, and African American studies departments should be immune from budgetary cuts. They are too important for the mental health of African American students, and to cut them is to ignore the needs of black students.

Lastly, colleges and universities need to fight for *hard* affirmative action policies, not soft. It is unacceptable for public universities, particularly flagship universities, to not be representative of the population. Schools without a critical mass of black students should declare an emergency and either demand changes in public policy or use their clout to influence future court and election battles. Too often, colleges and universities throw up their hands and claim to be powerless to fight for the rights of black students to attend their universities, even though they're quite aware of the K–12 disparity that exists in the United States and of how valuable a university education can be for transforming individual lives and communities.

As for African Americans, we need to stop sending our children to PWIs that are not proactive about ridding their campuses of racism. Those of us who are PWI graduates must rid ourselves of our blind loyalty to our alma maters, and understand that if our institutions don't believe that black lives matter, meaning that campus racism must be eradicated, then our alma maters shouldn't matter to us. Too often, we believe in the inevitability of campus racism, when in reality, it just hasn't been confronted effectively.

We must challenge campus racism wherever we find it.

Back in 2014, the cable network VH1 created a reality show about black sororities called *Sorority Sisters.* Thousands of black fraternity and sorority members were outraged by the program, but no one was doing anything effective about it. So I created a social media strategy to defeat the show. The strategy was simple: attack the advertisers, swamp social media with negativity about the show, and then drive down ratings. Thousands of black fraternity and sorority members followed my *Sorority Sisters* strategy, setting up websites and creating coalitions, and within weeks, *Sorority Sisters* was no more. Strategy and consistent, coherent pressure made a multibillion-dollar corporation ditch a television show.

We can do the same with campus racism.

African American graduates of PWIs need to break out beyond their own black alumni associations and work together to gather information about the status of black students on over 1,000 campuses. The collective action of black PWI alumni can place pressure on schools to change, while also rewarding others that are proactive. We also need to create a racial climate metric for every college and university in the United States, as a way for African American parents to help their children make decisions about which schools to attend. And African Americans need to leverage one of the most powerful chips we have for change . . . the African American high school athlete.

Too often, predominately white colleges and universities enter black communities and offer scholarships to our high school athletes without doing anything to reduce the racism on their campuses. It is classic exploitation, but African Americans can use this situation to change the campus racism dynamic. Simply make sure to inform all African American high school athletes about the racial conditions on campus, something that the University of Maryland's Colin Byrd attempted to do, and negatively recruit against any college or university that doesn't have an acceptable track record of deterring campus racism.

This is activism by African American alumni of PWIs. But those who can make the most difference are the African American students who are already on PWI campuses. Again, it's time for these students to reach beyond their own schools and work together with black college students nationwide. African American college students need to create a national Black Congress of Students, which would meet annually to identify issues that affect not just a handful of campuses but students throughout the country. Working as a collective effectively multiplies the power of black students, particularly on PWIs, where black student numbers are below critical mass.

More than anything, the black college students of today must learn how to confront, confront, and confront their universities' administrations about campus racism. Making the comfortable uncomfortable should be the mantra. You are *not* powerless, and confronting campus racism is about making those who think they have power understand that your moral power is not only greater but inherently predisposed toward victory. Protests, advocacy, and the use of strategy to eradicate campus racism means taking risks, pushing boundaries, and yes, making some people angry. Never compromise on principles, as you'll never get a second chance.

Also, African Americans need to take a second and third look at sending their children, the best and the brightest, to historically black colleges and universities. Too often, African American grads of PWIs look at HBCUs as schools that don't provide that real-world quotient. But isn't a quality education the African American college student's most important need?

As Nikki Giovanni said, she teaches at a PWI because "black students are there." And if those black students are going to be there, then my feeling is that these predominately white schools must not be allowed to treat racism as a normal aspect of college life. Eradicating campus racism produces better college students, both black and white, along with better Americans. And isn't that why we send our children to colleges in the first place?

NOTES

ACKNOWLEDGMENTS

1. Giovanni, N. (1995). *Racism 101*. New York: Quill, p. 111.

INTRODUCTION: A CENTURY OF ISOLATED INCIDENTS

1. Santayana, G. (1998). *The Life of Reason*. New York: Prometheus Books, p. 82.
2. Santayana, G. (1998). *The Life of Reason*. New York: Prometheus Books, p. 394.
3. Vidal. G. (2004, September 13). "The State of the Union." *The Nation*.
4. "More Americans View Blacks as Racist Than Whites, Hispanics." (2013, July 3). *Ramussen Reports*.
5. Press, A. (2011, March 11). "Fraternity in Racist Video Has Roots in Antebellum South." *The New York Times*. Retrieved February 1, 2015, from http://www.nytimes.com/aponline/2015/03/11/us/ap-us-sae-profile.html?_r=0.
6. "Sigma Alpha Epsilon Fraternity." (n.d.). Retrieved April 4, 2015, from https://www.sae.net/creed.
7. Greco, J. (2015, March 10). "Parker Rice: 'I Am Deeply Sorry for What I Did Saturday Night.'" KOCO 5. Retrieved March 15, 2015, from http://www.koco.com/news/parker-rice-i-am-deeply-sorry-for-what-i-did-saturday-night/31724874.
8. OU SAE Chant "There will never be a nigger in SAE." (2015, March 8). YouTube. Retrieved March 18, 2015, from https://www.youtube.com/watch?v=uDSffcVIVFg.
9. Zeliger, R. (2011, June 23). "Interview: Alice Walker: The Author and Activist, Who Is Setting Sail for Gaza on a Humanitarian Mission, Says Israel 'Is the Greatest Terrorist' in the Middle East." *Foreign Policy*. Retrieved from http://foreignpolicy.com/2011/06/23/interview-alice-walker/.
10. Bergum, K. (2015, January 15). "Unheard Members Discuss Grievances at Town Hall Meeting." *The Oklahoma Daily*. Retrieved March 12, 2015, from http://www.oudaily.com/news/unheard-members-discuss-grievances-at-town-hall-meeting/article_38a12c70-9d3d-11e4-b3ff-3b1c3849e853.html.
11. Quinn, A. (2013, March 22). "Chinua Achebe and the Bravery of Lions." NPR. Retrieved June 19, 2015, from http://www.npr.org/sections/thetwo-way/2013/03/22/175046327/chinua-achebe-and-the-bravery-of-lions.

CHAPTER 1: JIM CROW GREEK ROW

1. Lee, A. (1955). *Fraternities without Brotherhood: A Study of Prejudice on the American Campus.* Boston: Beacon Press.

2. Statement from President Boren. (2015, March 9). Retrieved March 16, 2015, from http://www.ou.edu/price/news_center/news_archive/2015/statementfrompresident.html.

3. Ohlheiser, A. (2015, March 9). "'Real Sooners Are Not Bigots.' How the University of Oklahoma Is Responding to a Racist Frat Video." *Washington Post.* Retrieved March 10, 2015, from http://www.washingtonpost.com/news/grade-point/wp/2015/03/09/real-sooners-are-not-bigots-how-the-university-of-oklahoma-is-responding-to-a-racist-frat-video/.

4. Schuppe, J. (2015, March 12). "Sigma Alpha Epsilon Has Worried about Frat House Culture for Years." NBC News. Retrieved March 12, 2015, from http://www.nbcnews.com/news/us-news/sae-history-n321651.

5. "SAE Identifies Beauton Gilbow as House Mother Who Appeared to Use Epithet." (2015, March 10). NBC News. Retrieved March 10, 2015, from http://www.nbcnews.com/news/us-news/sae-identifies-beauton-gilbow-house-mother-video-racial-epithet-n320936.

6. "Fraternity Headquarters Prepares for Hearing Process." (2015, March 14). Retrieved March 15, 2015, from http://www.sae.net/home/pages/news/news—media-statements—fraternity-leadership-closes-chapter-at-university-of-oklahoma.

7. Franklin, D. (2015, March 9). "Last Black Member from OU's 'Racist' Fraternity Talks about Time in SAE." News Channel 4. Retrieved March 11, 2015, from http://kfor.com/2015/03/09/last-black-member-from-ous-racist-fraternity-talks-about-time-in-sae/.

8. James, W. (2015, March 9). "There Will Never Be Another Black S-A-E." Retrieved March 9, 2015, from http://betweenthenotes.me/2015/03/09/there-will-never-be-another-black-s-a-e/.

9. William James, telephone conversation with author, May 30, 2015.

10. Glasspiegel, R. (2015, March 9). "Oklahoma LB Eric Striker's NSFW Response to Racist Video: 'These are the same MF'ers shaking our hands.'" Retrieved June 19, 2015, from http://thebiglead.com/2015/03/09/oklahoma-lb-eric-strikers-nsfw-response-to-racist-video-these-are-the-same-mfers-shaking-our-hands/.

11. Eric Striker, telephone interview with author, May 27, 2015.

12. Bergum, K. (2015, January 15). "Unheard Members Discuss Grievances at Town Hall Meeting." *The Oklahoma Daily.* Retrieved March 12, 2015, from http://www.oudaily.com/news/unheard-members-discuss-grievances-at-town-hall-meeting/article_38a12c70-9d3d-11e4-b3ff-3b1c3849e853.html.

13. Alexis Hall, telephone interview with the author, April 21, 2015.

14. Bergum, K. (2015, January 15). "Unheard Members Discuss Grievances at Town Hall Meeting." *The Oklahoma Daily.* Retrieved March 12, 2015, from http://www.oudaily.com/news/unheard-members-discuss-grievances-at-town-hall-meeting/article_38a12c70-9d3d-11e4-b3ff-3b1c3849e853.html.

15. "Sigma Alpha Epsilon." (2015). [Television series episode]. *Morning Joe,* Mika Brzezinski.

16. Williams, B. (2015, March 9). "Waka Flocka Flame Cancels University Of Oklahoma Concert: 'I Am Disgusted in the Actions of SAE." *Huffington Post.*

17. Graham, D. (2015, March 11). "Rap Lyrics and White Racism." *The Atlantic*.
18. (2015). Mika Brzezinski: "SAE Members Are 'Responsible.'" [Television series episode]. *In The Cycle*. Ari Melber.
19. Svrluga, S. (2015, March 10). "Fraternity Brothers Who Joined Racist Chant at University of Oklahoma Apologize." *Washington Post*. Retrieved March 11, 2015, from http://www.washingtonpost.com/news/grade-point/wp/2015/03/10/fraternity-brothers-who-joined-racist-chant-at-university-of-oklahoma-apologize/.
20. Wilonsky, R. (2015, March 24). "Highland Park's Levi Pettit Apologizes for Role in Racist SAE Video, Says It Was 'Disgusting.'" *Dallas Morning News*.
21. Wilonsky, R. (2015, March 24). "Highland Park's Levi Pettit Apologizes for Role in Racist SAE Video, Says It Was 'Disgusting.'" *Dallas Morning News*.
22. Pierce, M. (2015, March 25). "Expelled Oklahoma Fraternity Member Says He's 'Deeply Sorry' for Racist Song." *Los Angeles Times*. Retrieved March 26, 2015, from http://www.latimes.com/nation/la-na-oklahoma-fraternity-student-20150325-story.html.
23. Bush, R. (2015, March 27). "We Should All Be Grateful for Pettit's Chance to Right a Wrong." *Dallas Morning News*. Retrieved March 28, 2015, from http://www.dallasnews.com/opinion/editorials/20150326-editorial-after-racist-sae-chant-a-chance-for-redemption.ece.
24. Hutchinson, E. (2015, March 30). "Why I Applaud Ex-Oklahoma University Frat Levi Pettit for Confronting Racism." *Huffington Post*. Retrieved April 3, 2015, from http://www.huffingtonpost.com/earl-ofari-hutchinson/why-i-applaud-ex-oklahoma-university-frat-levi-pettit-for-confronting-racism_b_6959900.html.
25. Chelsea Davis, telephone interview with author, April 21, 2015.
26. Savali, K. (2015, March 30). The Root.com. Retrieved April 2, 2015, from http://www.theroot.com/articles/culture/2015/03/levi_pettit_why_should_black_people_forgive_racist_and_hateful_behavior.html.
27. Fisherman, T. (2015, March 28). "My Radio Interview of Why I Accepted This Young Man's Apology!" Retrieved March 29, 2015, from https://www.facebook.com/PittmanOK.
28. Adams, S. (2015, March 28). "My Radio Interview of Why I Accepted This Young Man's Apology!" Retrieved June 17, 2015, from https://www.facebook.com/PittmanOK.
29. Porter, C. (2015, March 28). "My Radio Interview of Why I Accepted This Young Man's Apology!" Retrieved June 17, 2015, from https://www.facebook.com/PittmanOK.
30. Chelsea Davis, telephone interview with author, April 21, 2015.
31. Chelsea Davis, telephone interview with author, April 21, 2015.
32. Kingkade, T. (2015, March 27). "SAE Fraternity Members Learned Racist Song at National Leadership Event, University Finds." *Huffington Post*. Retrieved April 4, 2015, from http://www.huffingtonpost.com/2015/03/27/sae-fraternity-racist-song_n_6956790.html.
33. William James, telephone conversation with author, May 30, 2015.
34. Syrett, N. (2009). *The Company He Keeps: A History of White College Fraternities*. Chapel Hill: University of North Carolina Press.
35. Syrett, N. (2009). *The Company He Keeps: A History of White College Fraternities*. Chapel Hill: University of North Carolina Press.
36. Brooks, F., and Starks, G. (2011). *Historically Black Colleges and Universities: An Encyclopedia*. Santa Barbara, Calif.: Greenwood, p. xxi.

37. Brooks, F., and Starks, G. (2011). *Historically Black Colleges and Universities: An Encyclopedia.* Santa Barbara, Calif.: Greenwood, p. xxi.

38. "The Berea Story." (n.d.). Retrieved February 10, 2015, from http://www.berea.edu/about/history/.

39. West, E. (1971, February 23). "Black History at Harvard." Retrieved March 19, 2015, from http://www.thecrimson.com/article/1971/2/23/black-history-at-harvard-pit-becomes/.

40. Snibbe, K. (2011, February 4). "A Window into African-American History." Retrieved March 23, 2015, from http://news.harvard.edu/gazette/story/2011/02/a-window-into-african-american-history/.

41. Du Bois, W., and Dill, A. (1910). *The College-bred Negro American: Report of a Social Study Made by Atlanta University under the Patronage of the Trustees of the John F. Slater Fund; Together with the Proceedings of the 15th Annual Conference for the Study of the Negro Problems, Held at Atlanta University on Tuesday, May 24th, 1910.* Atlanta, Ga.: Atlanta University Press.

42. Keylor, W. (2013, March 4). "The Long-forgotten Racial Attitudes and Policies of Woodrow Wilson." Professor Voices. Boston University. Retrieved February 17, 2015, from http://www.bu.edu/professorvoices/2013/03/04/the-long-forgotten-racial-attitudes-and-policies-of-woodrow-wilson/.

43. Du Bois, W., and Dill, A. (1910). *The College-bred Negro American: Report of a Social Study Made by Atlanta University under the Patronage of the Trustees of the John F. Slater Fund; Together with the Proceedings of the 15th Annual Conference for the Study of the Negro Problems, Held at Atlanta University on Tuesday, May 24th, 1910.* Atlanta, Ga.: Atlanta University Press.

44. Du Bois, W., and Dill, A. (1910). *The College-bred Negro American: Report of a Social Study Made by Atlanta University under the Patronage of the Trustees of the John F. Slater Fund; Together with the Proceedings of the 15th Annual Conference for the Study of the Negro Problems, Held at Atlanta University on Tuesday, May 24th, 1910.* Atlanta, Ga.: Atlanta University Press.

45. Mitchell, K. (2010, July 3). "Jack Johnson Was a Pioneer Who Gave Hope to Black Boxers Everywhere." *The Guardian.* Retrieved February 1, 2015, from http://www.theguardian.com/sport/blog/2010/jul/04/jack-johnson-pioneer-black-boxer.

46. Du Bois, W., and Dill, A. (1910). *The College-bred Negro American: Report of a Social Study Made by Atlanta University under the Patronage of the Trustees of the John F. Slater Fund; Together with the Proceedings of the 15th Annual Conference for the Study of the Negro Problems, Held at Atlanta University on Tuesday, May 24th, 1910.* Atlanta, Ga.: Atlanta University Press.

47. "Harvard to Bar None because of Race or Religion." (2015, April 23). *The Norwalk Hour.*

48. "Harvard to Bar None because of Race or Religion." (2015, April 23). *The Norwalk Hour.*

49. Kimbrough, W. (2003). *Black Greek 101: The Culture, Customs, and Challenges of Black Fraternities and Sororities.* Madison, N.J.: Fairleigh Dickinson University Press, p. 23.

50. Ross, L. (2000). *The Divine Nine: The History of African American Fraternities and Sororities.* New York, N.Y.: Kensington Books.

51. Pruitt, B. (n.d.). Sigma Gamma Rho Sorority History. Retrieved January 6, 2015.

52. Donohue, K. (2012). *Liberty and Justice for All?: Rethinking Politics in Cold War America.* Amherst: University of Massachusetts Press, p. 218.

53. Donohue, K. (2012). *Liberty and Justice for All?: Rethinking Politics in Cold War America.* Amherst: University of Massachusetts Press, p. 218.

54. Lee, A. (1955). *Fraternities without Brotherhood: A Study of Prejudice on the American Campus.* Boston: Beacon Press, p. 136.

55. "Fraternity Agency Asked to Take a Stand on Racism." (1949, November 26). *Baltimore Afro American.*

56. Stout, D. (2001, July 19). "Elmer Henderson, 88, Dies; Father of Major Rights Case." *The New York Times.* Retrieved February 23, 2015, from http://www.nytimes.com/2001/07/19/us/elmer-henderson-88-dies-father-of-major-rights-case.html.

57. "Fraternity Agency Asked to Take a Stand on Racism." (1949, November 26). *Baltimore Afro American.*

58. "Frats Are Told New Challenge Is Main Goal." (1949, February 5). *Gettysburg Compiler.*

59. Lee, A. (1955). *Fraternities without Brotherhood: A Study of Prejudice on the American Campus.* Boston: Beacon Press.

60. Lee, A. (1955). *Fraternities without Brotherhood: A Study of Prejudice on the American Campus.* Boston: Beacon Press.

61. Lee, A. (1955). *Fraternities without Brotherhood: A Study of Prejudice on the American Campus.* Boston: Beacon Press.

62. Donohue, K. (2012). *Liberty and Justice for All?: Rethinking Politics in Cold War America.* Amherst: University of Massachusetts Press, p. 218.

63. Syrett, N. (2009). *The Company He Keeps: A History of White College Fraternities.* Chapel Hill: University of North Carolina Press.

64. "Black Alumnus Recalls Fraternity's Bold Stand." (2006, January 26). *Hartford Courant.* Retrieved January 11, 2015, from http://articles.courant.com/2006-01-26/news/0601260936_1_fraternity-black-students-phi-epsilon-pi.

65. Applebome, P. (2002, December 13). "Lott's Walk Near the Incendiary Edge of Southern History." *The New York Times.* Retrieved February 10, 2015, from http://www.nytimes.com/2002/12/13/politics/13RACE.html.

66. "TKE at Arizona State Official Statement." (2014, January 21). Retrieved January 17, 2015, from http://www.tke.org/news/2014/01/21/tke_at_arizona_state_official_statement.

67. Syrett, N. (2009). *The Company He Keeps: A History of White College Fraternities.* Chapel Hill: University of North Carolina Press.

68. "Negro Frat Admits 'White Brother.'" (1946, October 1). *Ebony* magazine 24–26.

69. "Negro Frat Admits 'White Brother.'" (1946, October 1). *Ebony* magazine 24–26.

70. "An Ordinary Hero." (n.d.). Retrieved February 7, 2015, from http://anordinaryhero.com/.

71. Terry, C. (1988, May 10). "The 'Frontline' of Campus Race Relations." *Chicago Tribune.* Retrieved February 3, 2015, from http://articles.chicagotribune.com/1988-05-10/features/8803150956_1_racial-brawl-slurs-black-enrollment.

CHAPTER 2: THE MACHINE

1. (2005). Professor and minister Michael Eric Dyson on the state of the country: "Some of Us Are in First Class, but the Plane Is in Trouble." Radio series installment. In *Democracy Now!* Amy Goodman, host.

2. Chang, C. (2014, August 12). "Separate but Unequal in College Greek Life." The Century Foundation. Retrieved February 5, 2015, from http://www.tcf.org /work/education/detail/separate-but-unequal-in-college-greek-life/.

3. Soldner, A. (2014, April 29). "University of Alabama's Sororities Still Resist Integrating." BuzzFeed. Retrieved February 8, 2015, from http://www.buzzfeed .com/annasoldner/university-of-alabamas-sororities-remain-mostly-segregated# .khr94Dp7m.

4. Weiss, P. (1992, April 1). "The Most Powerful Fraternity in America." *Esquire.*

5. Jacobs, P. (2013, October 3). "10 Stories That Show the Power of 'The Machine.'" *Business Insider.*

6. Cabaniss, W. (1928, March 29). "To the Student Body." *Crimson White.*

7. Wickham, D. (2001, October 12). "Jim Crow Sentries Patrol Greek Houses at Alabama." *USA Today.* Retrieved February 18, 2015, from http://usatoday30 .usatoday.com/news/comment/columnists/wickham/2001-10-12-wickham .htm.

8. Flowers, S. (2007, December 19). "UA's Machine Produced Many Political Figures." *The Atmore Advance.* Retrieved February 7, 2015, from http://www .atmoreadvance.com/2007/12/19/uas-machine-produced-many-political-fig ures/.

9. Zengerle, J. (2002, February 4). "Alabama's New Schoolhouse Door: Sorority Row." *The New Republic.*

10. "Confirmed Facts about the Machine." (2011, November 29). *Crimson White.* Retrieved March 20, 2015.

11. "Confirmed Facts about the Machine." (2011, November 29). *Crimson White.* Retrieved March 20, 2015.

12. Tucker, W. (2011, November 15). "SGA Executive Speaks Out against Machine." *Crimson White.* Retrieved February 12, 2015.

13. "The University of Alabama: Where Racial Segregation Remains a Way of Life." (2001, Summer). *The Journal of Blacks in Higher Education* 32, 22–24.

14. "The University of Alabama: Where Racial Segregation Remains a Way of Life." (2001, Summer). *The Journal of Blacks in Higher Education* 32, 22–24.

15. Melanie Gotz, telephone interview with author, May 6, 2015.

16. Tucker, W. (2011, November 15). "SGA Executive Speaks Out against Machine." *Crimson White.* Retrieved February 12, 2015.

17. Weiss, P. (1992, April 1). "The Most Powerful Fraternity in America." *Esquire.*

18. Weiss, P. (1992, April 1). "The Most Powerful Fraternity in America." *Esquire.*

19. Weiss, P. (1992, April 1). "The Most Powerful Fraternity in America." *Esquire.*

20. Jones, A. (2006, November 22). "Time Out with Cleo Thomas." *Tuscaloosa News.* Retrieved March 4, 2015, from http://www.tuscaloosanews.com/apps/ pbcs.dll/article?AID=/20061122/TMAG07/61120011.

21. Jones, A. (2006, November 22). "Time Out with Cleo Thomas." *Tuscaloosa News.* Retrieved March 4, 2015, from http://www.tuscaloosanews.com/apps/pbcs.dll /article?AID=/20061122/TMAG07/61120011.

22. Cabell, B. (1999, March 15). "University of Alabama Election Sparks Racist Threats." CNN. Retrieved March 1, 2015, from http://www.cnn.com/US /9903/15/racial.campus.politics/.

23. Arrington, J. (2003). "Change Not Welcomed in SGA?" Retrieved January 8, 2015, from http://www.welcometothemachine.info/media.php?ID=71.

24. Elliot Spillers, telephone interview with author, May 26, 2015.

25. Brown, M. (2015, April 15). "More Than Just Child's Play: University of Alabama SGA Blocks New President from Picking Own Staff." AL.com. Retrieved April 19, 2015, from http://www.al.com/news/tuscaloosa/index.ssf/2015/04/university_of_alabama_sga_bloc.html.

26. Brown, M. (2015, April 15). "More Than Just Child's Play: University of Alabama SGA Blocks New President from Picking Own Staff." Retrieved April 19, 2015, from http://www.al.com/news/tuscaloosa/index.ssf/2015/04/university_of_alabama_sga_bloc.html.

27. Brown, M. (2013, August 28). "Sorority Offered Free Drinks to Members to Vote in Tuscaloosa City Board of Education Race." AL.com. Retrieved from http://blog.al.com/tuscaloosa/2013/08/sorority_offered_free_drinks_t.html.

28. "Suspected Voter Fraud." (2013, August 24). Television broadcast. WVUA.com.

29. Brown, M. (2013, August 29). "Alabama Law Professor's Letter to Faculty Senate Calls Greek Relationship Unhealthy, University 'Corrupt.'" AL.com. Retrieved from http://blog.al.com/tuscaloosa/2013/08/professors_letter_to_alabama_f.html.

30. Weiss, P. (1992, April 1). "The Most Powerful Fraternity in America." *Esquire.*

31. Wickham, D. (2001, October 12). "Jim Crow Sentries Patrol Greek Houses at Alabama." *USA Today.* Retrieved February 18, 2015, from http://usatoday30.usatoday.com/news/comment/columnists/wickham/2001-10-12-wickham.htm.

32. Melody Zeidan, telephone interview with author, May 13, 2015.

33. Webley, K. (2014, August 6). "Revolution on Sorority Row." *Marie Claire.* Retrieved http://www.marieclaire.com/culture/news/a10379/revolution-on-sorority-row-september-2014/.

34. Borger, J. (2001, September 10). "Secret Network Keeps Sororities White." *The Guardian.* Retrieved January 9, 2015, from http://www.theguardian.com/world/2001/sep/11/usa.julianborger.

35. "Woman Says She Broke Sorority Race Bar." (2001, September 9). *The New York Times.* Retrieved March 11, 2015, from http://www.nytimes.com/2001/09/09/us/woman-says-she-broke-sorority-race-bar.html.

36. Tucker, W. (2011, September 14). "Barriers Still Stand in Rush Process." *Crimson White.* Retrieved February 3, 2015.

37. "Campus Life: Alabama; Integration Is at Hand for Fraternity System." (1991, August 25). *The New York Times.* Retrieved February 7, 2015, from http://www.nytimes.com/1991/08/25/nyregion/campus-life-alabama-integration-is-at-hand-for-fraternity-system.html.

38. Zengerle, J. (2002, February 4). "Alabama's New Schoolhouse Door: Sorority Row." *The New Republic.*

39. Zengerle, J. (2002, February 4). "Alabama's New Schoolhouse Door: Sorority Row." *The New Republic.*

40. "Campus Life: Alabama; Integration Is at Hand for Fraternity System." (1991, August 25). *The New York Times.* Retrieved February 7, 2015, from http://www.nytimes.com/1991/08/25/nyregion/campus-life-alabama-integration-is-at-hand-for-fraternity-system.html.

41. Reeves, S. (2001, August 28). "Campus NAACP Leader Stands behind Remarks on Integration." *Tuscaloosa News.* Retrieved February 13, 2015, from http://www.tuscaloosanews.com/article/20010828/NEWS/108280342.

42. "The University of Alabama: Where Racial Segregation Remains a Way of Life." (2001, summer). *The Journal of Blacks in Higher Education* 32, 22–24.

43. Baklanoff, E. (2001, September 4). "Dave Washington's Stand Praised." *Tuscaloosa News.* Retrieved March 3, 2015, from http://www.tuscaloosanews.com /article/20010905/NEWS/109050304.

44. Tucker, W. (2011, September 14). "Barriers Still Stand in Rush Process." *Crimson White.* Retrieved February 3, 2015.

45. Beadle, N. (2003, September 25). "Officials Question Charges." *Crimson White.*

46. Jacobs, P. (2013, October 3). "10 Stories That Show the Power of 'The Machine.'" *Business Insider.* Retrieved from http://www.businessinsider.com/the-ma chine-university-alabama-all-white-secret-society-2013-10.

47. Tucker, W. (2011, September 14). "Barriers Still Stand in Rush Process." *Crimson White.* Retrieved February 3, 2015.

48. Melanie Gotz, telephone interview with author, May 6, 2015.

49. Brown, M. (2014, January 18). "University of Alabama Sorority Segregation Whistle-Blower Awarded 'Legacy' Award." *AL.com.* Retrieved January 9, 2015, from http://blog.al.com/tuscaloosa/2014/01/university_of_alabama_sorority_1 .html.

50. Crain, A. (2013, September 11). "The Final Barrier: 50 Years Later, Segregation Still Exists." *Crimson White.* Retrieved February 6, 2015.

51. Scherker, A. (2013, August 12). "University of Alabama Sorority Allegedly Discriminates against Black Women." *Huffington Post.* Retrieved January 22, 2015, from http://www.huffingtonpost.com/2013/09/12/university-alabama-sororiti es-black_n_3909348.html.

52. "President Bonner Progress Report on Sorority Integration." (2013, September 23). *Crimson White.* Retrieved March 9, 2015.

53. Webley, K. (2014, August 6). "Revolution on Sorority Row." *Marie Claire.* Retrieved http://www.marieclaire.com/culture/news/a10379/revolution-on-soror ity-row-september-2014/.

54. Crain, A. (2013, September 11). "The Final Barrier: 50 Years Later, Segregation Still Exists." *Crimson White.* Retrieved February 6, 2015.

55. Ferguson, L. (2013, November 13). "UA Employee Retires after Recruitment Allegations." *Crimson White.*

56. Owens, E. (2013, September 16). "Alabama Sorority Sisters Blame Racist Alumnae after Black Candidates Rejected." *The Daily Caller.* Retrieved http:// dailycaller.com/2013/09/16/alabama-sorority-sisters-blame-racist-alumnae -after-black-candidates-rejected/.

57. Jones, A. (2014, August 19). "UofA Girl Kicked Out of Sorority after 'NO Niggas!!!!!' Snapchat." Gawker. Retrieved February 3, 2015, from http://gawker .com/uofa-girl-sends-no-niggas-snapchat-gets-kicked-1623769925.

58. Bryant, J. (2001, March 14). "The Machine." *Crimson White.* Retrieved February 12, 2015.

CHAPTER 3: NOT BITTER, NO APOLOGIES

1. Patricia Gyi, telephone interview with author, April 16, 2015.

2. Keni Washington, telephone interview with author, April 19, 2015.

3. Burwell, F. (2011, January 13). "Fridays with Fred: Velma Bell and Beloit." Retrieved March 13, 2015, from https://www.beloit.edu/campus/news/fwf/?story _id=305678.

4. Young, D. (1961, February 28). "Young's Folly." *Daily Illini.*

5. "Girl Pledge Stirs Ruckus in Sorority." (1962, April 28). *Sarasota Herald-Tribune*.
6. Krombein, L. (1997, March 18). "Theta Pi Gamma Sorority History." Retrieved February 12, 2015, from https://sites.google.com/site/thetapigamma/history.
7. "Negress Pledged, Sorority Punished." (1962, April 30). *Milwaukee Sentinel*.
8. "Stanford Fraternity That Pledged Negro Fights Suspension." (1965, April 14). *The New York Times*.
9. "Stanford Fraternity That Pledged Negro Fights Suspension." (1965, April 14). *The New York Times*.
10. Antonucci, M. (2014, March 1). "What They Stood For." *Stanford Alumni Magazine*.
11. "Stanford Fraternity That Pledged Negro Fights Suspension." (1965, April 14). *The New York Times*.
12. Krombein, L. (1997, March 18). "Theta Pi Gamma Sorority History." Retrieved February 12, 2015, from https://sites.google.com/site/thetapigamma/history.
13. Sauer, M. (1962, May 3). "DGs Say 'Still No Comment': Wisconsin Reviews Pledging." *Daily Illini*.
14. Antonucci, M. (2014, March 1). "What They Stood For." *Stanford Alumni Magazine*.
15. Antonucci, M. (2014, March 1). "What They Stood For." *Stanford Alumni Magazine*.
16. Antonucci, M. (2014, March 1). "What They Stood For." *Stanford Alumni Magazine*.
17. Hathaway, J. (2014, December 12). "Sorority Girl Celebrates 21st Birthday with Racist Three-layer Cake." Gawker. Retrieved February 15, 2015, from http://gawker.com/sorority-girl-celebrates-21st-birthday-with-racist-thre-1670470468.

CHAPTER 4: THE GREAT AMERICAN HALF-BAKED SALE

1. Yan, H., and Martinez, M. (2011, September 28). "A Cupcake Sellout at 'Inherently Racist' Bake Sale by UC Berkeley Republicans." CNN. Retrieved January 8, 2015, from http://www.cnn.com/2011/09/27/us/california-racial-bake-sale/.
2. Yan, H., and Martinez, M. (2011, September 28). "A Cupcake Sellout at 'Inherently Racist' Bake Sale by UC Berkeley Republicans." CNN. Retrieved January 8, 2015, from http://www.cnn.com/2011/09/27/us/california-racial-bake-sale/.
3. King, M. L. (1963, August 28). "I Have a Dream." March on Washington for Jobs and Freedom. *American Rhetoric*.
4. King, M. L. (1963, August 28). "I Have a Dream." March on Washington for Jobs and Freedom. *American Rhetoric*.
5. King, M. L. (1964). *Why We Can't Wait*. New York: Harper & Row, p. 159.
6. Johnson, L. (1965). *Public Papers of the Presidents of the United States: Lyndon B. Johnson*, pp. 301.
7. X, M. (1964). "If You Stick a Knife in My Back." Television series episode.
8. Goodman, A. (2015, March 3). "Noam Chomsky: White America's Cruelty to Black People Far Worse Than South Africa." Alternet. Retrieved from http://www.alternet.org/news-amp-politics/noam-chomsky-white-americas-cruelty-black-people-far-worse-s-africa.
9. Leonhardt, D. (2007, September 30). "The New Affirmative Action." *The New York Times*. Retrieved February 9, 2015, from http://www.nytimes.com/2007/09/30/magazine/30affirmative-t.html?pagewanted=all&_r=0.

10. Hardisty, J. (1999). *Mobilizing Resentment: Conservative Resurgence from the John Birch Society to the Promise Keepers.* Boston: Beacon Press.

11. Goldfarb, C. (1944, November 18). "Antioch College, Ohio, Calls for More Colored Students." *The Afro American.*

12. Battelle, P. (1950, January 8). "Mrs. Schwartz Helps Increase the Negro Students in College." *St. Petersburg Times.*

13. Nemy, E. (1996, February 10). "Felice N. Schwartz, 71, Dies; Working Women's Champion." *The New York Times.* Retrieved January 8, 2015, from http://www.nytimes.com/1996/02/10/world/felice-n-schwartz-71-dies-working-women-s-champion.html.

14. Bearak, B. (1997, July 27). "Questions of Race Run Deep for Foe of Preferences." *The New York Times.* Retrieved January 27, 2015, from http://www.nytimes.com/1997/07/27/us/questions-of-race-run-deep-for-foe-of-preferences.html.

15. "Ward Connerly's Falling Star." (2004). *The Journal of Blacks in Higher Education* 43 (Spring 2004), pp. 26–29.

16. "Ward Connerly's Falling Star." (2004). *The Journal of Blacks in Higher Education* 43 (Spring 2004), pp. 26–29.

17. Limbaugh, R. (2013, August 5). "The Soft Bigotry of Low Expectations." Retrieved February 20, 2015, from http://www.rushlimbaugh.com/daily/2013/08/05/the_soft_bigotry_of_low_expectations.

18. Beamon, T., and Bachman, J. (2013, March 22). "Thomas Sowell to Newsmax: GOP Outreach to Blacks 'Most Unpromising.'" Newsmax. Retrieved from http://www.newsmax.com/Newsfront/sowell-gop-blacks-unpromising/2013/03/22/id/495990/.

19. "CA Secretary of State—Vote96—Proposition 209." (1996). Retrieved March 6, 2015, from http://vote96.sos.ca.gov/Vote96/html/BP/209.htm.

20. "Public Strongly Backs Affirmative Action Programs on Campus." (2014, April 22). Pew Research. Retrieved February 18, 2015, from http://www.pewresearch.org/fact-tank/2014/04/22/public-strongly-backs-affirmative-action-programs-on-campus/.

21. Hardisty, J. (1999). *Mobilizing Resentment: Conservative Resurgence from the John Birch Society to the Promise Keepers.* Boston: Beacon Press, p. 154.

22. Bearak, B. (1997, July 27). "Questions of Race Run Deep for Foe of Preferences." *The New York Times.* Retrieved January 27, 2015, from http://www.nytimes.com/1997/07/27/us/questions-of-race-run-deep-for-foe-of-preferences.html.

23. Pitts, L. (1999, March 18). "On Affirmative Action, Black Hens Shouldn't Cater to White Foxes." *The Spokesman Review.*

24. Hardisty, J. (1999). *Mobilizing Resentment: Conservative Resurgence from the John Birch Society to the Promise Keepers.* Boston: Beacon Press, p. 127.

25. Connerly, W. (1997, April 9). "Race Preferences Lose in Court—Again." *The Los Angeles Times.* Retrieved February 1, 2015, http://articles.latimes.com/1997-04-09/local/me-46801_1_racial-preferences.

26. Bearak, B. (1997, July 27). "Questions of Race Run Deep for Foe of Preferences." *The New York Times.* Retrieved January 27, 2015, from http://www.nytimes.com/1997/07/27/us/questions-of-race-run-deep-for-foe-of-preferences.html.

27. Allen-Taylor, J. (2013, November 6). "Why Black Students Are Avoiding UC Berkeley." *East Bay Express.* Retrieved from http://www.eastbayexpress.com/oakland/why-black-students-are-avoiding-uc-berkeley/Content?oid=3756649.

28. Allen-Taylor, J. (2013, November 6). "Why Black Students Are Avoiding UC Berkeley." *East Bay Express*. Retrieved from http://www.eastbayexpress.com /oakland/why-black-students-are-avoiding-uc-berkeley/Content?oid=3756649.

29. Allen-Taylor, J. (2013, November 6). "Why Black Students Are Avoiding UC Berkeley." *East Bay Express*. Retrieved from http://www.eastbayexpress.com /oakland/why-black-students-are-avoiding-uc-berkeley/Content?oid=3756649.

30. Allen-Taylor, J. (2013, November 6). "Why Black Students Are Avoiding UC Berkeley." *East Bay Express*. Retrieved from http://www.eastbayexpress.com /oakland/why-black-students-are-avoiding-uc-berkeley/Content?oid=3756649.

31. "Cal Day 2015." (2015, April 18). University of California at Berkeley. Retrieved April 5, 2015, from http://calday.berkeley.edu/find.php.

32. Asimov, N. (2015, March 17). "UC Berkeley Black Students Demand Fixes to 'Hostile' Climate." *San Francisco Chronicle*. Retrieved April 6, 2015, from http:// www.sfgate.com/bayarea/article/UC-Berkeley-black-students-demand-fixes -to-6139786.php.

33. "The Black Student Union at UC Berkeley Shuts Down Sather Gate at #Black-AtCalDay." (2015, April 18). Storify. Retrieved April 21, 2015, from https:// storify.com/B_A_Simons/black-students-shutdown-sather-gate-at-blackatcald #publicize.

34. Sharp, S. (2004, November 18). "In Silence, Black Students Make Voices Heard." *Daily Cal*. Retrieved February 13, 2015, http://archive.dailycal.org/ar ticle.php?id=16967.

35. Destiny Iwuoma, telephone interview with author, April 23, 2015.

36. Hardy Nickerson NFL Football Statistics. (n.d.). Pro-Football-Reference .com. Retrieved June 19, 2015, from http://www.pro-football-reference.com /players/N/NickHa00.htm.

37. Amy Nickerson, telephone interview with author, May 21, 2015.

38. Ashleigh Nickerson, telephone interview with author, May 19, 2015.

39. Haleigh Nickerson, telephone interview with author, May 21, 2015.

40. Gabe King, telephone interview with author, May 27, 2015.

41. Nickerson, A., "Concerns about African American numbers at Cal!" Email to Chancellor Birgeneau, February 29, 2012.

42. Long, K. (2015, March 13). "Black Students Seek UW Admission-policy Changes." *Seattle Times*. Retrieved from http://www.seattletimes.com/seattle -news/black-students-seeks-uw-admission-policy-changes/.

43. Wu, M. (2009, April 2). "Affirmative Action Stigmatizes Minority Students, Study Finds." *Daily Princetonian*. Retrieved April 26, 2015, from http://daily princetonian.com/news/2009/04/affirmative-action-stigmatizes-minority-stu dents-study-finds/.

44. Wu, M. (2009, April 2). "Affirmative Action Stigmatizes Minority Students, Study Finds." *Daily Princetonian*. Retrieved April 26, 2015, from http://daily princetonian.com/news/2009/04/affirmative-action-stigmatizes-minority-stu dents-study-finds/.

45. Darity, W., Aja, A., and Hamilton, D. (2014, September 27). "Why We're Wrong about Affirmative Action: Stereotypes, Testing and the 'Soft Bigotry of Low Expectations.'" *The Huffington Post*. Retrieved March 5, 2015, from http:// www.huffingtonpost.com/william-a-darity-jr/why-were-wrong-about-affirma tive-action_b_5613026.html.

46. Wu, M. (2009, April 2. "Affirmative Action Stigmatizes Minority Students, Study Finds." *Daily Princetonian*. Retrieved April 26, 2015, from http://daily princetonian.com/news/2009/04/affirmative-action-stigmatizes-minority-stu dents-study-finds/.

47. Darity, W., Aja, A., and Hamilton, D. (2014, September 27). "Why We're Wrong about Affirmative Action: Stereotypes, Testing and the 'Soft Bigotry of Low Expectations.'" *The Huffington Post*. Retrieved March 5, 2015, from http:// www.huffingtonpost.com/william-a-darity-jr/why-were-wrong-about-affirma tive-action_b_5613026.html.

48. Kilborn, P. (2000, February 4). "Jeb Bush Roils Florida on Affirmative Action." *The New York Times*. Retrieved February 13, 2015, from http://www.nytimes .com/2000/02/04/us/jeb-bush-roils-florida-on-affirmative-action.html.

49. Samuels, R. (2015, April 6). "After Bush Order, Florida Universities Cope with Shrinking Black Enrollment." *Washington Post*. Retrieved from http:// www.washingtonpost.com/politics/after-bush-order-florida-universities-cope -with-shrinking-black-enrollment/2015/04/06/82d1e574-bcfe-11e4-bdfa-b8e 8f594e6ee_story.html.

50. Leonhardt, D. (2007, September 30). "The New Affirmative Action." *The New York Times*. Retrieved February 9, 2015, from http://www.nytimes.com/2007 /09/30/magazine/30affirmative-t.html?pagewanted=all&_r=0.

51. Morrison, P. (2014, April 30). "Janet Napolitano, UC's Flak Catcher, on Admis-sions Policy, Tuition Hikes and More." *Los Angeles Times*. Retrieved February 1, 2015, from http://www.latimes.com/opinion/op-ed/la-oe-0430-morrison-na politano-20140430-column.html#page=1.

52. Mitchell, K. (2013, November 8). "Student Posts Video to Spark Discus-sion about Lack of Diversity at UCLA." *Daily Bruin*. Retrieved February 13, 2015, from http://dailybruin.com/2013/11/08/student-posts-video-to-spark-dis cussion-about-lack-of-diversity-at-ucla/.

53. "UCLA Has More NCAA Championships Than Black Male Freshmen." (2013, November 8). *Huffington Post*. Retrieved January 4, 2015, from http://www .huffingtonpost.com/2013/11/08/ucla-black-enrollment-freshmen_n_4242213 .html.

54. Mitchell, K. (2013, November 8). "Student Posts Video to Spark Discus-sion about Lack of Diversity at UCLA." *Daily Bruin*. Retrieved February 13, 2015, from http://dailybruin.com/2013/11/08/student-posts-video-to-spark-dis cussion-about-lack-of-diversity-at-ucla/.

55. "UCLA Has More NCAA Championships Than Black Male Freshmen." (2013, November 8). *Huffington Post*. Retrieved January 4, 2015, from http://www .huffingtonpost.com/2013/11/08/ucla-black-enrollment-freshmen_n_4242213 .html.

56. Adamczyk, A. (2013, November 19). "#BBUM Goes Viral on Twitter." *Michi-gan Daily*. Retrieved April 6, 2015, from http://michigandaily.com/news /black-student-union-gains-national-attention-bbum-twitter-campaign.

57. "Choice without Equity: Charter School Segregation and the Need for Civil Rights Standards." (2009). Civil Rights Project. Retrieved February 3, 2015, from http://civilrightsproject.ucla.edu/research/k-12-education/integration-and -diversity/choice-without-equity-2009-report.

58. "Ward Connerly's Falling Star." (2004). *The Journal of Blacks in Higher Educa-tion* 43 (Spring 2004), pp. 26–29.

59. Kennedy, R. (2013). *For Discrimination: Race, Affirmative Action, and the Law.* New York: Pantheon, p. 7.

60. X, M. (1964, December 3). Oxford Union Debate on Integration. Oxford University, UK.

CHAPTER 5: THE JOKE'S ON YOU, BLACK

1. Syrett, N. (2009). *The Company He Keeps: A History of White College Fraternities.* Chapel Hill: University of North Carolina Press.

2. *Dear White People* (2014). (Motion picture.) United States: Code Red.

3. Lena Waithe, telephone interview with author, May 24, 2015.

4. Sue, D., and Rivera, D. (2010, October 5). "Racial Microaggressions in Everyday Life." *Psychology Today.* Retrieved January 14, 2015, from https://www.psychologytoday.com/blog/microaggressions-in-everyday-life/201010/racial-microaggressions-in-everyday-life.

5. Terry, C. (1988, May 10). "The 'Frontline' of Campus Race Relations." *Chicago Tribune.* Retrieved January 26, 2015, from http://articles.chicagotribune.com/1988-05-10/features/8803150956_1_racial-brawl-slurs-black-enrollment.

6. Terry, C. (1988, May 10). "The 'Frontline' of Campus Race Relations." *Chicago Tribune.*

7. Curwood, S. (1987, January 4). "The New Rise of Racism in America." *Boston Globe.* Retrieved March 15, 2015.

8. "Group Says Reagan Partly to Blame for Rise in Campus Racism." (1990, May 31). Associated Press. Retrieved February 21, 2015, from http://www.apnewsarchive.com/1990/Group-Says-Reagan-Partly-To-Blame-for-Rise-in-College-Racism/id-2c98139cf531d0fc7dac9717e7bebde6.

9. Mitgang, L. (1987, March 15). "Bigotry Is Unwelcome New Trend." Associated Press. Retrieved February 28, 2015.

10. "Group Says Reagan Partly to Blame for Rise in Campus Racism." (1990, May 31). Associated Press. Retrieved February 21, 2015, from http://www.apnewsarchive.com/1987/Bigotry-Is-Unwelcome-New-Campus-Trend/id-da0707ea3663537f769c5eaf9ff32df7.

11. Mitgang, L. (1987, March 15). "Bigotry Is Unwelcome New Trend." Associated Press. Retrieved February 28, 2015, from http://www.apnewsarchive.com/1987/Bigotry-Is-Unwelcome-New-Campus-Trend/id-da0707ea3663537f769c5eaf9ff32df7.

12. "Penn Ousts Fraternity." (1981, November 12). Associated Press. Retrieved March 2, 2015.

13. "University Trying to Heal Scars from 'Ghetto Party.'" (1982, December 14). Associated Press.

14. Mitgang, L. (1987, March 15). "Bigotry Is Unwelcome New Trend." Associated Press. Retrieved February 28, 2015, from http://www.apnewsarchive.com/1987/Bigotry-Is-Unwelcome-New-Campus-Trend/id-da0707ea3663537f769c5eaf9ff32df7.

15. Mitgang, L. (1987, March 15). "Bigotry Is Unwelcome New Trend." Associated Press. Retrieved February 28, 2015, from http://www.apnewsarchive.com/1987/Bigotry-Is-Unwelcome-New-Campus-Trend/id-da0707ea3663537f769c5eaf9ff32df7.

16. Mitgang, L. (1987, March 15). "Bigotry Is Unwelcome New Trend." Associated Press. Retrieved February 28, 2015, from http://www.apnewsarchive.com

/1987/Bigotry-Is-Unwelcome-New-Campus-Trend/id-da0707ea3663537f7
69c5eaf9ff32df7.

17. Yamane, D. (2001). *Student Movements for Multiculturalism: Challenging the Curricular Color Line in Higher Education.* Baltimore: The Johns Hopkins University Press. See also Mitgang, L. (1987, March 16). "Colleges Blame Themselves and National Climate for Rise in Campus Bigotry." Associated Press. Retrieved March 23, 2015, from http://www.apnewsarchive.com/1987/Colleges-Blame -Themselves-and-National-Climate-for-Rise-in-Campus-Bigotry/id-4966157 71f34addd09e0243c6027b648.

18. "Campus Racism Explored." (1988, April 15). Associated Press. Retrieved February 3, 2015.

19. "Suspect Arson, Offer Award." (1988, August 5). United Press International. Retrieved February 11, 2015.

20. Mitgang, L. (1987, March 15). "Bigotry Is Unwelcome New Trend." Associated Press. Retrieved February 28, 2015.

21. "Colleges Battling New Wave of Campus Racism." (1988, October 31). Associated Press. Retrieved March 2, 2015.

22. "Fraternity Apologies for 'Ghetto Party,' Faces Disciplinary Proceedings." (1988, October 17). Associated Press. Retrieved February 14, 2015.

23. Mitgang, L. (1987, March 15). "Bigotry Is Unwelcome New Trend." Associated Press. Retrieved February 28, 2015, from http://www.apnewsarchive.com /1987/Bigotry-Is-Unwelcome-New-Campus-Trend/id-da0707ea3663537f7 69c5eaf9ff32df7.

24. Shuffleton, A. (1988, November 5). "Frat Fundraiser Called Racially Insensitive." *Harvard Crimson.* Retrieved May 5, 2015, from http://www.thecrimson .com/article/1988/11/5/frat-fundraiser-called-racially-insensitive-pstudents/.

25. Shuffleton, A. (1988, November 5). "Frat Fundraiser Called Racially Insensitive." *Harvard Crimson.* Retrieved May 5, 2015, from http://www.thecrimson .com/article/1988/11/5/frat-fundraiser-called-racially-insensitive-pstudents/.

26. Jones, R. (1988, May 15). "Lesson in Racism: UW Blacks Tell of Insults, Isolation." *Milwaukee Journal.* Retrieved February 7, 2015.

27. Syrett, N. (2009). *The Company He Keeps: A History of White College Fraternities.* Chapel Hill: University of North Carolina Press.

28. Chang, C. (2014, August 12). "Separate but Unequal in College Greek Life." The Century Foundation. Retrieved April 2, 2015, from http://www.tcf.org /work/education/detail/separate-but-unequal-in-college-greek-life.

29. Crain, A. (2013, September 20). "U.S. Attorney's Office Monitors UA Segregation Allegations." *Crimson White.* Retrieved February 2, 2015, from http://www.cw.ua .edu/article/2013/09/u-s-attorneys-office-monitors-ua-segregation-allegations.

30. Kimbrough, W. (2003). *Black Greek 101: The Culture, Customs, and Challenges of Black Fraternities and Sororities.* Madison, N.J.: Fairleigh Dickinson University Press, p. 23.

31. Chang, C. (2014, August 12). "Separate but Unequal in College Greek Life." The Century Foundation. Retrieved April 2, 2015, from http://www.tcf.org /work/education/detail/separate-but-unequal-in-college-greek-life.

32. Schafler, K. (2014, October 1). "Confederate Battle Flag Causes Controversy during UH Football Game." *Daily Cougar.* Retrieved February 7, 2015, from http://thedailycougar.com/2014/10/01/confederate-battle-flag-causes-contro versy-uh-football-game/.

33. "Frat Inspired by Robert E. Lee Bans Rebel Uniforms." (2010, April 22). *Herald-Dispatch.* Retrieved May 5, 2015, from http://www.herald-dispatch.com /news/briefs/x1196514825/Frat-inspired-by-Robert-E-Lee-bans-Rebel-uni forms; Glenn, L. (2001, November 9). "Auburn Fraternities' Costumes Cause Tension." *The Auburn Plainsman.* Retrieved April 11, 2015.

34. "'Old South' Fraternity Targeted over Confederate Event." (2009, May 13). Fox News. Retrieved February 7, 2015, from http://www.foxnews.com/story /2009/05/13/old-south-fraternity-targeted-over-confederate-event.html.

35. "Frat Inspired by Robert E. Lee Bans Rebel Uniforms." (2010, April 22). WDBJ 7. Retrieved March 9, 2015, from http://articles.wdbj7.com/2010-04-22/uni forms_24088278.

36. "Racial Hatred and Higher Education." (2013). *The Journal of Blacks in Higher Education.* Retrieved January 6, 2015, from http://www.jbhe.com/2013/09 /racial-hatred-and-higher-education/.

37. Fox, R. (2013). *A Guide to the Racist Rager.* Total Frat Move. Retrieved February 17, 2015, from http://totalfratmove.com/how-to-throw-a-racist-rager/.

38. "Black Students Not Surprised Banned Fraternity Returns." (2002, May 18). Associated Press. Retrieved March 11, 2015.

39. Page, C. (2001, November 18). "Blackface Students Need Better Schooling." *Chicago Tribune.* Retrieved March 14, 2015, from http://articles.chicago tribune.com/2001-11-18/news/0111180081_1_alpha-tau-omega-chapter-black face-fraternity.

40. Tucker, C. (2001, November 11). "Halloween Frat Party Offers Sad Lesson in Racism." *Atlanta Journal Constitution.* Retrieved February 10, 2015.

41. Pilgrim, D. (2000, September 1). "Who Was Jim Crow?" Ferris State University. Retrieved April 10, 2015, from http://www.ferris.edu/jimcrow/who.htm.

42. Kemp, E. (2011, November 15). "Blackface 'Cosby' Costume Draws Southern Miss. Sorority Penalty." *USA Today.* Retrieved February 7, 2015, from http://usatoday30.usatoday.com/news/education/story/2011-11-15/black face-cosby-sorority/51214224/1.

43. "Syracuse Suspends Fraternity after Blackface Incident." (2002, June 6). *The Journal of Blacks in Higher Education.* Retrieved May 3, 2015.

44. Woo, M. (2013, May 1). "Lambda Theta Delta, Asian-American Fraternity at UC Irvine, Suspends Itself over Blackface Video." *OC Weekly.* Retrieved January 14, 2015, from http://blogs.ocweekly.com/navelgazing/2013/05/lambda _theta_delta_blackface_suspension.php.

45. "Washington University in St. Louis' Sigma Alpha Epsilon Chapter Suspended for Alleged Racist Pledge Activity." (2013, February 27). *Huffington Post.* Retrieved March 9, 2015, from http://www.huffingtonpost.com/2013/02/27 /sigma-alpha-epsilon-racism_n_2776707.html.

46. Shavell, S. (2012, October 26). "Community Reacts to Blackface Incident." *The Independent Florida Alligator.* Retrieved March 8, 2015, from http://www.alliga tor.org/news/campus/article_638083b4-1f27-11e2-a242-0019bb2963f4.html.

47. Woodhouse, K. (2013, October 31). "Offensive Fraternity Party Invite Prompts Reprimand from University of Michigan." *MLive.* Retrieved March 21, 2015, from http://www.mlive.com/news/ann-arbor/index.ssf/2013/10/university_of _michigan_fratern_2.html.

48. Cubbison, G. (2010, February 18). "'Compton Cookout' Creates Campus Uproar." NBC San Diego. Retrieved February 18, 2015, from http://www.nbcsan

diego.com/news/local/Compton-Cookout-Creates-Campus-Uproar-84648212
.html.

49. Grega, K. (2014, January 21). "ASU Tau Kappa Epsilon Fraternity Causes
Outrage after MLK-themed Party." *The State Press*. Retrieved March 29,
2015, from http://www.statepress.com/article/2014/01/asu-tau-kappa-epsilon
-fraternity-causes-outrage-after-mlk-themed-party/.

50. Munzerieder, K. (2012, October 30). "UF Frat Boys in Blackface for Halloween Cause Campus Controversy." *Miami New Times*. Retrieved March 22, 2015,
from http://www.miaminewtimes.com/news/uf-frat-boys-in-blackface-for-hallo
ween-cause-campus-controversy-6549612.

51. Jacobs, P. (2013, August 14). "Dartmouth Fraternity Criticized for Racially
Themed 'Bloods and Crips Party.'" *Business Insider*. Retrieved March 20, 2015,
from http://www.businessinsider.com/dartmouth-fraternity-bloods-crips-party
-2013-8.

52. Asch, J. (2013, August 14). "Breaking: Of Crips and Bloods and Memories of
Ghetto Parties." Dartblog. Retrieved April 18, 2015, from http://www.dartblog
.com/data/2013/08/010998.php.

53. Farberov, S. (2013, August 16). "Dartmouth Fraternity and Sorority under Fire
for Throwing 'Crips and Bloods' Party Where 200 Guests Dressed Up Like
Gang Members." *The Daily Mail*. Retrieved February 11, 2015, from http://
www.dailymail.co.uk/news/article-2395400/Dartmouth-fraternity-sorority
-throwing-Crips-Bloods-party-200-guests-dressed-like-gang-members.html.

54. Asch, J. (2013, August 14). "Breaking: Of Crips and Bloods and Memories of
Ghetto Parties." Dartblog. Retrieved April 18, 2015, from http://www.dartblog
.com/data/2013/08/010998.php.

55. Kalsi, D. (2015, April 6). "Clemson's SAE Fraternity Activities Suspended after 'Cripmas' Party." Fox Carolina. Retrieved April 14, 2015, from http://www
.foxcarolina.com/story/27568067/clemson-president-on-cripmas-party-clemson
-is-better-than-this.

56. Williams, D., and Annarino, L. (2013). "Ohio University's Students Teaching
about Racism in Society." Ohio University. Retrieved March 18, 2015, from
http://www.ohio.edu/orgs/stars/Home.html.

57. Brouillette, J. (2015, February 9). "Guests Wear Ponchos, Sombreros and Construction Gear at 'Border Patrol' Fraternity Party." *The Daily Texan*. Retrieved
March 11, 2015, from http://www.dailytexanonline.com/2015/02/09/guests
-wear-ponchos-sombreros-and-construction-gear-at-border-patrol-fraternity
-party.

58. Maly, D. (2012, September 26). "Fraternity Cancels Event after Being Accused
of Bias." *The Daily Texan*. Retrieved April 20, 2015, from http://www.dailytexan
online.com/news/2012/09/26/fraternity-cancels-event-after-being-accused-of
-bias.

59. Konopasek, M. (2015, March 13). "UW Investigates Allegations of SAE Fraternity Racism." Retrieved March 18, 2015, from http://www.king5.com/story
/news/local/seattle/2015/03/12/uw-investigates-sae-fraternity-racism-allega
tions/70240858/.

60. Brown, R. (2015, March 9). "UA Student Released from Sorority for Snapchat Containing Racial Slur." King 5. Retrieved April 18, 2015, from http://
www.cw.ua.edu/article/2015/03/student-released-from-sorority-for-snap
chat-containing-racial-slur.

61. Hathaway, J. (2014, December 12). "Sorority Girl Celebrates 21st Birthday with Racist Three-layer Cake." Gawker. Retrieved February 18, 2015, from http://gawker.com/sorority-girl-celebrates-21st-birthday-with-racist-thre-16704 70468.

62. Beusman, C. (2013, June 13). "Frat Plays Humiliating, Racist, Homophobic 'Prank' on Mailman." Jezebel. Retrieved March 18, 2015, from http://jezebel .com/frat-plays-humiliating-racist-homophobic-prank-on-m-513192536.

63. "Division of Diversity and Community Engagement." (n.d.). University of Texas. Retrieved March 13, 2015, from http://www.utexas.edu/diversity/cam pus-culture/campus-climate-response-team/about.php.

64. "Williams Cancels Classes to Reflect on Hate Speech." (2011, November 15). InsideHigherEd. Retrieved February 11, 2015, from https://www.insidehighered .com/quicktakes/2011/11/15/williams-cancels-classes-reflect-hate-speech.

65. "Racist Graffiti Written on a Greenhouse at Southern Illinois University Car-bondale." (2012, December 14). The Journal of Blacks in Higher Education. Re-trieved March 13, 2015, from http://www.jbhe.com/2012/12/racist-graffiti-writ ten-on-a-greenhouse-at-southern-illinois-university-carbondale/.

66. Kingkade, T. (2012, October 17). "'White History Month' Flier on Mercer University Campus Causes Outrage." Huffington Post. Retrieved April 27, 2015, from http://www.huffingtonpost.com/2012/10/17/white-history-month-flier -mercer-university_n_1974736.html.

67. "Racial Incidents on the Campus of the University of Nebraska Lincoln." (2013, November 27). The Journal of Blacks in Higher Education. Retrieved March 25, 2015, from http://www.jbhe.com/2013/11/racial-incidents-on-the -campus-of-the-university-of-nebraska-lincoln/.

68. Blau, M. (2012, December 21). "Emory TV Show Apologizes for Racist Joke Made by Student Anchor." Creative Loafing. Retrieved May 15, 2015, from http://clatl.com/freshloaf/archives/2012/12/21/emory-tv-show-apologizes-for -racist-joke-made-by-student-anchor.

69. Coker, M. (2013, May 10). "UC Irvine Says 'Go Back 2 Africa Slave' Note Was Left in Student's Backpack in Lab: Update." OC Weekly. Retrieved February 6, 2015, from http://blogs.ocweekly.com/navelgazing/2013/05/charity_lyons_uci _african_slav.php.

70. "UVA Groups Respond to Racial Graffiti on Beta Bridge." (2013, May 16). NBC. Retrieved May 13, 2015, from http://www.nbc29.com/story/22144229 /uva-groups-respond-to-racial-graffitti-on-beta-bridge.

71. Kinzie, S. (2005, September 17). "Racist Incidents Unnerve U-Va." The Wash-ington Post. Retrieved February 26, 2015, from http://www.washingtonpost .com/wp-dyn/content/article/2005/09/16/AR2005091601896.html.

72. Joy Omenyi, telephone interview with author, May 23, 2015.

73. Friedman, J. (2012, December 19). "6 Campus Protests That Captured the Na-tion's Attention in 2012." USA Today. Retrieved January 22, 2015, from http:// college.usatoday.com/2012/12/19/6-campus-protests-that-captured-the-nations -attention-in-2012/

74. "Ole Miss Chancellor Denounces Campus Protests Sparked by Obama Re-election." (2012, November 7). Democratic Underground. Retrieved February 15, 2015, from http://www.democraticunderground.com/10021756167.

75. Ladd, D. (2014, February 17). "After Racist Attack on James Meredith Statue, Ole Miss Offers $25,000 Reward for Info." Jackson Free Press. Retrieved April

6, 2015, from http://www.jacksonfreepress.com/weblogs/jackblog/2014/feb/17/ole-miss-responds-to-racist-attack-on-james-meredi/.

76. "African American Ole Miss Student Is a Victim of a Race-related Attack." (2014, February 22). *Journal of Blacks in Higher Education.* Retrieved March 23, 2015, from http://www.jbhe.com/2014/02/african-american-ole-miss-student-is-a-victim-of-a-race-related-attack/.

77. Helm, M. (2012, December 16). "North Alabama Player Tweets Racist Obama Comment after Speech Pre-empted NFL Game, Now Gone from Team." Al.com. Retrieved June 18, 2015, from http://www.al.com/sports/index.ssf/2012/12/north_alabama_player_tweets_ra.html.

78. Schweers, J. (2013, October 28). "UF President Condemns ATO for Racial, Sexual Taunts." *The Gainesville Sun.* Retrieved February 18, 2015, from http://www.gainesville.com/article/20131028/ARTICLES/131029579.

79. Coscarelli, J. (2012, May 8). "Cornell Frat Accused of Calling Black Students 'Trayvon' after Throwing Bottles at Them [Updated]." *New York Magazine.* Retrieved June 18, 2015, from http://nymag.com/daily/intelligencer/2012/05/cornell-frat-trayvon-marton-bottles-black-students.html.

80. Hennessy-Fiske, M. (2012, March 29). "Trayvon Martin Case: Texas Student's Cartoon Causes Controversy." *The Los Angeles Times.* Retrieved April 11, 2015, from http://articles.latimes.com/2012/mar/29/nation/la-na-nn-trayvon-cartoon-20120329.

81. "University of Wisconsin-Madison Investigating Fraternity after Racial Slur Incident." (2012, March 28). *Huffington Post.* (VIDEO). Retrieved March 24, 2015, from http://www.huffingtonpost.com/2012/03/27/university-wisconsin-madison-racial-slur-incident_n_1381165.html.

82. Martese Johnson, telephone interview with author, June 13, 2015.

83. Shapiro, T. (2015, June 12). "Martese Johnson, Free of Charges, Seeks Racial Harmony on U-Va. Campus." *The Washington Post.* Retrieved June 13, 2015, from http://www.washingtonpost.com/local/education/martese-johnson-free-of-charges-seeks-racial-harmony-on-u-va-campus/2015/06/12/35ead544-112d-11e5-9726-49d6fa26a8c6_story.html.

84. Joy Omenyi, telephone interview with author, May 23, 2015.

85. Shapiro, T. (2015, June 12). "Martese Johnson, Free of Charges, Seeks Racial Harmony on U-Va. Campus." *The Washington Post.* Retrieved June 13, 2015, from http://www.washingtonpost.com/local/education/martese-johnson-free-of-charges-seeks-racial-harmony-on-u-va-campus/2015/06/12/35ead544-112d-11e5-9726-49d6fa26a8c6_story.html.

86. Kaplan, T., and Murphy, K. (2014, March 20). "San Jose State Hate Crime Case: Black Student Files $5 Million Claim." *Mercury News.* Retrieved February 25, 2015, from http://www.mercurynews.com/crime-courts/ci_25387139/san-jose-state-hate-crime-black-student-files.

87. Kaplan, T., and Murphy, K. (2014, March 20). "San Jose State Hate Crime Case: Black Student Files $5 Million Claim." *Mercury News.* February 25, 2015, from http://www.mercurynews.com/crime-courts/ci_25387139/san-jose-state-hate-crime-black-student-files.

88. Kaplan, T. (2013, November 20). "San Jose State Students Accused of Tormenting Black Roommate Are Charged with Hate Crimes." *Mercury News.* Retrieved February 25, 2015, from http://www.mercurynews.com/crime-courts/ci_24566367/san-jose-state-students-charged-hate-crime.

CHAPTER 6: HONORING THE DISHONORABLE

1. Johnson, H. (1903). *The Nations from a New Point of View*. National Baptist Publishing Board.
2. Colin Byrd, telephone interview with author, May 23, 2015.
3. "All About Testudo." (n.d.). University of Maryland. Retrieved April 14, 2015, from http://www.umd.edu/testudo.html.
4. Galitsky, D. (2015, February 12). "What's in a (Facility) Name? Racism." *The Diamondback*. Retrieved May 13, 2015, from http://www.diamondbackonline .com/opinion/article_a46b9b50-b252-11e4-b926-b3b8f8da0694.html.
5. "Donald Gaines Murray and the Integration of the University of Maryland School of Law." (n.d.). University of Maryland School of Law. Retrieved April 15, 2015, from https://www.law.umaryland.edu/marshall/specialcollections /murray/.
6. McKenna, D. (2013, October 31). "76 Years Later, Maryland Tries to Right a College Football Wrong." *Deadspin*. Retrieved March 7, 2015, from http://dead spin.com/76-years-later-maryland-tries-to-right-a-college-footb-1455976233.
7. Kirshner, A. (2013, November 8). "University Officials Make Amends for 76-year-old Racial Slight." *The Diamondback*. Retrieved April 18, 2015, from http://www.diamondbackonline.com/news/campus/article_b32b1470-4842 -11e3-90f2-0019bb30f31a.html.
8. McKenna, D. (2013, October 31). "76 Years Later, Maryland Tries to Right a College Football Wrong." Deadspin. Retrieved March 7, 2015, from http://dead spin.com/76-years-later-maryland-tries-to-right-a-college-footb-1455976233.
9. Galitsky, D. (2015, February 12). "What's in a (Facility) Name? Racism." *The Diamondback*. Retrieved May 13, 2015, from http://www.diamondbackonline .com/opinion/article_a46b9b50-b252-11e4-b926-b3b8f8da0694.html.
10. Durr, K. (2003). *Behind the Backlash: White Working-class Politics in Baltimore, 1940–1980*. Chapel Hill: University of North Carolina Press.
11. Kingkade, T. (2015, March 13). "UMD Frat Brother Allegedly Sent Racist Email, Signed Off with 'F*** Consent.'" *The Huffington Post*. Retrieved May 18, 2015, from http://www.huffingtonpost.com/2015/03/13/umd-racist-frat-email _n_6863386.html.
12. Wells, C., and Wood, P. (2015, March 13). "UM College Park Investigating Email Containing Racial, Ethnic Slurs." *The Baltimore Sun*. Retrieved April 18, 2015, from http://www.baltimoresun.com/news/maryland/bs-md-umd-email -20150313-story.html.
13. "SGA and MICA Town Hall with President Loh." (2015, April 2). YouTube. Retrieved May 17, 2015, from https://www.youtube.com/watch?v=vVGJgB3 OgV8.
14. "SGA and MICA Town Hall with President Loh." (2015, April 2). YouTube. Retrieved May 17, 2015, from https://www.youtube.com/watch?v=vVGJgB3 OgV8.
15. Lyman, B. (2015, June 4). "Ala. Senate Votes to Rename Edmund Pettus Bridge." *Montgomery Advertiser*. Retrieved June 9, 2015, from http://www .montgomeryadvertiser.com/story/news/politics/southunionstreet/2015/06/03 /ala-senate-votes-rename-edmund-pettus-bridge/28409105/.
16. Svrluga, S. (2015, April 8). "U-Md. Student Government Endorses Demand That Byrd Stadium Be Renamed, Citing Racist Legacy." *The Washington Post*.

Retrieved April 19, 2015, from http://www.washingtonpost.com/news/grade
-point/wp/2015/04/08/u-md-students-demand-byrd-stadium-be-renamed
-citing-racist-legacy/.

17. Byrd, C. (2015, March 29). "An Open Letter to Prospective Black Athletes at
the University of Maryland, College Park by Colin Byrd." Bmorenews.com. Retrieved May 18, 2015, from http://www.bmorenews.com/blog/oped-an-open
-letter-to-prospective-black-athletes--print.shtml.

18. Moredock, W. (2014, February 4). "Ben Tillman Was a Racist, Terrorist, and
Murderer: It's Time to Take Down His Statue." *Charleston City Paper.* Retrieved
February 3, 2015, from http://www.charlestoncitypaper.com/charleston/ben
-tillman-was-a-racist-terrorist-and-murderer-its-time-to-take-down-his-statue
/Content?oid=4857402.

19. Waldrep, C. (2001). *Local Matters: Race, Crime, and Justice in the Nineteenth-
Century South.* Athens: University of Georgia Press.

20. Budiansky, S. (2008). *The Bloody Shirt: Terror after the Civil War.* London: Pen-
guin, p. 236.

21. Simkins, F. (1944). *Pitchfork Ben Tillman, South Carolinian.* Baton Rouge: Louisiana State University Press, p. 218.

22. Norrell, R. (2009). *Up from History: The Life of Booker T. Washington.* Cam-
bridge, Mass.: Belknap Press of Harvard University Press, p. 246.

23. Cary, N. (2015, February 12). "Clemson Won't Rename Tillman Hall, Board
Chair Says." Greenville Online. Retrieved April 8, 2015, from http://www.green
villeonline.com/story/news/education/2015/02/11/clemson-rename-tillman
-hall-board-chair-says/23238993/.

24. Cary, N. (2015, February 12). "Clemson Won't Rename Tillman Hall, Board
Chair Says." Greenville Online. Retrieved April 8, 2015, from http://www.green
villeonline.com/story/news/education/2015/02/11/clemson-rename-tillman
-hall-board-chair-says/23238993/.

25. Kingkade, T. (2014, April 16). "Washington & Lee University Students Demand Removal of Confederate Flags." *The Huffington Post.* Retrieved January
8, 2015, from http://www.huffingtonpost.com/2014/04/16/washington—lee
-confederate_n_5161367.html.

26. Connor, R., and Poe, C. (1912). *The Life and Speeches of Charles Brantley Aycock.*
Garden City, N.Y.: Doubleday, p. 216.

27. Weinberg, C. (2014, May 5). "Duke and UNC Debate Changing Names of
Buildings That Honor Racists." *InsideHigherEd.* Retrieved February 2, 2015,
from https://www.insidehighered.com/news/2014/05/05/duke-and-unc-debate
-changing-names-buildings-honor-racists.

28. Smith, J. D. (2002). *Managing White Supremacy: Race, Politics, and Citizenship
in Jim Crow Virginia.* Chapel Hill: University of North Carolina Press.

29. Plecker, W. (1943, January). "Walter Plecker, M.D., to Local Registrars, Phy-
sicians, Health Officers, Nurses, School Superintendents, and Clerks of the
Court." Disappearing Indians? Retrieved February 27, 2015, from http://www2
.vcdh.virginia.edu/lewisandclark/students/projects/monacans/Contemporary
_Monacans/letter.html.

30. Moxley, T. (2010, September 16). "White Supremacist's Name Removed from
Radford U. Building." *The Roanoke Times.* Retrieved March 7, 2015, from http://
www.roanoke.com/news/white-supremacist-s-name-removed-from-radford-u
-building/article_af83347d-350c-5ec3-b480-4f70d0cb9460.html.

31. Moxley, T. (2010, September 16). "White Supremacist's Name Removed from Radford U. Building." *The Roanoke Times*. Retrieved March 7, 2015, from http://www.roanoke.com/news/white-supremacist-s-name-removed-from-radford-u-building/article_af83347d-350c-5ec3-b480-4f70d0cb9460.html.

32. Jordan, H. (1912). *Science*, 151, 152.

33. Lamm, S. (2015, February 2). "Activists Continue the Fight to Rename Saunders Hall." *The Daily Tar Heel*. Retrieved March 18, 2015, from http://www.dailytarheel.com/article/2015/02/activists-continue-the-fight-to-rename-saunders-hall.

34. Weinberg, C. (2014). "Ugly History on Tobacco Road." *Inside Higher Education*.

35. Prince, R. (2015). "N.C., Texas Schools Confront Confederate Iconography." *Richard Prince's Journal-isms*.

36. Priestland, D. (2015, April 13). "The University of Cape Town Is Right to Remove Its Cecil Rhodes Statue." *The Guardian*. Retrieved May 17, 2015, from http://www.theguardian.com/commentisfree/2015/apr/13/cape-town-remove-cecil-rhodes-statue.

37. Barnett, R. (2015, March 12). "Thurmond's Biracial Granddaughter on Tillman Hall: Changing Name 'Won't Change Hearts.'" *The Greenville News*. Retrieved from http://www.greenvilleonline.com/story/news/local/pickens-county/2015/02/04/thurmonds-biracial-granddaughter-tillman-hall-changing-name-change-hearts/22898171/.

38. Klein, R. (2014, January 23). "Yes, Schools in the U.S. Still Bear the Names of White Supremacists." *The Huffington Post*. Retrieved March 20, 2015, from http://www.huffingtonpost.com/2014/01/15/white-supremacist-schools_n_4509352.html.

39. Hoenig, C. (2014, January 17). "White Supremacists Honored with School Names." Diversity Inc. Retrieved February 9, 2015, from http://www.diversityinc.com/news/white-supremacists-honored-school-names/.

40. Egan, T. (2006). *The Worst Hard Time: The Untold Story of Those Who Survived the Great American Dust Bowl*. Boston: Houghton Mifflin, p. 108.

41. Murray, W. (Director). (1906, November 20). "Proceedings of the Constitutional Convention of the Proposed State of Oklahoma Held at Guthrie, Oklahoma." Lecture conducted from Oklahoma Territory, Muskogee, Indian Territory.

42. Murray, W. (Director) (1906, November 20). "Proceedings of the Constitutional Convention of the Proposed State of Oklahoma Held at Guthrie, Oklahoma." Lecture conducted from Oklahoma Territory, Muskogee, Indian Territory.

43. Egan, T. (2006). *The Worst Hard Time: The Untold Story of Those Who Survived the Great American Dust Bowl*. Boston: Houghton Mifflin, p. 108.

44. Tolnay, S., and Beck, E. (1995). *A Festival of Violence: An Analysis of Southern Lynchings, 1882–1930*. Urbana: University of Illinois Press.

45. Martin, H. (2013, October 9). "Racial Climate Report Released." *The Daily Mississippian*. Retrieved January 5, 2015, from thedmonline.com/racial-climate-report-released.

46. Knef, A. (2014, August 1). "Chancellor Jones Announces Plan for Leadership on Race Issues and Diversity." *Hoddy Toddy*. Retrieved from http://hottytoddy.com/2014/08/01/chancellor-jones-announces-plan-for-leadership-on-race-issues-and-diversity/.

47. Maffly, B. (2013, December 6). "Amid Name Debate, Dixie Removes Confederate Statue." *Salt Lake Tribune*. Retrieved from http://archive.sltrib.com/article.php?id=24417674&itype=storyID.

48. Martin, M. (2013, May 7). "FBI Most Wanted Terrorists List: Who Is Assata Shakur?" NPR. Retrieved May 18, 2015, from http://www.npr.org/2013/05/07/181914429/fbi-most-wanted-terrorists-list-who-is-assata-shakur.

49. Glick, B. (1989). *War at Home: Covert Action against U.S. Activists and What We Can Do About It.* Boston: South End Press, p. 77.

50. Martin, M. (2013, May 7). "FBI Most Wanted Terrorists List: Who Is Assata Shakur?" NPR. Retrieved May 18, 2015, from http://www.npr.org/2013/05/07/181914429/fbi-most-wanted-terrorists-list-who-is-assata-shakur.

51. Martin, M. (2013, May 7). "FBI Most Wanted Terrorists List: Who Is Assata Shakur?" NPR. Retrieved May 18, 2015, from http://www.npr.org/2013/05/07/181914429/fbi-most-wanted-terrorists-list-who-is-assata-shakur.

52. Goodman, A. (2013, May 2). "Former Black Panther Assata Shakur Added to FBI." Democracy Now. Retrieved June 9, 2015, from http://www.democracynow.org/blog/2013/5/2/ex_black_panther_assata_shakur_added_to_fbis_most_wanted_terrorist_list.

53. Kaminer, A. (2013, October 21). "Protests as City College Closes a Student Center." *The New York Times.* Retrieved from http://www.nytimes.com/2013/10/22/nyregion/protests-as-city-college-closes-a-student-center.html?_r=0.

54. Baker, D. (2015, March 27). "Berkeley Students Outrage Police with Demand to Honor Cop Killer." *San Diego Union-Tribune.* Retrieved from http://www.sandiegouniontribune.com/news/2015/mar/27/berkeley-students-building-renamed-assata-shakur/.

55. Willgress, L. (2015, March 20). "UC Berkeley Students Want to Rename a Campus Building after a Notorious Cop Killer Who Was the First Woman on the FBI's Most Wanted Terrorists List." *The Daily Mail.* Retrieved from http://www.dailymail.co.uk/news/article-3004033/UC-Berkeley-students-want-rename-campus-building-notorious-cop-killer-woman-FBI-s-wanted-terrorists-list.html.

56. O'Flynn, E. (2015, April 9). "Furious White Groups Say South African University's Decision to Remove Statue of British Colonialist Cecil Rhodes Following Black Student Protests Is 'Racism in Disguise.'" *The Daily Mail.* Retrieved from http://www.dailymail.co.uk/news/article-3031543/Cape-Town-university-votes-remove-Cecil-Rhodes-statue.html.

57. "College Students Want to Name a Building after a Convicted Cop Killer." (2015, March 19). Fox News. Retrieved from http://www.foxnews.com/us/2015/03/20/student-group-demands-california-university-rename-building-after-convicted-cop/.

58. Eromosele, D. (2015, March 20). "Black Students at UC Berkeley Want a Hall Renamed after Assata Shakur." The Root.com. Retrieved from http://www.theroot.com/articles/news/2015/03/black_students_at_berkeley_want_a_hall_renamed_after_assaka_shakur_and_the.html.

59. Delong, K. (2015, May 19). "Mural Featuring FBI Most Wanted Terrorist Removed at MU, Sorority Says Proper Research Wasn't Done." Fox6Now.com. Retrieved from http://fox6now.com/2015/05/18/mural-featuring-one-of-fbis-most-wanted-terrorists-removed-at-mu-sorority-says-proper-research-wasnt-done/.

60. Izadi, E. (2015, May 20). "After Outcry, Marquette University Removes Campus Mural of Assata Shakur." *Washington Post.* Retrieved from http://www

.washingtonpost.com/news/grade-point/wp/2015/05/19/after-outcry-mar
quette-university-removes-assata-shakur-campus-mural/.

61. Izadi, E. (2015, May 20). "After Outcry, Marquette University Removes Campus Mural of Assata Shakur." *Washington Post.* Retrieved from http://www
.washingtonpost.com/news/grade-point/wp/2015/05/19/after-outcry-mar
quette-university-removes-assata-shakur-campus-mural/.

62. Izadi, E. (2015, May 20). "After Outcry, Marquette University Removes Campus Mural of Assata Shakur." *Washington Post.* Retrieved from http://www
.washingtonpost.com/news/grade-point/wp/2015/05/19/after-outcry-mar
quette-university-removes-assata-shakur-campus-mural/.

63. Friedorsdorf, C. (n.d.). "Stripping a Professor of Tenure over a Blog Post." *The
Atlantic.* Retrieved from http://www.theatlantic.com/education/archive/2015
/02/stripping-a-professor-of-tenure-over-a-blog-post/385280/.

64. Jaschick, S. (2015). "Firing a Faculty Blogger." *Inside Higher Education.* Retrieved
from https://www.insidehighered.com/news/2015/02/05/marquette-moves-fire
-controversial-faculty-blogger.

65. Jaschick, S. (2015). "Firing a Faculty Blogger." *Inside Higher Education.* Retrieved
from https://www.insidehighered.com/news/2015/02/05/marquette-moves-fire
-controversial-faculty-blogger.

66. McAdams, J. (2015, February 4). "Marquette to Warrior Blogger: We're Going to Fire You." Marquette Warrior. Retrieved February 21, 2015, from http://
mu-warrior.blogspot.com/2015/02/marquette-to-warrior-blogger-were-going
.html.

67. "Texas Students Take Aim at Jefferson Davis Campus Statue." (2015, May 8).
The New York Times. Retrieved May 18, 2015, from http://www.nytimes.com
/aponline/2015/05/08/us/ap-us-confederate-symbols-davis-statue.html?_r=0.

68. McCann, M. (2015, May 29). "Written in Stone: History of Racism Lives on
in UT Monuments." *The Austin Chronicle.* Retrieved from http://www.austin
chronicle.com/news/2015-05-29/written-in-stone/.

69. Samuels, A. (2015, May 12). "No Decision Made on Removal of Jefferson
Davis Statue from U. of Texas Campus." *USA Today.* Retrieved from http://
college.usatoday.com/2015/05/12/no-decision-made-on-removal-of-jefferson
-davis-statue-on-u-of-texas-campus/.

70. Herrera, S. (2015, April 17). "Jefferson Davis Statue Vandalized Once Again,
This Time with Spray Paint." *Daily Texan.* Retrieved from http://www
.dailytexanonline.com/2015/04/17/jefferson-davis-statue-vandalized-once
-again-this-time-with-spray-paint.

71. X, M. (1963, October 11). "If Someone Sics a Dog on You, Kill That Dog."
YouTube. Retrieved March 19, 2015, from https://www.youtube.com/watch
?v=o7f5NTLgtEA.

72. Shakur, A. (1987). *Assata: An Autobiography Chicago,* Ill.: L. Hill, p. 262.

CHAPTER 7: WE'RE MAD AS HELL . . .
AND WE'RE TAKING OVER THE BUILDING

1. New, J. (2014). "Can You Hear Us Now?" *Inside Higher Education.*

2. Stone, A. (2014, February 24). "Racist Posts on Yik Yak Prompt Student Protest at Colgate University." *The Huffington Post.* Retrieved May 15, 2015, from

http://www.huffingtonpost.com/2014/09/24/colgate-university-protest-racist
-yik-yak_n_5875106.html.

3. Stone, A. (2014, February 24). "Racist Posts on Yik Yak Prompt Student Protest at Colgate University." *The Huffington Post*. Retrieved May 15, 2015, from http://www.huffingtonpost.com/2014/09/24/colgate-university-protest-racist
-yik-yak_n_5875106.html.

4. Arenson, K. (2001, November 27). "Racial Tensions Lead to Student Protest at Colgate." *The New York Times*. Retrieved March 12, 2015, from http://www
.nytimes.com/2001/11/28/nyregion/racial-tensions-lead-to-student-protest-at
-colgate.html.

5. Arenson, K. (2001, November 27). "Racial Tensions Lead to Student Protest at Colgate." *The New York Times*. Retrieved March 12, 2015, from http://www
.nytimes.com/2001/11/28/nyregion/racial-tensions-lead-to-student-protest-at
-colgate.html.

6. "Racist Comments on Social Media Attributed to American University Students." (2015). *The Journal of Blacks in Higher Education*. Retrieved from http://www.jbhe.com/2015/03/racist-comments-on-social-media-attributed
-to-american-university-students/.

7. Vega, T. (2014, February 24). "Colorblind Notion Aside, Colleges Grapple with Racial Tension." *The New York Times*. Retrieved January 11, 2015, from http://
www.nytimes.com/2014/02/25/us/colorblind-notion-aside-colleges-grapple
-with-racial-tension.html.

8. Vega, T. (2014, February 24). "Colorblind Notion Aside, Colleges Grapple with Racial Tension." *The New York Times*. Retrieved January 11, 2015, from http://
www.nytimes.com/2014/02/25/us/colorblind-notion-aside-colleges-grapple
-with-racial-tension.html.

9. Adamczyk, A. (2013, November 19). "#BBUM Goes Viral on Twitter." *Michigan Daily*. Retrieved April 6, 2015, from http://michigandaily.com/news/black
-student-union-gains-national-attention-bbum-twitter-campaign.

10. Byng, R. (2013, November 20). "#BBUM Hashtag Sparks Dialogue about Diversity at the University of Michigan." *The Huffington Post*. Retrieved June 18, 2015, from http://www.huffingtonpost.com/2013/11/20/bbum-university-of
-michigan-black-students_n_4310790.html.

11. Byng, R. (2013, November 20). "#BBUM Hashtag Sparks Dialogue about Diversity at The University of Michigan." *The Huffington Post*. Retrieved June 18, 2015, from http://www.huffingtonpost.com/2013/11/20/bbum-university-of
-michigan-black-students_n_4310790.html.

12. Press, A. (2015, March 31). "'Black People Should Be Dead': Bucknell Students Expelled for Racist Radio Rant." *The New York Post*. Retrieved May 16, 2015, from http://nypost.com/2015/03/31/black-people-should-be-dead
-bucknell-students-expelled-for-racist-radio-rant/.

13. "Racial Incidents at the University of Massachusetts." (2014). *The Journal of Blacks in Higher Education*. Retrieved from http://www.jbhe.com/2014/10
/racial-incidents-at-the-university-of-massachusetts/.

14. Wojcik, S. (2013, November 29). "Lehigh University Alumna Files Complaint with Feds, Says Discrimination Not Taken Seriously at School." *Lehigh Valley Live*. Retrieved from http://www.lehighvalleylive.com/bethlehem/index
.ssf/2013/11/lehigh_university_alumna_files.html.

15. "Lehigh University Avoids Sanctions in Federal Investigation of Racist Incidents." (2014). *Huffington Post*. Retrieved from http://www.huffingtonpost.com/2014/10/02/lehigh-federal-investigation-racism_n_5922080.html.

16. Templeton, J. (1829, July 22). "The Claims of Liberia." *Chillicothe Gazette.*

17. Kendi, I. (2012). *The Black Campus Movement: Black Students and the Racial Reconstitution of Higher Education, 1965–1972.* New York: Palgrave Macmillan.

18. Morehouse, H. (1896). "The Talented Tenth." *The American Missionary,* pp. 181–182.

19. Du Bois, W.E.B. (1903). "The Talented Tenth." *The Negro Problem: A Series of Articles by Representative Negroes of To-day.* London: Forgotten Books.

20. Kendi, I. (2012). *The Black Campus Movement: Black Students and the Racial Reconstitution of Higher Education, 1965–1972.* New York: Palgrave Macmillan.

21. "Students Force Out Gordon: Resignation of President of Howard Is Accepted." (1905, December 28). *The New York Times.*

22. Kendi, I. (2012). *The Black Campus Movement: Black Students and the Racial Reconstitution of Higher Education, 1965–1972.* New York: Palgrave Macmillan.

23. "Map of 73 Years of Lynchings." (2015, February 10). *The New York Times.* Retrieved from http://www.nytimes.com/interactive/2015/02/10/us/map-of-73-years-of-lynching.html?_r=0.

24. Du Bois, W.E.B. (1919, May 1). "Returning Soldiers." *The Crisis,* p. 13.

25. Kendi, I. (2012). *The Black Campus Movement: Black Students and the Racial Reconstitution of Higher Education, 1965–1972.* New York: Palgrave Macmillan.

26. Nicholson, C. (2011). "To Advance a Race: A Historical Analysis of the Intersection of Personal Belief, Industrial Philanthropy and Black Liberal Arts Higher Education in Fayette McKenzie's Presidency of Fisk University, 1915–1925." (Dissertation). Chicago: Loyola University Chicago.

27. Nicholson, C. (2011). "To Advance a Race: A Historical Analysis of the Intersection of Personal Belief, Industrial Philanthropy and Black Liberal Arts Higher Education in Fayette McKenzie's Presidency of Fisk University, 1915–1925." (Dissertation). Chicago: Loyola University Chicago.

28. Kendi, I. (2012). *The Black Campus Movement: Black Students and the Racial Reconstitution of Higher Education, 1965–1972.* New York: Palgrave Macmillan.

29. Aptheker, H. (1969). "The Negro College Student in the 1920s—Years of Preparation and Protest: An Introduction." *Science and Society,* pp. 150–167.

30. Painter, N. (1971, December 1). *New England Quarterly,* 64–4.

31. Painter, N. (1971, December 1). *New England Quarterly,* 64–4.

32. Painter, N. (1971, December 1). *New England Quarterly,* 64–4.

33. Painter, N. (1971, December 1). *New England Quarterly,* 64–4; Du Bois, W. (1922, August 1). *The Crisis,* 153.

34. Painter, N. (1971, December 1). *New England Quarterly,* 64–4.

35. Sollors, W. (1993). *Blacks at Harvard: A Documentary History of African-American Experience at Harvard and Radcliffe.* New York: New York University Press.

36. Painter, N. (1971, December 1). *New England Quarterly,* 64–4.

37. "Ewart Guinier, 79, Who Headed Afro-American Studies at Harvard." (1990, February 7). *The New York Times.*

38. Kendi, I. (2012). *The Black Campus Movement: Black Students and the Racial Reconstitution of Higher Education, 1965–1972.* New York: Palgrave Macmillan.

39. Kendi, I. (2012). *The Black Campus Movement: Black Students and the Racial Reconstitution of Higher Education, 1965–1972.* New York: Palgrave Macmillan.

40. "Woolworth's Lunch Counter—Separate Is Not Equal." (n.d.). American History. Retrieved March 18, 2015, from http://americanhistory.si.edu/brown/history/6-legacy/freedom-struggle-2.html.

41. Leifermann, H. (1967, December 9). "Fisk, Central State Adjusting to New Students' Demands." *The Baltimore Afro American*.

42. Williamson, J. A. (1999). "In Defense of Themselves: The Black Student Struggle for Success and Recognition at Predominantly White Colleges and Universities." *The Journal of Negro Education* vol. 68, no. 1 (Winter), pp. 92–105.

43. Williamson, J. A. (1999). "In Defense of Themselves: The Black Student Struggle for Success and Recognition at Predominantly White Colleges and Universities." *The Journal of Negro Education* vol. 68, no. 1 (Winter), pp. 92–105.

44. "Young Negroes in SC Demonstrate." (1968, November 26). *Danville Register*.

45. Henderson, K. (1993, December 13). "A Place of Their Own Helps Black Students Tune In to Academics." *Christian Science Monitor*.

46. Bradley, S. (2003). "'Gym Crow Must Go!' Black Student Activism at Columbia University, 1967–1968." *The Journal of African American History* Vol. 88 (2).

47. "Armed Black Students." (1969, April 30). *New York Post*.

48. "The Root 100: Phillip Agnew." (2013). TheRoot.com. Retrieved March 10, 2015, from http://www.theroot.com/articles/lists/2013/10/theroot_100/phillip_agnew.html.

49. Chin, M. (2015, January 19). "Phillip Agnew, Dream Defender." *In These Times*. Retrieved February 18, 2015, from http://inthesetimes.com/article/17543/phillip_agnew_dream_defender.

INDEX